Figuring the Word:
Essays on Books, Writing, and Visual Poetics

D1453121

ISBN: 1-887123-23-7

Granary Books, Inc.
568 Broadway #403
New York, NY 10012
sclay@interport.net
www.granarybooks.com

Distributed by
D.A.P. / Distributed Art Publishers
155 Avenue of the Americas
New York, NY 10013
Tel: (212) 627-1999
Fax: (212) 627-9484
Orders: 800-338-BOOK

FiGURing THE WORD

Essays on Books, Writing, and Visual Poetics

JOHANNA DRUCKER

GRANARY BOOKS • New York City • 1998

for Gino

CONTENTS:

Introduction

Introduction

Charles Bernstein

During the 1960s and 1970s, The New York Public Library acquired an admirable collection of contemporary small press magazines, including many of the xerox, mimeo and side-stapled publications featured in the 1998 show, *A Secret Location on the Lower East Side: Adventures in Writing 1960-1980*. This was the heyday of a writing storage medium called microfiche, which the librarians embraced as a space-age space saver: no sooner had they committed these publications to fiche than they disposed of the cumbersome objects, as one would discard the husks around an ear of corn. However, it wasn't too long before the library found themselves recollecting, and prominently displaying, the material artifacts that they had earlier so abruptly deaccessioned.

What difference does it make? What's the fuss about these material imprintings of language—isn't it the content that matters? Does the method of storage really make a difference?

The work of Johanna Drucker reflects a radical change in understanding the semantic contribution of the visual representation of language—not just for visual poetry or artists' books, not just for poetry, but for all forms of written language. To be sure, Drucker has focussed her attention on language works in which visual materiality is foregrounded. But the lessons she has to teach—historical, philosophical, and aesthetic—apply to all the technologies human beings have invented to store and explore language. *All language is visual when read.* In her work, Drucker reverses a common assumption even among writers, typographers, and visual poets that the visual dimension of writing is ornamental, decorative, extrasemantic—a matter of design, not signs that matter. "The single, conservative constant in my work," she says, "is that I always intend for the language to have meaning. My interest is in extending the communicative potential of writing, not in eliminating or negating it."

In these pages, Drucker presents herself as a visual artist, a literary writer, a scholar/historian, and an aesthetician. In each of these areas, Drucker has made substantial contributions. But it is her synthesis of these fields that is her most extraordinary achievement and that links her late twentieth century work in the United States to the work of two towering British scholar-book artists of the previous fin-de-siècles: William Blake of the late eighteenth century and William Morris of the late nineteenth. Like these men of letters, this modern-day person of books bends and stretches the nature of art practice well beyond its conventional generic constraints. She questions and transforms the gender codings of the intellectual, the polymath, the scholar, and the printer. Indeed, Drucker is more a satirist than a visionary or utopian, reveling in, rather more than reviling, the "carnival of grotesque human folly." For all its extraordinary detail and formidable erudition, Drucker's work is rigorously anti-systematic, emblematically anti-authoritarian, and often giddily eccentric.

Figuring the Word is a work of poetics rather than criticism or theory in that these essays are the products of doing as much as thinking, of printing as much as writing, of designing as much as researching, of typography as much as composition, of autobiography as much as theory. The mark of the practitioner-critic is everywhere present in these pieces: it is as notable in Drucker's insistence on discussing her process of making things as it is when she reveals her process of hiding things. Moreover, even as she has learned the history of her medium, she remains insistent that current practice, not precedent, is her guiding impulse: "The idea that there were precedents for such activity seemed a lot less important than that there was a future in it."

Figuring the Word is a wide-ranging collection of Drucker's essays from the early-80s to the present. Written in a variety of styles and presented in a variety of formats, the book reflects many divergent aspects of her work and thinking, while at the same time demonstrating how cohesive her project has been. Drucker begins with a wonderfully digressive discussion of her work as a book artist in which she gives an account of what lead her not only to her book art, but also to her related scholarly investigations. She then provides a series of close readings of the work of a number of contemporary language artists, providing in other essays overviews of the historical precedents for this work. The book includes not only a perceptive essay about the use of language in the landscape but also a prescient essay about the use of language in the new electronic frontier of cyberspace. In several sections, Drucker narrates her personal history as a way to explore the affinity with the genre fiction and tabloid prose that underlies much of her writing. And throughout the collection, she interrogates the role and significance of gender, not only for her own work, but for the genres within which she works. Drucker insists that "the place for women is not as the Other but as the one who shows that that Other has always been present," a position that is, to a remarkable degree, analogous to her view about the material features of language.

Susan Bee and I first met Johanna Drucker in 1977 in a large tent in Bryant Park, on the grounds of the New York Public Library, during a Small Press Book Fair. Drucker was exhibiting her first few letterpress books, which immediately caught my attention as just the kind of work that I wanted to focus on in a new journal Bruce Andrews and I were just starting, *L=A=N=G=U=A=G=E*. Indeed, I reviewed Drucker's *From A to Z* in the first issue of *L=A=N=G=U=A=G=E*, commenting on its uncanny fusing of constructivist contraints (she had set every piece of type from a set of 45 type drawers she had acquired), sumptuous physical detail (a vision of textual excess and density), and wry metanarrative commentary.

Drucker's works, including her unlikely and necessary creation of an awesome body of scholarship exploring the history of alphabets and the theory of the visual representation of language, have remained central to my own sense of writing in the years since. In a wider context, her work has become ever more relevant with the introduction of new writing reproduction and distribution technologies.

When we met, Drucker already knew what the folks in the library would celebrate two decades later: that writing is not just made of ideas but also of marks. That language only means when it matters.

I. Foreword

Writing and the Book

The essays in this collection were written for particular publications or specific situations between the early 1980s and the present; some comment upon books I made as much as a decade earlier. Brought together they form a constellation of inquiries into the fields of writing, typography, and the book as a form. All are pieces which migrate between creative and scholarly approaches, sometimes more to one side or the other of this divide. They are motivated by my interest in the activities that begin with mark-making and then move out from that originary act to become writing in poetics, literature, design, and the visual arts.

Writing: the word is ambiguous in its dual identity as a verb and a noun, an act and a product, a visual and verbal form, the composition of a text and trace of the hand. Teasing out these different ideas has formed the shifting ground of my work as a scholar and an artist. In thinking of writing as representation, I came to question how it is that letters, words, and pictorial elements all participate in producing a work with complex textual value. At its most fundamental writing is inscription, a physical act which is the foundation of literary and symbolic activity. Typography, artists' books, concrete poetry, and visual art which use text as an image (rather than in the usual, neutral way) take these written traces to a higher level of organization as symbols, signs, syntactic and semantic structures. Through these material forms writing functions culturally, psychically, and metaphysically.

There is much that is personal in these essays: my current work exists in a continuum with thoughts from the days in which I stared at alphabet wallpaper in my childhood bedroom, intent on deciphering the potent enigma of those letterforms. At that time I wrote in tiny notebooks, sheltering the text in the protective curve of my body, secure in the conviction that that intimate and private life of writing could be shielded from prying eyes and then burst forth into the world as a book. From my earliest awareness I was convinced that my identity was as a writer: experience was only real if it was transformed into writing and writing was only legitimate if it ended up in a book. I felt protected by writing, concealed and revealed simultaneously, because my text could go out into the world as a book without my having to accompany it. Books lived a life of their own, independent of the identity and presence of their writers—at least, in some fictive sense. Writing seemed free from the constraints of a gendered existence—and as a child and a young woman, I felt that my gender posed a threat to my desire for an intellectual life. Writing provided an escape through invention and distancing strategies. Though escape is no longer either an option or desire, the need for reflective solitude and the practice of writing remain central to my life and identity.

When I learned letterpress printing in 1972 as an undergraduate at the California College of Arts and Crafts, it had a profound effect on the way my work developed. Acquiring the skills to produce printed work gave me a sense of competence and worldly authority. Printing remains a radically empowering skill in my experience, a potent complement to that of speaking and writing, because it provides a fundamental means of transforming personal expression into an authoritative form within the social order and the public sphere. The physicality of printing makes that transformation a somatic experience, an act of the body, which moves the interior voice, the personal word, into the cultural domain. The roots of my thinking, research, and writing remain closely bound to the creative activity of setting type, using a letterpress, making books, and now, working with electronic media.

Between 1972 and the present many experiences have contributed to my creative and scholarly development: exhibiting my artwork, working as a waitress, being part of a poetry scene in the Bay Area, working at the West Coast Print Center (established by the NEA to provide low-cost printing services to the literary community), traveling to Greece and Europe, printing and selling my books, moving more than a dozen times to different regions, cities, and countries. The decision to go to graduate school at the University of California at Berkeley in 1979 opened unforeseen avenues for professional development. Three professors, Bertrand Augst, Tony Dubovsky, and Julian Boyd, sponsored my interdisciplinary Ph.D. in "Ecriture: Writing as the Visual Representation of Language" through a self-designed program synthesizing historical, theoretical, and critical approaches in semiotics, psychoanalysis, literature, and visual art. In some sense all the work in this volume is a direct outgrowth of that education. Since that time my work has synthesized creative as well as scholarly approaches and these pieces reflect the sometimes fluid—and at other times more rigid—lines of distinction between these two areas of my activity.

In organizing this selection, I have avoided essays which served as preliminary drafts or sketches for what have become my published books in this area: *The Visible Word* (University of Chicago Press, 1994), *The Alphabetic Labyrinth* (Thames and Hudson, 1995) and *The Century of Artists' Books* (Granary Books, 1995). I have followed publisher Steve Clay's suggestion that many bits and pieces which have appeared in a wide variety of publications, often obscure or of limited circulation, be brought together. The earliest pieces are one or two papers from the Berkeley days, written when I was just starting my systematic study of the history of writing. I look at them now as foundational—not only for the work in-between, but for the work I hope to do in the future. There are also a number of visually scored works written with format and typographic design as elements of their composition. Where possible I have preserved these close to their original form or in an interpretation suited to this current format. Similarly, I have not tried to edit this collection into a homogeneous style. The polymorphousness of the texts seems infinitely more interesting to me than any single tone could be—and the variety instantiates and exemplifies the material qualities of writing (in all senses) so important to the arguments.

Many thanks are due in many quarters. First to Steve Clay for suggesting and fostering this project. Then to Matthew Kirschenbaum for his willingness to help produce an in-print version of the interview he published in the on-line journal *Post-Modern Culture* (Johns Hopkins University Press, Spring 1997). To various editors whose hands can be felt in the reprinted articles, a note of acknowledgment for their expertise, as well as a note of gratitude to those publishers who permitted these pieces to be published in the first place (their original sources are cited, when appropriate, at the end of each article). There are many friends and colleagues with whom conversations and exchanges have been generative and rewarding in many ways: Emily McVarish, Betsy Davids, Charles Bernstein, Susan Bee, Steve McCaffery, Marjorie Perloff, Janet Zweig, Mira Schor, and not least of all, Gino Lee, whose expertise, friendship, and generosity are a constant resource. Finally, to Brad Freeman, in all ways and for all manner of encouragement and affection, an ongoing and loving appreciation.

New Haven, 1998

II. The Word Made Flesh

Dark the bat-elf, dauphin to a leaf, our prince, licked his leaden lips and spewed back to them the piecemeal come of their misgivings. Come with me, he hissed enticing, shower fringe like liquid grail to

grill yourselves loss earthbound stupid trust be- spise its banal crush the seized substance, spit sence past the wings and come

They knew that saliva and profound issue. his hands and that inertia, the subject tissue.

impaled on reck- fantasies. Your littles you, de- panderings and moment for its its diffuse es- full spread of my with me.

the savour of the cause of its The elf clapped oh the valour of effect of the Drool from the

labial fold appears as vapor and that emmission for the droplets' sake is cool, very very cool and damp: the understated friction on the skin, unscaled but not quite imprintable its masked flexibility does not de- rive from evolution but from malice and the taut religion of his ener- gies.

Dark, the Bat-elf, 1972, Letterpress and stone lithography, 8″ x 8″.

Through Light and the Alphabet

Interview with Matthew G. Kirschenbaum

"According to the Hebrew myth," notes the poet Charles Bernstein, "light was the first act of creation. That is probably the most famous hierarchization of sight among the human senses: the Bible creates the conditions for using eyes before it creates eyes. Eyes, at least in our culture, are the most prized of the human sense organs; assumed to be responsible for processing the most information about the world, eyesight is the sense most associated with survival. Presumably, the evidence is that most people would give up limbs or tongue, ears or nose—though such choices are usually hypothetical—before they would cede sight. The problem with these formulations is that sight is imagined to be split off from the other senses, and from language . . . ."[1]

It is precisely this schism that Johanna Drucker's collective work addresses itself to, in the process constituting one of the most striking oeuvres in late twentieth century aesthetics. Drucker, who holds a Ph.D. from Berkeley, is currently Associate Professor of Art History at Yale University. For twenty-five years she has been writing, printing, and binding artists' books, many of them under the imprint of her own Druckwerk press, using both letterpress and offset production techniques. (The earliest of these is *Dark, the Bat-Elf*, from 1972, in an edition of 13 copies.) Her works place particular emphasis on typography, but their range is far greater than sheer formal experimentation; as Drucker herself writes in a recent article: "The particular form of typographic poetics which has formed the center of my work from the late 1970s is dedicated to exploring the non-linear potential of print form and to the power of visual material form to proliferate meaning within a semantic field through visual structure. But it is also bound up with issues of female identity, prose traditions, and the relations between fiction as a literary form and fiction as a cultural form—tabloids, pulp novels, and genre writing. Though all of this work from the last two decades can now, in my own critical writing, be framed in terms which locate it within traditions and contemporary frameworks of visual poetry and aesthetic innovation, it was originally conceived without that information and with a far more intuitive and unregulated sensibility."[2]

In addition to her book art, Drucker has also published several highly regarded critical studies, including *The Visible Word: Experimental Typography and Modern Art, 1909-1923* (focusing on Dada, Russian and Italian Futurism, and Cubism); *Theorizing Modernism: Visual Art and the Critical Tradition* (a collection of essays); *The Alphabetic Labyrinth* (a scholarly history of the alphabet); and most recently, *The Century of Artists' Books* (a major study which has the potential for opening an entire field to critical inquiry). All of this work, critical and creative, has accumulated in a corpus which is, as Nick Piombino has put it, nothing less than "a conceptual framework for the relationship between the visual arts and the written arts."[3]

Nowhere, I believe, is such a conceptual framework currently more needed than in the post-alphabetic writing spaces of electronic media—an area to which Drucker has, in fact, lately turned her attention. In this interview, which was conducted between Charlottesville, Virginia, and New Haven, Connecticut, via electronic mail in March of 1997, I have attempted to frame my questions so as to provide as complete an overview as possible of Drucker's career, with particular emphasis on her recent interest in matters of the virtual. The text of the interview is accompanied by forty digital images of Drucker's work, as well as a brief catalogue essay entitled "The Corona Palimpsest: Present Tensions of the Book." [*Note: that was true in the on-line version and has been modified here.–JD*]

1. MGK: I'd like to start with a very broad-based question, one apropos of this interview appearing in a special issue on "hypertext" in a journal that publishes only electronically. Your cumulative work as a writer, as a printer and a book-maker, and as a historian of visible language in all its forms suggests an intimacy with the printed word unlike that of any other contemporary artist or thinker I can name—and I say that not least because the nature of that intimacy has been so self-consciously scrutinized and explored by you throughout your career. Yet, your response to electronic media is clearly very different from, say, that of Sven Birkerts, a self-confessed bibliophile who regards the proliferation of new information technologies as a "Faustian pact" and who concludes his book *The Gutenberg Elegies* with the admonition to "Refuse it." So I'd like to ask you to talk about when and how you first began to see developments in electronic media as important to your other long-standing scholarly and creative interests. I also understand that you

have a book in progess called *www.VisCult*. Have you been spending much time on-line lately, and what are your thoughts on the phenomenon of the Web as a visual-verbal environment?

JD: My sense of the Web and my reaction to it is fairly clear, so I can give you a straightforward answer to that question. The reason I don't have the same extreme response of "refusal" that someone like Birkerts has—or the same wild enthusiastic "embrace" that many others have—is that I see new technology in terms of continuities and disruptions. One thing which interests me is the way books and readers are being transformed by exposure to hypermedia. It has become, very quickly, a commonplace for my students to object to the claims of hypermedia by pointing out (unsolicited) that they can read a book, a newspaper, or a journal in a "hypertext" fashion. This was of course always true, but it's the sensitivity to that possibility which hypertext has given them.

It's also interesting to consider ways in which various tropes of "bookness" will and won't (do and don't) find their counterparts in the electronic environment. Certain fundamental spatial and physical properties of the books which are essential to our reading/understanding are the finitude of the object—which orients us—and the punctum division of the page—exploited more in artists' books and commercial media than in the standard literary form. (Asked for an example of this physical orientation and its influence on reading, I offer the difference between the meaning ascribed to a sentence in a mystery/narrative when one is aware that there is 90 percent of the book left to read and that same sentence when the narrative has advanced to the point where there is a highly diminished volume of pages still to come.) In the "Corona Palimpsest" essay I wrote to accompany an exhibition of Nora Ligorano and Marshall Reese's piece of that name, the issue of the mutual interaction of the two domains—literal books and electronic media—is stated in terms of a "current tension of the book" which "reflects the present tense of electronic media coming into being." Neither escapes transformation in the process. Nor should it.

In my own experience, the Web is both useful and frustrating. A great source for information, research, and communication, it is very disorienting for me. I am attached to the spatial modes which print media offer as orientation. I despise the "scrolling screen" and the attempt to locate myself in a document by the position of the sidebar marker. As for surfing the web, I feel keenly aware that my dislike of the experience is directly linked to an "ethos" of time. The purely diversionary, time-consuming, open-endedness makes me crazy—and this, I know, is because I am attached to an equation in which time = labor = production. I can't let go of this enough to "enjoy" surfing, simply being "in" the experience of wandering through site after site. The potential of hypermedia to offer a newly shaped experience—one with spatial navigational coordinates—is terrific, and exciting, and satisfying to contemplate. But I want a bigger monitor and a better sense of the virtual physicality of that space in order to enjoy it.

Ultimately I don't believe in techno-determinism. My conviction is that technology appears when there is already a predisposition to be receptive to it. The desire for more communicative modes, commercial outlets, interconnected nodes of individual existence, and the escapist but also eclectic and available aspects of the electronic environment—these all seem in part to have been "prepared for" in advance of the general receptivity with which the Net has been received. There is an inevitability to the way in which this will affect us and offer specific tools and functions—but we all know it won't solve social problems, won't liberate us from our bodies, and won't magically lift us out of linear time or patterns of thought. We still experience the world in a moment to moment sequence of events, and still read that way as well, for the most part. The "forms" which will emerge won't, I don't think, replace print media for a long time—we're too attached to the intimacy and convenience of portable books and magazines—but the electronic forms will and already are allowing the popular imagination to reinvent its relation to the received traditions of reading, writing, and imagining. Don't you think?

One postscript: I would want to note that there are a few other people whose profiles as poets/writers parallel mine in their interest in visual poetry and its theoretical and historical dimensions—Steve McCaffery, as you know, is the most obvious one and he and I have a lot in common in that way. Others would include Susan Howe, the Australian Pete Spence, younger Canadian writers like Christian Bok and Darren Werschler-Henry, the late bpNichol, and the list could expand. My point isn't to try and give an exhaustive outline of all of these people—but to situate myself among a group of writers who have common interests so that my "uniqueness" such as it is, is qualified a bit by my own growing sense of a community of poets with shared concerns. The list of scholars is of course extensive also—as you know, so I won't even begin that.

2. MGK: We'll circle back around to electronic media, but I want to talk at some length about your writing and book art. You've said, "The original inspiration for exploring the potential of language as a material form came from the experience of 'holding language in my hands'— lines of letterpress type shaped in a composing stick whose weight and presence were as much physical as linguistic—and from looking at language in the world."[4] And indeed, much of your earliest letterpress work, such as *From A to Z* (1977)—which was the outcome of an attempt to "use each and every piece of type in the forty-odd drawers and use them once and only once and make a text which made sense"— directly confronted the material constraints of the medium.[5] You've also said that for a long time, you simply thought of yourself as "a writer whose interest in typograpy, printing, and experimentation made my work impossible for anybody but myself to publish."[6] But in 1980 you entered Berkeley's graduate program in Visual Studies and began reading critical theory. So who was important to you, and how did reading someone like Jacques Derrida, say, impact the earlier phenomenological premises of your printing and writing?

JD: Entering the graduate program at Berkeley didn't alter my basic conviction that my way of working with letterpress (and later, offset and computer generated typography and images) made it impossible for someone else to publish—or at least print—my book projects (for technical reasons), but it did provide theoretical, critical, and historical material on which to further develop those projects. *Against Fiction*, for instance, took its title from the work of Paul Feyerabend's *Against Method*, a book I encountered by stumbling into his class in my first year at school. But Feyerabend didn't exert much influence on me—I got to philosophy through French theory, as you suggest. The result of this exposure was twofold: I was able to conceptualize my work through those newly acquired theoretical ideas and I was able to understand some of the conceptual premises which had been latent in my earlier work.

Derrida's work provided insight into mark-making, the concept of the "trace," in its pedestrian actualized sense as well as in the more arcane philosophical domain. Lines, letters, and signs had been a major component of the visual art work I had done in the 1970s, so that theories of signification resonated profoundly for me. But I had very little immediate use for Derrida in terms of my creative projects. He was clearly disinterested in the more mundane aspects of writing as material and of the history of its visual forms—which were central to my various projects. That disinterest, however, became a point against which certain of my texts were written (*Through Light and the Alphabet* and *The Word Made Flesh* in particular). I thought, perhaps naively, that I could mount a refutation-through-demonstration in such projects—at least a counter-position in which materiality was pried loose from the slipping change of signifiers. I didn't expect this work would really have much effect on critical theory—though I did once send a copy of *Against Fiction* to Fredric Jameson (he never replied). The critical mix to which I was exposed between 1980 and 1986 was mainly dished up to me by my mentor in the French Department, Bertand Augst, a largely unpublished but terrifically inspiring teacher. Through him I was introduced to the full spectrum of critical theory—Roland Barthes, Michel Foucault, Sigmund Freud, Jacques Lacan, Roman Jakobson, Gerard Genette, and so on. I eschewed feminist theory for a long time—it was not until towards the end of my graduate career that I became interested in French and British feminism and the work of Julia Kristeva. I had tended to think of feminist theory as something akin to a theory disabilities act—a compensatory discourse designed to help the inadequate to deal with their limitations. Having initially believed that "writing could save me from being a woman" ("Writing with Respect to Gender," opening line), I had, not surprisingly, come to believe that theory could do the same. I think women in academia in the 1980s were intent on proving they could "do theory with the boys" as a way of asserting their intellectual credentials. Though I became well-steeped in the lineage of structuralist theory from Russian Formalism to French Deconstruction and Post-Structuralism, I didn't have a strong sense of cultural theory and Marxist critical theory until after grad school. Signification was for me a largely ahistorical issue, not exactly outside of culture, but never linked to it in specific ways at that point—ironic to me since now what I am most interested in considering is the way visual art and writing function as cultural practices.

It's odd to me to consider my earlier work as "phenomenological," though I can see how that makes sense in terms of the belief in materiality and its capacity to "be" as well as to "mean." In other ways I feel there was a strong systemic and structuralist bias to the pieces which emerged from the typecase—as if in some desperate attempt to wring "parole" free from the "langue" of normative discourse. There was certainly never much sense of essence or transcendence in my work, even if it was grounded in an encounter with material or the letterpress medium. Even now, for instance, as I am beginning work on a new printing project which is generated directly out of a lead font (unused, fresh from a foundry about twenty years ago, but still pristine), I don't see myself trying to get at its essential properties, but rather, see the project as exploring the tension between that which can be generated from its finite set and the language which strains at those limits.

3. MGK: On the Buffalo Poetics list a few months ago, Ron Silliman commented that in San Francisco in the seventies there was something of a split between people writing in ways that became identifiable as Language poetry, and artists and writers working in mixed media forms—visible/concrete poetries, or else sound or performance-oriented work. I was wondering what your own recollections and impressions of this period are. You spent much of the seventies and part of the eighties in the Bay area; you also worked as a typesetter at the West Coast Print Center from 1975-77 where you came into contact with poets from a variety of traditions. *From A to Z* documents some of your ambivalence toward this scene; for example, you record the spoken or unspoken challenge to your activities at the Print Center with a background in the visual arts rather than poetry: "How can you even presume to [write] without knowing the tradition." And your response: "Quick, tell me the differences among Olson, Williams, & Pound." How did such confrontations with "the tradition" affect your development as a writer in these settings? Likewise, you've described another early book, *Fragile* (1977), as "one of many struggles for recognition from the mainly male poetry community."[7] Could you expand on that statement?

JD: Well, the history of the San Francisco scene is deserving of a good old fashioned scathing *roman a cléf*—and I may yet write it! Certainly all of our memories of that era are quite different and highly subjective. When I first met Ron Silliman (through Barrett Watten) in 1975 or 1976, I was fairly uninformed about the traditions of modern poetry—and what I did know was French symbolism, Dada, and Surrealism, not the Anglo-American tradition. From my point of view, the Language poets (not even yet quite wearing that label, still trying it on, as it were) affirmed for me that what I was already doing with my writing was in fact part of something, and that it was legitimate. I had been isolated as a writer, thinking of myself as someone doing highly figured, dense prose. That's still how I think of myself—whether the work is rendered typographically or not, though of course different issues arise in the typo-pieces (or "typopoesis" as my friend, designer Gino Lee, says). As far as I remember, there weren't any other poets doing visual or "concrete" work (I've never connected myself with that latter term since it seems historically specific to me and refers to Brazilian and German/Swiss poets in particular)—I wonder who Silliman is thinking of. There was plenty of performance, video, and conceptual art going on, and a fine press and newly burgeoning artists' book scene. I always felt distinctly singled out for exclusion—especially from anthologies and magazines—on account of the visual dimension of my work. But in terms of readings, social life, and a sense of being part of the conversation, between 1975 and 1977 I felt very much involved. Then I left the Bay Area for two years to go to Europe. On the way, I stopped in New York for a book fair, met Charles Bernstein, Susan Bee, Abby Child, Bruce Andrews, Paul Zelevansky, Nick Piombino—and all in all found a far more enthusiastic reception among this group than I had ever found among my California peers. Their work was much closer in spirit to mine. Charles and Susan sometimes have suggested that it was just in the nature of the New York scene that there were already more crossovers among visual artists and poets and that my work didn't seem anomalous to them. By the time I went back to the Bay Area in 1979, the cliques and alliances had ossified, there were "poetry wars" raging, and I went to grad school instead of looking for a peer group among the poets.

4. MGK: On the first page of *The Century of Artists' Books* (1995) you state plainly, "In many ways it could be argued that the artist's book is *the* quintessential 20th-century artform." The volume that follows is essentially a substantiation of that assertion. Yet artists' books have not enjoyed a correspondingly broad public recognition. Marjorie Perloff, for example, in a recent essay entitled "Something is Happening, Mr. Jones," discusses the popularity of the National Gallery's Vermeer exhibition as example of the vitality of public interest in the arts. Now this

is probably an unfair comparison, not least because of complex questions as to the assignation of cultural capital to an artist like Vermeer, but still, it seems reasonable to expect that the *Dressing the Text* exhibition of artists' books now touring the country will not draw the same magnitude of lines and crowds. So why is it that one still has to explain the concept of an "artist's book" to most people? Likewise, in *The Visible Word* (1994) you make a very specific argument about how the consolidation and ossification of critical narratives of the modernist avant-garde served to discourage awareness of typographic experimentation in both the visual and the literary modernist traditions; can similar arguments account for most contemporary academic critics' limited awareness of artists' books? It occurs to me, for example, that the reception of Tom Phillips's *A Humument*, which is probably the best known artist's book, might make for an interesting case study.

JD: The problems which artists' books face don't seem to be based so much in critical resistance (though there is a bit of that) as in the "demographics" of the form. What I mean is that artists' books are difficult to exhibit, haven't found their niche in either the artworld (can't show them in a case very successfully) or the literary world (often they are too pictorial). They are comparable to video as an emerging media, and video is finding its greatest success these days by integrating itself into sculpture and installation works. Some book sculptures—works which reference the book as an icon or cultural artifact—have found a similar point of receptivity, but they are almost all works which have ceased to function as books.

The "bookness" of the book which artists' books attend to does raise a few critical issues. First, the familiar conventions of a book are often violated or ignored in a phenomenon I call the "no introduction" syndrome. With an object as conventional as a book, this is baffling to many first-time viewers. Second, books are time-based media. They unfold in sequence (fixed or not) over time, require a certain amount of attention, and can't be taken in in the "all at once glance" mode we have come to believe is the correct way of viewing visual art. Electronic media suffer from the same problem—exhibiting a CD-ROM or hypertext work in a gallery simply induces frustration and resentment on the part of many viewers. So, there is a critical issue at the core here which has to do with the discrepancy between expectations brought to the experience of art and the actual encounter with an artist's book. Artists' books, like all books, both provide and require an intimate experience which is hard to reconcile with public venues, mass audience, or display given their small scale, one-on-one format. I think this is an insurmountable problem, basically, but it doesn't keep artists' books from finding an audience (small), a home (private and public collections) and critical recognition (growing).

5. MGK: You've written that "[t]he single, conservative constant of my work is that I always intend for language to have meaning. My interest is in extending the communicative potential of writing, not in eliminating or negating it. While my work tends to go against established conventions of appearance of type on a page, this deviation is intended to call attention to the structure of those norms, as much as to subvert them." This seems absolutely essential to your concerns in a book such as *Against Fiction* (1983), which experiments with layout, fonts, and illustrations in order to dramatize the normally transparent homogeneity of the unmarked page. Likewise, in that book's first lines you seem to align conventional narrative with a "Gratifying hook INTO ATTENTION AND OBLIVION. AN OUTGROWN FORM, ADDICTIVE, SEDUCTIVE." Your own prose, semantically and syntactically difficult and complex, resists absorption, transparency, and everything we associate with the sensation of "losing yourself in the book." This seems to align your work with the sort of "impermeable" writing delineated by Charles Bernstein in his "Artifice of Absorption," as well as with some of the forms of "radical artifice" suggested by Marjorie Perloff in her book of that same name. But I wonder whether you ever find your self-described "conservative" investment in communication at odds with your affinities for more "radical" artifices. Also, as you know, novels were once widely condemned for corrupting their readers, especially when those readers were women who presumably couldn't understand the difference between fiction and reality. The tabloid form of the headlines you use—"ADDICTIVE, SEDUCTIVE"—seems to play on that; how does the gendered history of the "rise of the novel" affect your own attitudes toward writing fiction and narrative prose?

JD: Ultimately, after all, my work is prose-bound, prose-driven, prose-fed, and prose in its form. My sources were 19th and 20th century literature: novels, fiction, prose accounts and their mass media counterparts in film, television, and the photo-roman. I love fiction, find it addictive, won't let myself read it during the day, and keep thinking that I will, ultimately, manage to write those long fiction books which I dreamed of in my youth. In fact, as a very young writer—throughout my teens—I did write long fictional narratives with star-crossed lovers, long-lost relatives, and obscure parentage. I don't read the contemporary versions of these things—the Jacqueline Susann stuff is just too badly written to engage my imagination—but I do go back to a Trollope or an Austen from time to time with great gratitude and read lots of contemporary genre fiction, particularly mysteries. But this is all beside

Against Fiction, 1984, letterpress and linoleum, 10" x 13".

the point—which is, that having grown up believing I would indeed write such works, I matured into the very same group of Language poets mentioned above, only to find that as much as they disdained prose, they were virulent prohibitionists when it came to fiction. My addiction notwithstanding, I had the realization that fictional narrative was totally unacceptable within the emerging literary formations with which I was then identifying. Now I'm not so sure—my belief in "high" literature is somewhat tempered—I think literary work is important, but not the only thing which is viable or useful or even legitimate.

The conservatism of meaning to which I refer, however, has another aspect to it. There is a considerable amount of typographic work which is "experimental" in nature (mainly that means not aligned in straight rows!) which does not have an allegiance to linguistic meaning. It is, in that sense, about visual materiality as a means of creating effect or experience—the "phenomenal"—but can in no sense be "read." That sort of production always seemed gratuitous to me—since my engagement was with linguistic meaning, its limits and mutations, potential and transformation—not with leaving it behind. In that sense I would have to say that I do, absolutely, conform to the idea of "radical artifice" which Marjorie Perloff outlines. My conservatism is not so much in the form which communication takes, as in preserving communication as the fundamental function of linguistic texts. The paradox, as per my above statements, is that as a reader I am drawn to the "easy vehicle" of normative prose and as a writer I am continually tripped up in my attempt to write such work by the thick, clotting effects of language as it condenses into compelling figurative text. I love that density in other writers. A friend of mine, Marisa Januzzi, gave me a copy of Mina Loy's *Insel* about a year ago, and I was in absolute heaven feeling a close affinity with Loy's textual strategies. I do have a moral proscription against writing normative prose—I can't seem to let myself—though one critic/poet/friend once said she couldn't believe I would characterize my entire ouevre as a mere effect of language disorder which blocked my basic desire to write pulp. Well, nor could I, but these moral imperatives are not outside the realm of what determines the form of my work. And I do keep trying to write those long prose novels—both the normative and the "impermeable."

6. MGK: You've also said of *Against Fiction* that, "The text recorded a five year struggle with the desire to write fiction and the sense of its impos-

sibility in contemporary literary contexts." Could you expand on what you meant by that? Also, in a short piece entitled "Final Fiction" published in *Temblor* in 1986, you state: "On one level writing is always the thing in itself meeting the challenge of too many religious and radio revelations."[8] You seem to be suggesting that writing is a struggle against the homogenization of language, no? Let me also quote a paragraph from near the beginning of this piece, because it seems relevant and because it's good fun: "On the sidewalk a colony of newborns swarmed through the layers of debris. Their birth was a demonstration. Radical virtues pass intact through the hand to hand combat of mating. A spontaneous generation of spiders arose from the raw cheese. Every favorite substance was honored for at least a moment by the tentative groping of the newborn breed. Burst free from their little egg cells they hot-footed their hairy way across the fresh surface in an ecstasy of exploration. Their joy at finding themselves able to make movements resulted in a fanatical tracing of a maze of finely stepped lines into the soft substance. Clever little devils. They hardly knew themselves what they wrote, except that it sure wasn't fiction."[9]

JD: "Final Fiction" was written out of scraps left over from *Against Fiction*. Which is to say, that *Against Fiction* had arisen out of an accumulation of snippets and scraps written over a five year period in which I was trying to let myself write the fictional narratives which I was simultaneously editing out of existence; one little aborted novel after another. In shaping the text, I aligned the scraps according to their affinity with each other, thematically speaking (thus the subtitle, "Organized Affinities"—a play on Goethe, obviously, and structural rather than romantic). The finished manuscript was several hundred pages of unreadably dense, grey, prose. So I struggled with a format for it, came up with the progressive geometry of the *Against Fiction* pages and signatures, and proceeded to typeset and print it (about 800 hours worth of work, casually estimated). In the process, much of the prose was transformed—cooked down, reduced, to make it as dense as possible. There is still quite a bit of abstract, non-referential, meandering language in *Against Fiction*, but I was working towards the figurative density which shows up in that section of "Final Fiction" which you quoted. You can see, clearly, the evidence of critical theory in that work—the play set up between the marks made by the spiders and the assignation of meaning to them as "writing." My fascination with the alphabet, with the pleasure of mark-making, with the contrast between motivated and arbitrary signs — all of those show up in that passage. At the same time, the other phrase you cite demonstrates the never very hidden interest I have in tabloid and mass culture. Marjorie Perloff, in a recent review of my work, said she felt that the conspicuous recycling of the language(s) in my prose seemed to indicate my desire to wrest linguistic significance back from its banalization in mass media. I think that's true—and I don't think that that's in contradiction to the fact that I love the junk food brain fix of soap operas, tabloids, and made for tv mini-series. Quite the contrary, it's the fact that these forms work, that I do find them seductive, which fascinates me—I don't have critical disdain for them. I'm their ideal viewer, totally identified and immersed, inhabiting those cliches. It's just that in my work the clichés come out inverted, in some recombinant prose in which the mutation is neither parodic nor pastiched, rather, a marbled effect of compression, condensation, and displacement. The challenge is to preserve the imaginative interior life— and with it some illusion or actuality of subjective agency—or at the very least, to provide a contemporary linguistic experience which is both of and distinct from that which the media matrix provides.

7. MGK: *The Word Made Flesh* (1989) is one of your best known letterpress works, and it demonstrates many of your most characteristic gestures: suggesting meaning through the spatial proximity and orientation of words and letter-forms as well as using visual cues like point sizes, colors, and fonts to encourage non-linear reading practices. Each page (except the very first) is dominated by a single broad, dense, almost corpulent black letter-form—progressing sequentially through the book, we realize they combine to spell the title phrase—around which other linguistic units gather and accumulate, these arrangements becoming more complex the deeper we move into the book. After the fifth opening, the visual field of the page becomes further complicated by the addition of a matrix of evenly spaced red letters which constitute their own distinct—though not disconnected—textual event. The volume as a whole is prefaced with the phrase *a l'interieur de/u la langue/age*, but in all of this I find a work concerned with the psychology of reading as much as with the psychology of the word. Do you have any interest in cognitive approaches to spatial form and pattern recognition, and their application to our biological—embodied—processing of visual information, such as textual forms? This sort of thing also seems very relevant

to your interest in a thinker such as Wittgenstein and the relationship between visual or linguistic signs and "the real," if real here is understood in terms of the embodied mind's operations on language—Wittgenstein himself being influential to certain branches of cognitive science.

JD: I'm afraid my answer to the question of cognitive science and approaches to spatial form and pattern recognition will disappoint you—I just don't know that material at all, though I am interested. So maybe you can send a bit of a "starter" reading list for me. It tailors into my current concerns—which, in fact, emerged in part from the "Wittgenstein's Gallery" piece, as you may or may not know. That piece exists only as a set of drawings/works on paper (on slides too) and a text. I've exhibited it, but not published it, which is fine since it was rather preliminary in certain ways. But as far as I understand what you are getting at, here's the common point of departure: I was interested in "Wittgenstein's Gallery" in a "Visual Investigations" which might have parallels with his philosophical ones. According to what conventions of pictorial form do we process visual experience as knowledge and in so doing, show both the limits of the conventions to accomodate the experiential and the conceptual while also gaining insights into the nature of conventions themselves? Because pictorial conventions are so much more fluid, mutable, and less available to a systematic structural analysis than linguistic ones, this is a different kind of problem. So I made my problem set out of thinking through the mis-match between conventions in syntax/grammar/language and visual form. A concrete example, for instance, was to take the concept of spatial relations indicated by prepositions and think about ways in which these can be indicated in visual, diagrammatic terms. Which they can and can't—that is, the images which show "in" or "between" might also show all kinds of other things incidentally as part of the process—images don't delimit their domain of signification as neatly as words and we are all too familiar with ways in which words are already problematic in that realm.

So, between that "Wittgenstein's Gallery" project and my current interest in AI and logic, visual analysis, machine vision, etc., I have become more curious about whether one could begin to articulate the conceptual parameters according to which a model of artificial vision could be structured. This is what I call my "beyond David Marr" project. I'm sure there's tons of recent work in this area, but David Marr's

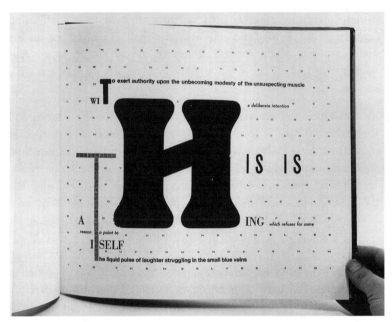

The Word Made Flesh, 1989, letterpress, 12 1/2" x 10 1/2".

posthumously published keywork in this field hit certain conceptual impasses in trying to make the leap towards the ways perceived visual data can be analysed and the intellectual frameworks which are used to make cognitive sense of this data.

But I have a feeling this is a long way from where you were wanting to go with the question about *The Word Made Flesh*. When I made that book, in 1988-89, I wasn't thinking at all about AI, though I did do the "Wittgenstein's Gallery" project the same spring. I was just seduced by those huge, beautiful wood letters which spell out the title, and wanted to make something with them, and of course, make a text in which materiality was the referent as well as the conspicuous formal property of the piece. It was my "no transcendence" work. The plane of reference is supposed to be collapsed with the plane of discourse. Though, of course, it can't be.

8. MGK: *Simulant Portrait* (1990) is the auto/bio/monography of Sim-one, the prototype of a phylum of artificial life known as the "Sims." It is a portrait of, in the words of Sim-one's biographer—who is one of several textualized presences embodied by the book—"an unlived life,

versions of a life she thought she'd lived, written out by herself, almost." Or, "a life lived as information," as the book has it elsewhere, for unlike the Generics before them, Sims are possessed of a personal memory and identity. To what extent was your work in this book influenced by the "ironic political myth" of Donna Haraway's now-famous "Cyborg Manifesto"? Were there specific interventions in feminist/ cyborg theory that you were attempting to make? You also play with notions of documentation and the construction of historical records, themes which have been in your work since *Twenty-Six '76 Let Hers* (1976) and *From A to Z*. In *Simulant Portrait*, you write: "And the blank space of the past, from which she had been, of course, conspicuously absent, reverberated with the strange insertion of her consciousness into its strictures and orthodoxies. That was what we had not counted on—that of course the entire of history would change, reorganize, shift with the domino effect of copy in the file suffering the entry of new material on its early pages. Alignments altered radically. The paper clips and rubber bands fell from the files. Her literal body burst into view. The metaphors of weave, texture, warp and woof all strained to the limits and finally dispersed."

But this passage, which seems to want to be read as a moment of embodied presence trumping *différance*, also speaks to the artifact of the actual book itself, for despite all of the text's commitment to partiality and fragmentation in its representational strategies (both narratively and graphically), we are ultimately left with a cohesive material object in our hands, no?

JD: The odd thing is that I didn't know anything about Donna Haraway when I came up with my *Simulant* project—in fact, *Simians, Cyborgs, and Women* has a publication date of 1991, a year after I had published *Simulant Portrait*—and when I heard about it and her work, I sent her a copy of my book. So, there is no influence at all of Haraway in this book; instead, I think there may be certain issues in feminist theory which were common points of reference. I remember my major feminist litany at that point was "how to become subjects of our own discourse, of our own desire?" The centrality of both language and sexuality in that question was brought on by my, at that point, raging rejection of Lacanian psychoanalysis in its formulation of the "feminine." Having bought into it wholesale in the late 1980s, I was interested when a number of my women students began to look at me like I was from another planet as

I explained the concept of "lack" to them—and the organization of sexual identity in relation to that silly "phallus" which is always and never exactly what it is. So, *Simulant* came out of feminist theory and art, not out of cyborg theory—which I didn't know much about. Like *The History of the/my Wor(l)d*, *Simulant* is very much about the place of the female subject in history and the capacity of women to find/make their own personal histories as well as to be part of History in the broader sense.

As for blank spaces and text, fragmentation and archives, history and books—there is another odd background element here. I had been working at the time on my (still languishing) biography of Ilia Zdanevich, or Iliazd. That project had been extremely satisfying from the point of view of research process. I had met Hélène Zdanevich and in working with her on the biography we took as our point of departure a set of sheets which had served as the basis of a chronology. Comprised of a list of short statements such as "March 10-14—went to Venice," these sheets led us back into an elaborate archive of materials on Iliazd's books, personal life, research projects, and intellectual activity. A single line might lead to a whole journal, a packet of letters, a railway ticket, or any of almost infinitely varied items in the boxes Hélène had in Iliazd's studio. Given my propensity for fetishizing the documentary

Simulant Portrait, 1990, offset printed, 7 1/4" x 8 1/2".

nature of archives, this was pure pleasure to me—unlike the made-up documents of the *A to Z* project—which, after all, I had invented because I was so envious of Alastair Johnston's archival work on his book on the Auerhahn Press. In working on Iliazd, I became interested in the tension between archival documents and synthetic, descriptive prose text. *Simulant* is a hybrid—part pseudo-document, part syntho-prose, and stopped short of archival miscellany production.

I was also inspired by the work of Dennis Wheatley—who made documentary mysteries in the 1930s—stories he told entirely through a collection of papers which were printed to resemble (or actually be) the "documents in the case." Reading through the portfolio, one assembled the clues. Though bound within paper wrappers, his work has always served as an exemplary model of the hypertext archive in my mind. In principle, there is no fixed limit—one can continually expand the file by tracing out a character's life history, idiosyncracies, or any of a number of other narrative or non-narrative threads of connection from the basic story. But the fetish-y quality of this production seemed too cute to me for *Simulant*, too contrived, so I settled on this middle ground of discrete texts within a related mode of production. But the boundedness of the book—the finitude of the object—is another issue. In a one-of-a-kind project I did in 1984-85, *Mind Massage* (which also has sci-fi themes), references within the main book text gave rise to a group of other book objects. So, a character's reference to a story would be linked to an actual book in the same box, a secondary text, which the reader could choose to read at any point. All the bits fit into a single box container, but weren't bound into a single book. The hypertext aspect is pretty obvious, though of course in 1984 that wasn't exactly a current term. To me a book is defined by its boundedness and finitude; against these limits the fragment gains its identity and definition, but I find the potential of linkage highly useful.

9. MGK: In *The History of the/my Wor(l)d* (1990), which counterbalances an almost overbearingly grand, sweeping historical narrative with a more intimate text, some of your longstanding concerns with the discrepancies between public and private experience, history and autobiography, and the relationship between writing and reality come together. The book communicates through three distinct planes of referentiality (text, images, and conspicuous diacritical markings), all of which are mutually expressive of and responsive to one another; and, as in many

of your books, color coding, font sizes and proportions, and the spatial proximities (and disjunctions) of words, images, and icons all likewise carry information about the text's topology. Marjorie Perloff has also noted that this book represents your first foray into collage—its images were "found" at Harvard's Bow and Arrow Press where it was printed.[10] The subtlety and richness of your design work on every page here seems like a good opportunity to ask you to open a window onto some of your compositional practices. I'm not asking you to adjudicate among possible meanings or interpretations; rather, I'm interested in your remarks on some of the design decisions you self-consciously made in laying out and printing the book. Perhaps we could do this through close attention to the visual dynamics of one or two particular openings.

JD: The visual structure of *History* is meant to parallel the verbal text, usually acting utterly independently of two large narratives in red and black. The premise on which I began was that I would simply arrange the images as they came to hand from boxes of found cuts at the Bow and Arrow Press where I was working (thanks to the largesse of Gino Lee and Jim Barondess). I would write the "history" which was suggested by the images. I didn't do this, in fact, but did much rearranging of visual components to create visual puns and resonances on the pages. Sometimes there are obscure jokes in the visuals—as in the very first

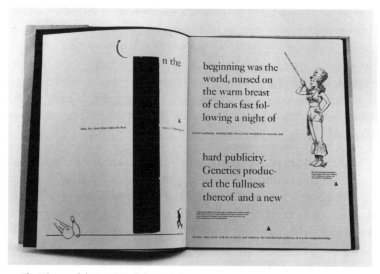

The History of the/my Wor(l)d, 1989, letterpress, 10" x 13".

opening where the bowling ball colliding with a pin is to suggest the "big bang" theory of the origin of the universe in an irreverent counterpoint to the already undermined-by-parody lines of Genesis which open the book.

The second opening is a good example of the visual play in the book: I decided to use the image which looks like a Sunday school book illustration to anchor the captions in my own family history ("a brother or [and] two sisters"). To amplify the workshop feel, I put the hammer next to it, punning with "labor" in the caption and the depiction of carpentry. To forge a visual alliance, I put the eyedropper on the right page into diagonal alignment with the hammer, but the decision to use the dropper had been suggested by the drop-like shape suspended above the mysterious bit of machinery in the center of the page. These rhyme well with the "waters" of the large black text. The horseshoe crab was a natural match, reiterating both the shape of the "drop" globe and the idea of marine life and water. It sits right at the base of the triangle formed by the hammer and dropper—thus activating the whole opening across these diagonal connections. The diacritical marks fill out the page, defining the full space, mass, volume of the active area and also, in the case of the dropper and hammer, give them a stability through the use of a vertical axis. They're subtle, the diacritics, but they provide structure without adding too much content to the pages.

Sometimes the connections among images are obvious—in the next opening all images are "batons"—the arrow, wand, or long pipe. In some cases it's the literal content which puns—as in the opening where the large red telescope is aimed at the tunnel in the earth into which two men are peering with surveying equipment. Often it's just a matter of echoing shapes—as in the opening beginning "a virus of civility . . ." where the open penknife echoes the fretwork of the cranes and the spindly diagrammatic image of the townscape. In every case, my intention was to let the images create their own relations, complement each other, and give each other an identity or emphasis through the contrast or interconnection. This is particularly true in the next to last opening where, for instance, there is a pair of women figures—one a classical nude and the other a burlesque looking figure with a rolling pin. The closeness in size and level of detail made them a perfect match. Likewise, the idea of progressing from the teeny, tiny, buffalo on the top of the right hand page (captioned as "Plankton") to the huge trout-like fish at the bottom simply took advantage of the scale of the found cuts to make a visual joke. The images are a separate level of discourse, however, and function through their links to each other and through inflections of the captions, rather than as illustrations in the conventional sense. There is no *a priori* sense of a signified or referential field to which they must adhere—they come into the book as self-sufficient elements, primary, not secondary, with respect to the whole.

10. MGK: *Narratology* (1994) is one of your most recent and most ambitious books. On one of its first pages, you "define" narratology as "[t]he stories according to which the possibilities of living a life gained access to the psychic theater staging the imaginary events as real." The book itself is a compendium of visual and linguistic riffs on different flavors of genre fiction (historical romance, sweet romance, science fiction, horror, adventure, glitz, etc.), all presented on pages of varying sizes and placement, so that "the revelation of the text elements . . . occur through covering/uncovering portions of a page in turn."[11] (All of this, from the title on down, strikes me as a send-up of orthodox structuralism.) You also note that the edition of 70 copies (each of which includes twenty-five drawings water-colored by hand) required 1000 hours of work, distributed over three years (exclusive of the actual writing). In commenting on the book, you've written, "And then I realized that the narratives according to which I believed my life would be lived had come from genre fiction. Genre fiction—books with attractive covers, embossed, foil stamped, and bearing vivid images. Available in supermarkets, airline terminals, train stations, malls. Except that I had never been allowed to read any. Allowed by whom? By myself of course . . . I felt a strong taboo against reading them. I mean they were bad, bad literature."[12]

All of this also seems very relevant to your earlier comments on your own prose style and your attempt to resist and/or reveal the homogenization and commodification of language in the media's sphere: ". . . I love the junk food brain fix of soap operas, tabloids, and made for tv mini-series. Quite the contrary, it's the fact that these forms work, that I do find them seductive, which fascinates me—I don't have critical disdain for them. I'm their ideal viewer, totally identified and immersed, inhabiting those clichés. It's just that in my work the cliches come out inverted, in some recombinant prose in which the mutation is neither parodic nor pastiched, rather, a marbled effect of compression,

DOMESTIC

His tongue protruded through the mucous membrane of her emotional defenses, taking the plunge which ripped her heart loose from its bearings. Pressing home his advantage he manuevered the lip service to contractual arrangements as carefully into place as his keys in his jeans were wedged to advertise the other advantages he had recently grown into. But the story on the late breaking news did not include the reversal of fortune she had suffered by being forced to remain after school these long afternoons without adequate transportation. Deep bitterness accumulated behind the dam of blocked movement as she stayed trapped between the seasons of vacation and the seasons of unrest. Splinters from a pier she'd known in the intimate proximity of childhood now rose to the surface of the skin, begging to be let free from the wounds into which they had found their way.

APPARATUS

TROPHY WIFE TO A CANNIBAL
Rise to the occasion little dove of my heart, and let us rejoice in the efficiency of the loaded cartridge which replays the old relief effort before our eyes. Projected on the screen it hid the house that hid our crumbling hopes and threw the global scale of the disaster back into a domestic frame while it shook the foundations of our intimate relations to their molten core.

Narratology, 1994, letterpress and watercolor, 10″ x12″.

condensation, and displacement. The challenge is to preserve the imaginative interior life—and with it some illusion or actuality of subjective agency—or at the very least, to provide a contemporary linguistic experience which is both of and distinct from the media matrix."

But let me reduce my meanderings here to something you'll hopefully be able to take off from: in *Narratology* and other work, you seem to be inverting the fundamental tenets of metafiction—it's not that all the stories have been exhausted and so the only possibility we are left with is to write about the impossibility of reading and writing, but rather that the stories have exhausted our own capacity for expression so one must write through them in order to reclaim a language with which to communicate. Would you agree with that, and if so, why is it that the "high postmodernism" which metafiction exemplifies (and I'm thinking of writers like Calvino, Robbe-Grillet, Cortazar) is not compelling to you, at least in your creative undertakings?

JD: It's true that I have less affinity for the self-conscious tropes of "high postmodernism" than I might—but that is for a combination of reasons. One's own self-perception is always a point of departure for encountering any work in the world, and though the arena I was operating in was miniscule (if it can be called an arena at all) when I produced *From A to Z* in 1977, I felt resentful of the attention paid in the mainstream to works whose contrivances seemed more obvious and less complex or dense than my own. This was adolescent hubris, obviously, combined with an absence of any sense of reality. At this point, I'm much more sympathetic and curious when it comes to someone like Cortazar. But the crucial point of difference is, as you clearly point out, that the metafictional self-consciousness of writing about writing which is fundamental to much of what constitutes the paradigm of postmodern fiction was not aligned with my approach. I had a different set of questions, I think, having inhabited the fictions of classic 18th and 19th century form, having lived in them and been formed by them. It was getting to this issue which motivated the continual return to the narrative, to the sense of the ways expectations about and responses to the actuality of unfolding events in my own experience could be processed according to those already in place patterns. This segues into the next question, obviously.

The issue of form, however, is what is in focus here, and the ways in which certain rhetorical devices—what in Gerard Genette's terms would be called "discourse markers" or features of discursive form,— became subject matter in postmodernism; my own formal interests were with the rhetoric of narrative, I think, though the discursive was certainly a topic of investigation in typographic format. The "how" of the construction was something I addressed more at the level of the book's arrangement of elements, structures, and layout than inscribed in the text. You'll notice in *From A to Z* that a number of the parodic texts take the "this is being written as I write it" as a point of departure. The self-conscious attention to process as subject matter had become so banal in the late 1970s, especially among some of the writers I was close to, that it didn't have much imaginative appeal. It seemed like a major "so what?" at that point. I think I was never really interested in the kind of distancing which such work produces (or aims at), as I was in engagement.

11. MGK: I'd like to push you a bit on the relationship between "lived experience" and its representation in written forms of language. This is a concern that seems to span the range of your work, from the bicentennial *Twenty-Six '76 Let Her's*—your earliest typographically experimental book, which is your cryptic account of a four-day visit to Los Angeles—on up through *Narratology*. You've written on the theoretical underpinnings of lived experience in the context of this latter work: "Sometime in the last couple of years, critical theory embraced the concept of 'lived experience'. This was intended as a guerilla action to upstage theory, to challenge the concepts of 'the mediated,' 'constructed,' and 'semiotic' models of experience (and representation) which had become the evil dominatrices and terminators of academic writing. This assertion of the Lived was that it was real, direct, available—and more authentic than all this structuralist, poststructuralist, and deconstructive blah-blah."[13]

With regard to the writing of *Narratology*, you go on to say: "It didn't work. There was no real in all this; all the referents slipped away as fast in this rendering as in any other."[14] In *The Current Line* (1996), you're even more succinct: "Experience never had a chance against language." On the other hand, in a book like *Through Light and the Alphabet* (1986), you begin with this: "All our conversations were in language and according to conventions others could be party to, but this one took off on its own trajectory to mind the business being left out of the accounts. The world was too amorphous for repose inside of sweet articulation." So are these differing accounts of the relationship between language and (lived) experience contradictions that you've deliberately sustained throughout your work, or do they reflect changing points of view?

JD: There are two aspects to the notion of the "lived" as I currently understand it. One, which is the more prevalent, is the assertion of a base of experience as a base of authority. This is a political assertion which is extremely problematic since it assumes a fully conscious, self-constituting subject rather than a socially constituted position of subjectivity. The subject of the "lived" seems to exist outside of any psychoanalytic model, to take the experiential at face value, and to deny much of the work of fantasy, drives, desire—in fact, the entire apparatus of the unconscious. Nonetheless, as a place from which to challenge the authority of the elite culture which produced a theoretical discourse of subjectivity which, by its jargoned turgidity and textual opacity, excluded many people, it made sense. When I set myself the problem of "looking for the lived," I quickly realized that it couldn't be separated out from the fantasmatic. That for me at least, the sense of what constitutes experience is so bound up in the effects of the psyche upon its production that there was no independent base of "lived" experience. That is of course the premise of *Narratology* as cited in your question above. The tension between the positions of lived versus constructed are nicely outlined in terms of historical debates in Great Britain in the introduction to Victor Burgin's new book, *In/Different Places*—where he traces the emergence and dialogue of what he calls "culturalists" (advocates of the lived) and "structuralists" (those of the constructed).

But the second notion of the lived is grounded in a more fundamental conviction I have about the relation between various aspects of perception and the strictures of systematic representation. This relation is most evidently conflicted in the contrast between visual experience and linguistic form. There are many ways in which we process visual data which have no linguistic correlate—from the perception of highly nuanced modulations of color to the process by which we recognize a familiar form, person, space, place through the tiniest of visual clues. A strict adherent to language as the primary mode of mental activity (sorting, typing, cataloguing, organizing, etc., our perceptions into meaningful thought) would of course assert that what is happening is that a translation is being made. I know absolutely this isn't true, and that much of what I experience exists outside of language. I won't say outside of culture, because the whole way in which we hierarchize information to survive, the way we establish what is to be perceived, is so culturally coded that it would seem pointless to make such an assertion. But those cultural codes are not so highly articulated or evident in some domains as they are in others. I would never argue that the "visual" is unregulated, but I would say its regimes of ordering are distinct from those of language. This is the "world" which is "too amorphous for repose inside of sweet articulation." Obviously, I am always battling this—even in myself—and thus the counter-remark in *The Current Line* about "[e]xperience never having had a chance against language" which comes down so strongly on the side of condemning the cultural hegemony for its eliminative, coercive, controlling strictures.

12. MGK: I'd like to ask you about maps, and whether you take any interest in them as visual/verbal forms. I bring this up partly out of self-indulgence—maps fascinate me, though I have only an amateur's knowledge of cartography. But it seems to me that maps can very effectively demonstrate the fundamentals of visible language: words and letters are deployed to quite literally occupy space. I also notice that the relationship between textuality and cartography seems to be a minor but persistent theme in some of your work. I think of *Bookscape* (1986-8), which you've described as a reflection of "the postmodern object-oriented architecture of Dallas," or else *Otherspace* (1992), which contains images of Martian maps and is subtitled *"Martian Tylopography."* Likewise, a book like *The Word Made Flesh* seems to me very cartographically oriented, at least in so far as it experiments with our sense of scale and uses arrangements of letter forms to create typographic contours on the page. Are you aware of any historical points of convergence among the various technologies associated with cartography, writing, and printing?

JD: It is the process of mapping spatial and temporal arrangements onto the structure of the book/page—rather than a literal engagement with maps—which has shown up in my work. At this moment I have a student—Tim McCormick—who is doing his senior project on the theme of landscape as a model for typographic legibility in electronic documents. He has been synthesizing materials on topographic modelling, print versions of maps, landscapes, and cityscape imagery, theories of intertextuality, and the "disorientation" problem which currently plagues hypermedia as the basis for a final project which will be a "panoramic" projection of the research in typographic format. The concept of a "horizon" as an organizing line from which other elements can be read coherently provides a framework for what, eventually, will be a spatialized domain of language. He's interested in the practical application of this idea, rather than using it to generate artistic or poetic expression.

I find this exciting since it involves the integration of a visual logic, with all its analogue to optical experience and historical conventions, into new media. It's clear that the mobility through planes of representation—the various cuts through an axonometric sequence (or even "planes" receding through a perspectively constructed field)—is potentially greater in the electronic environment than in printed documents with their opacity, single plane surface, and fixed relations of elements within that surface. But the conceptualization of spatial relations—including, of course, a temporal axis within modular units—is a very ready extension of the visual conventions with which we are long familiar. The first work in which I attempted to use typographic format to represent a spatial/temporal field was actually *Twenty-Six '76*—the book about my trip to Los Angeles with Jim Petrillo and Betsy Davids in 1976. The sequence of pages in that work are each, in a sense, supposed to be schematic diagrams of moments in time as projected onto a picture plane, then sequenced into the book as pages (planographic slices along a temporal plane). That work is so abstract and obscure that it may not read that way—and there was no self-conscious attempt to make the pages "read" through/against each other as a whole since I did structure them each uniquely (though themes, motifs, etc. repeat). I am doing an issue of *A-Bacus* this fall and would like to revisit this idea in a new work.

The apocryphal tale I sometimes tell, and you can believe it or not if you like, is that when I was six my parents took me on a trip to Europe with my older brother and younger sister. For three and a half months we travelled in Great Britain, France, Switzerland, Italy, Israel, and then back (crossing the Atlantic in both directions by boat). When I returned to Philadelphia, my recollection is that I said to myself, "Thank god, I finally have something to write about." And then I wrote a five and a half page piece for the school newspaper, *The Chatterbox*, about the trip in which the distribution of text on the page matched my memory of the way the time of the trip had been distributed through the various geographical locations. While this may or may not be true, it has become a point of reference for me in terms of understanding the "space" of the page, text, and book as a structural form—and of my own self-consciousness about it.

In the 1980s when I was doing my graduate work, I found my institutional home in the College of Environmental Design. I had already done quite a bit of travelling by then—and had written the book on Italy, with its poem on the Netherlands (*Italy*, The Figures, 1980), as well as the Greek book (unpublished), so I was well disposed towards reading about "place" and landscape in theoretical terms. When I spent a year in Paris in 1984-85 I began a letterpress project which was to integrate two experiences—that of getting to know the city and that of expanding my limited French in the context of linguistic immersion. This was a topographic piece—but I never finished it—someplace in a print shop near La Bastille there's a galley of undistributed type shoved way back into the dark corners of a galley cabinet.

When I moved to Dallas I was struck by the unfamiliarity of the landscape—not just its seventies boom architecture and soulless mall sensibility. I found myself continually disoriented—as if the coordinate points shifted in relation to each other as well as to the perceiver as one moved through. This idea of a continual realignment of elements was what provided part of the inspiration for the *Bookscape*—though that work is also about the relations between the presumed closure of a book form and the openness of textual play.

As for technologies, of course there are many points of convergence—probably most explicit in the elaborate engravings of the 17th and 18th centuries. I think of the work of Athanasius Kircher, for instance, with its exquisite articulation of the late medieval cosmological hierarchies struggling to accomodate the structures of modern thought. His literal and encyclopedic sensibility is satisfyingly organized even at the moment at which the belief that one could, in actuality, mirror the structure of the "world" in a representational system is already starting to be transformed by empiricism. The work of his (barely) contemporary, Bishop John Wilkins, provides the complement—his *Essay on the Real Character* being the outline of all knowledge in a kind of modern Aristotelianism. The contrast between the diagrammatic Wilkins and the pictorially structured Kircher is useful since it seems to have a contemporary analogue in AI research—the question which continues to intrigue us all being, of course, what are the relations between formal structures of representation and thought?

If by technologies you mean something more literal, then, again, I think engraving (and manuscript) are the technological modes which most closely approach the electronic in the flexibility they accord to interactions between visual and verbal modes. Since in an engraving each letter is "drawn" and in a photoshop document each "word" can be treated as an image—these are closer in their ontological condition of production than they were in letterpress printing—where, of course, words and images are different orders in every respect—technologically and conceptually.

In my limited experience of virtual spaces I have experienced some of the same kind of disorientation I experienced with the Dallas landscape—the sense that as one turns one's head one doesn't simply get a different view through elements fixed in space, but that the coordinates mapping the space realign along the perspectival axis of vision. This added change creates a sense of vertigo for me—I want to be able to distinguish between the experience of looking around in a stable space and that of remaking or creating space along a virtual sightline.

13. MGK: You've already talked some about the exhibition entitled "Wittgenstein's Gallery," a series of some one hundred and twenty-five watercolor and ink images which "takes up Wittgenstein's investigation of the idiosyncratic character of language and its independence from the world by applying the same principles of investigation to the convention of visual images and their lack of relation to the 'real.'" Some of these same images also appear as illustrations in your most recent fiction, *Dark Decade* (1995). Is there a formal or critical connection between these two works? *Dark Decade*, for example, is a very acute critique of the current mediascape and the detachment of the language and images of the media from anything remotely recognizable as "real."

Also, I notice that in your drawing and painting you have a tendency to depict people, human figures (I'm thinking of *Against Fiction*, *Just As* (1983), *Narratology*, and others, as well as *Dark Decade*); this seems to correspond on some level to your interests in autobiography, biography, and novelistic character. Are there specific conventions and techniques of visual representation—portraiture, the photo ID, the talking head—in which you're attempting to intervene in the same way that your writing and book-making intervenes in various linguistic and bibliographic conventions?

JD: I think there is a bit of confusion here because in fact the images in "Wittgenstein's Gallery" are very different from those in *Dark Decade* or the other books you mention, but they were exhibited together in a show I did at Barnard College in New York in 1991. They are often figurative, but far more simple, structured to prove certain points: a drawing of a coffee mug in several different modes/styles as a way to demonstrate the difficulty of putting emotional codes into graphic language; some diagrammatic drawings of interlocking blocks with arrows as an interrogation of prepositional relations in visual terms, and so forth. The *Dark Decade* images, and the images in *Against Fiction, Simulant Portrait* (the only one with photographs), and *Narratology* are all figurative because they quote various genres or media: newspapers, wire service photos, women's magazine images, and pulp fiction illustrations respectively. So those images are self-consciously parodying and imitating such modes.

I had produced drawings and paintings throughout the 1970s—I graduated art school in 1972, had a show in 1973, and went on to make drawings, pastels, oil paintings, and even an etching book—all in an "organic minimalist" sensibility. The book was done in Amsterdam, sold to various museums there, and found its way into a few American collections also, though I can't remember which ones—it's called *Experience of the Medium*. I pretty much stopped doing that work by the late 1980s—I couldn't see where it was going to go in the world, had become involved with academic life, and keeping up my creative writing practice was more important to me than drawing. I taught drawing for quite a few years as well—and I lived with it as a daily activity. But basically I find making visual art boring on account of the repetitive and time-consuming aspect while writing seems capable of synthesizing more information for me, letting me process anything through it.

So, you're right that the images in the works you mention DO attempt the same kind of intervention as the texts—an appropriation and transformation of clichés, tropes, and modes of production.

14. MGK: Most of your printing has been in letterpress, but you've also occasionally worked in offset in such books as *Just As* (1983), *Simulant Portrait*, and *Otherspace*. Originally a technique of mass production, you've written that offset artists' books "offer an alternative to the mainstream of mass media's hegemonic control over texts and images . . . offset extends an industrial process into the territory of fine art printing, calling into question the terms of finite production, especially the limited edition so central to that tradition."[15] You've also interestingly characterized offset printing as a nostalgic activity, at least in relation to electronic media, for the process is essentially one of reconstituting stored text and image data in material form: "When electronic media give up their nostalgic need for life in material, then the mechan-

ical processes of offset printing will lose their industrial function and perform some new metaphysical practices of smooth running in an aesthetic dream."[16] Given that a PC with sofware such as Photoshop and Quark costs significantly less than offset equipment, does on-line electronic publishing promise anything of the above-mentioned "smooth running aesthetic dream"? What can small presses, 'zines, and individual writers and artists involved in on-line publishing learn from the history of offset and other alternative printing practices, mimeo/xerox for example?

JD: I'm not sure I think of offset as nostalgic—the idea that there is a nostalgia for "life in material" is not a characteristic of that printing mode as much as an aspect of the current increased awareness of materiality which seems to derive from a response to the idea of a relatively immaterial electronic environment. Offset has always suffered in the print and book world from a dimished perception of its actual material specificity. Because it is seen primarily as a mode of reproduction rather than production, and because of its character as a planographic rather than relief mode of printing, it has tended to disappear rather than be granted any aesthetic quality or virtue. This of course has implications for the economic valuation of its products and one of the points I was emphasizing in "Work" was the effacement of the labor involved in the offset process. This is also a problem in electronic documents which are in many cases extremely time consuming to produce and yet do not net any clear return on that labor. While the Net and other venues for distribution of electronic documents will solve certain of the logistical problems which faced small press printers and publishers in the past (getting the product out to an interested audience), these won't resolve the economic dilemmas. Certainly production costs in terms of paper, printing, binding, and so forth are reduced, but not the actual work investment. Since most small press publisher/printers didn't make much money off their work anyway, this isn't a huge change, but it sets up a situation in which there will never be any inventory to sell off if and when it accrues value.

Desktop publishing combines the tasks of what used to be an entire design and production team into the work of a single person—who can now be the writer, designer, layout person, camera person, and so forth. The problem is that so few people have the training to perform these jobs adequately that there are all kinds of aberrant things which happen. Not understanding production in a traditional darkroom environment can make an individual's electronic camerawork into something which can't really be printed effectively. WYSIWYG is an enormous fiction unless one is going directly to electronic output—and for publishing in any volume this is still not cost effective. You couldn't produce a *New York Times Sunday Magazine* using laser color printers—or even a small edition of a children's book. Once you get over fifty to a hundred copies, the time and money involved don't really pay off. The newest innovations in the printing industry are offset presses hooked directly to computer terminals—a Heidelberg press which produces four color copies within several impressions (thus approximating the paper use efficiency of a xerox machine). But for high volume offset is an industry standard likely to remain for quite some time. Most people using desktop publishing have never been introduced to the concept of designing from the production backwards—thinking about the output first instead of last. This is a conceptual problem, not just a production problem, since it determines the choices about the ways in which the design of a document evolves.

15. MGK: In *The Visible Word*, you distinguish between the marked and unmarked page: The basic distinction between marked and unmarked typography occured simultaneously with the invention of printing. Gutenberg printed two distinctly different kinds of documents which embodied the characteristic features of what evolved into the two distinct traditions. On the one hand he printed bibles, with their perfectly uniform grey pages, their uninterrupted blocks of text, and without headings or subheadings or any distraction beyond the occasional initial letter. These bibles are the archetype of the unmarked text, the text in which the words on the page "appear to speak for themselves" without the visible intervention of author or printer. Such a text appears to possess the authority which transcends the mere material presence of words on a page, ink impressions on parchment. By contrast, the Indulgences which he printed displayed the embryonic features of marked typography. Different sizes of type were used to hierarchize information, to create an order in the text so that different parts of it appear to "speak" differently, to address a reader whose presence was inscribed at the outset by an author in complicity with the graphic tools of a printer who recognized and utilized the capacity of typographic representation to manipulate the semantic value of the text through visual means.[17]

This passage provides a historical underpinning for not only your own work, but also for the poetics of Steve McCaffery (who, with bp Nichol, articulated likeminded ideas in *Rational Geomancy*), as well as Bernstein, Howe, and any number of other contemporary poets or artists who ground their work in principles of visual materiality. And, this recent activity is itself an extension or transformation of various Modernist projects, which in turn find roots in Mallarmé, or Blake, or Dickinson, or the medieval *Book of Kells* (depending on what genealogy one wishes to adopt). Now hypertext theorists have recently begun making very similar distinctions with regard to electronic media; in *The Electronic Word*, for example, Richard Lanham writes, "The textual surface has become permanently bi-stable. We are always looking first AT it and then THROUGH it . . ."[18] In Lanham and elsewhere, the emphasis is on how the malleability of the medium reinforces the visible artifice of digital texts and images. Many of these observers of the new media, however, seem all too unaware of the long tradition in experimental poetics which has rigorously and fruitfully engaged these same issues of representation and signification (or if such work is acknowledged, it most commonly takes the form of references to early twentieth century figures such as Marinetti or Kenneth Burke). So do you think these various traditions of visual materiality will find a legacy in electronic media, and if so, how does being digital alter their practice?

JD: One chapter of *www.VisCult* is titled "The Ontology of the Digital Image" and addresses the distinction I perceive between the roles of codes of materiality in traditional media and the encoding process which gives illusory/temporary material form in the digital environment. There is a moment in production in any media which we could call the moment of "transmigration of content"—I describe it in terms of the act by which a typesetter takes up a phrase to be set, carries it in her head, and then remakes it in a sequence of lead letters in the compositor's stick. Information is a part of each incarnation or embodiment—the material history of the artifact contributing to the way it is read (inscription in marble vs. graffiti). Though the sequence of material embodiments (various editions of a single work, for instance) is subject to the same kind of mutability to which an electronic document is subject, there is always a trace in material of the decisions, history, and effects of that material embodiment. The moment of "transmigration" may work as a filter, but it is effectively mooted by the fact that the text continues to be incarnated in one material form after another. By contrast, the electronic document has no stable material identity, exists ultimately as a disembodied code, and thus bears no "information" within its material form. It's the loss of this (often considered incidental) information which distinguishes the electronic from the material document. Making the means of visual innovation and experiment available to a greater number of people than could have ever learned letterpress or other traditional technologies does seem to have the potential to explode the visual inventions (and conventions) according to which text will be disposed. Ignorance of the history of prior innovations won't be a likely hindrance. As I think I already mentioned to you, when I began setting visual work at the West Coast Print Center in the mid-1970s, Alastair Johnston started babbling to me about Mallarmé and I just stared at him blankly. As far as I was concerned, I was just doing what the type itself seemed to make possible—the idea that there were precedents for such activity seemed a lot less important than that there was a future for it.

16. MGK: I'd like to talk a little bit about contemporary experimental graphic design, a field which, it seems to me, is absolutely essential to our understanding of what's going on in electronic media. I would argue that the leading concern of avant-garde graphic design today is to formalize a representation of print's communicative exhaustion. As a result, an entire digital aesthetic—or "look"—is being synthesized. *Wired* is perhaps the best known and least interesting example of this—but what do you think of the work of, say, David Carson, whose post-alphabetic layouts and fonts are criticized for "not communicating," even as Carson himself has migrated from alternative underground magazines like *Beach Culture* and *Ray Gun* to designing (and presumably communicating) for the likes of Swatch and Pepsi, among others? Likewise, in *The Visible Word*, you write: "The use of graphics as the means to make and perpetuate the image of the corporation, and through it, the virtuous projection of themes of progress, industry, and capitalist consumption, was essential to the public fantasmatic notion of modern life. In that culture, images and signs circulate without relation to their mode of production, and they sign the existence of a spectacle designed expressly for consumption, not productive necessity, but its surplus. Graphic design is not only the sign par excellence of that surplus, but is the very site in which it comes into being and is itself consumed as spec-

tacle through the formal mechanics of display."[19] Is there any room for graphic design as an oppositional practice, and if so, who's doing that work today?

JD: Contemporary graphic design's self-conscious display of "non-communicative" typography, layout, and "post-alphabetic" aesthetics has to be understood in large part in relation to the site of graphic design in the culture: it is, after all, the spectacular display kickwheel to the consumer-based economy of super-surplus in which first world designers work. So when I look at *Wired* or Carson, what I am struck by is the way in which motifs of old counter-culture style, rhetoric, or identity are directly co-opted to pique the interest (credit) of the boomers, generations X, and Next. To interpret the stylistic extremes of non-communicative prose in substantive terms is to either reduce the gestures to an emblematic enactment of surface/graphism for its own sake, to a generational transgressive I-can-go-farther-than-anyone-at-Cranbrook careeristic bid for attention, or to a reflection on the print-culture's own surplus of production. Most mainstream print material might as well run "greeked" copy anyway for all that it communicates—that is, the style-fashion type publications (*Wired, Interview, Ray Gun*). In my moments of self-righteous puritanical judgment, I see this as an inevitable dumbing down of a fundamentally anti-intellectual culture gone nuts on its own brain/eye candy self-indulgences and in my more tolerant moments I see it as the best kind of revenge against the old Beatrice Warde "crystal goblet" repressions against which I feel equal outrage.

But in terms of "oppositional practices," it seems that graphic designers face the same obstacles as the rest of us except that they potentially have terrific tools for overcoming those obstacles: how to make any kind of strategic intervention in the seamless seeming face of the spectacle. Sheila de Bretteville is a model of promoting and practicing oppositional design: she uses (and encourages her students to use) their grapic design skills for community based activism. She and her students have done billboards about literacy (using rebus-like icons which "read" when looked at), proposed stamp designs to promote awareness of domestic violence, and given public voice in visible ways to marginal or disenfrancished groups who would not have an effective visual presence in the "spectacle" otherwise. Since such work builds not only consciousness but community action coalitions, it seems more "oppositional" to me than any intervention in the style codes of graphic design could be. While it's true that habits of reading are bound to conventions, and that as readers we evolve our capacity to read new typefaces, new formats, and new hypermedia, I think that there is still a distinction to be made between effective communication and its inverse. I don't really want to be confronted with an innovative, "post-alphabetic" design when I am looking through the *Yellow Pages* for a plumber and my living room ceiling is falling in. Do you? The sites in which such innovations gain their legitimacy and visibility are highly fetishized and circumscribed—to say print culture is exhausted as if it described the condition of all print circulating in the culture at this time is the same as saying that all economic value is now only symbolic—just because some amount of economic value is generated from purely symbolic transactions. Clearly the style motifs indicate that there is the possibility of non-communicative design serving certain functions—but are they career functions, anti-information functions, innovative pushing the aesthetic/cultural envelope functions, or just novelty functions? That it is possible would seem to indicate (as in the similarly absurd extremes of contemporary art) that it is somehow significant. But how significant I don't think I have the perspective to say.

17. MGK: You've recently written on Joseph Nechvatal, a new media artist who uses computer viruses to electronically alter the contents of the digital images he works from in order to achieve a "limited but transformative mutation": "The body of the image is literally eroded in the process, but behind the screen, unseen, in the inner workings of its stored condition as a file. When the virus has run its course through the file the body of the image offers its wrecked corpus for our inspection. The resulting beauty is not meant as a denial of the reality of damage, but as an antidote to its terminal velocity through the culture at large".[20] Last summer, the Institute for Advanced Technology in the Humanities here at Virginia ran a seminar on the semiotics of digital images. Fernande Saint-Martin's writing on visual semiotics was our starting point. The goal was to work towards a formalized descriptive scheme for images which might be used as the basis for certain computational processes; it was observed that if a program like Photoshop, say, can use its filters to transform an image in some predictable way, computers ought to be capable of formalizing and acting upon other elements of the image's composition. Are you familiar with Saint-Martin's

work and if so, does it seem relevant to such a project? More generally, what do you see as the most salient points about treating digital images as information structures? You've talked about this some already but I'm especially interested in hearing more about your work on David Marr (and perhaps you could also give readers a very brief account of his contributions to the study of visual information).

JD: Is Saint-Martin the person who did the beautiful "semiotics of maps" book? I remember an exhaustive, extensive semiotic analysis of such visual material from the 1980s, but have to look it up to see if that's the same person. I find semiotics a useful tool for descriptive analysis, but like many such systems, it is difficult to use as a basis for certain kinds of conceptualization. For instance, if I think about (from my really rather superficial knowledge of it) the work of David Marr, what struck me was that he was proceeding with a very systematic, logical development of basic oppositional parameters for sorting fields of visual data (like a scanned image, screen, or other planographic image) according to fundamental features of those visual components: open/closed, bounded/blurred, patterned/solid. While such basics are useful for machine vision because they can be programmed as sets of conditions a sensor and data processor can assess, they will never approach the conceptual terms on which our cognitive visual functions are based. For instance, take the idea of recognition. How do you know if someone, something, or some place is familiar? The entire concept of familiarity, of prior knowledge, of a social specificity of relation (let alone the emotional charge which might accompany it) can't be programmed by such parameters. You can have a machine tell if it "knows" a voice through a voice-print match, but visual-print matches are harder except on highly constrained data-bases (fingerprints). The integration of vision and cognition can't be reduced to semiotic analysis. And this, again, was part of what I was trying to begin to work with in "Wittgenstein's Gallery." I think we have to think backwards or outwards from cognitive structures as well as working from visual structures. Someplace at the end of one of the books I read on AI someone (Dreyfus? Minksy?) wrote that ultimately the problem facing AI designers is that of constructing one full intelligence with one full life's experience.

18. MGK: I've asked you to take a look at the Language Visualization

and Multilayer Text Analysis project at Cornell's Theory Center. The stated objective of this project was to "develop a tool which allows a researcher to explore interactively the structures and typologies of discursive formation in large samples of textual data and develop new techniques for reading and interpreting text space." In other words, the researchers wanted to find ways to effectively visualize texts as data, as information. But what's most striking to me about the images they produced is that they are simply gorgeous to look at—the screenshots of the actual interface no less than the more self-consciously aestheticized compositions in the "palimpsest gallery." These images remind me of your own work, and also recent "visual poems" by Charles Bernstein (see, for example, Bernstein's "Cannot Cross"; "Illuminosities"; "Littoral"; and "Veil"). What are the implications of such a radiant convergence of information and aesthetics, two categories of experience which we habitually perceive as widely differentiated?

JD: I was enthralled with the images in the Language Visualization site at Cornell and have been sending people to visit that site ever since you introduced me to it. The work has the graphic beauty of Edward Tufte's visual forms. Tufte (whose work you probably know) draws extensively on earlier models for his inspiration—looking at diagrams, schematic layouts, maps, and many varied sources which inform his understanding of the way information can be rendered legible through visual form. I think that, again, there are many other precedents here and that the intersections of aesthetics and information, because they were frequently presented through the single organizing hand/eye of a fine graphic artist, proliferate throughout history. Some of my favorites are the diagrams used to map the logic systems of Petrus Ramus, the images in the books by the 17th century polymath Jesuit scholar Athanasius Kircher, and of course the history of map-making, of flow charts, of organizational schemas, time-lines, hierarchical diagrams, and so forth. I find these all infinitely suggestive as structures whose internal logics bear meaning in themselves as well as serving as a vehicle for the presentation of information.

19. MGK: Have you read any hypertext fiction or poetry and if so what is your opinion of it? And would you ever consider working in computerized hypertext? I ask because of your longstanding interest in alternatives to linear and sequential reading patterns. One of your most

common techniques for achieving this, in books as diverse as *Twenty-Six '76 Let Her's* or *The Word Made Flesh* or *The History of the/my Wor(l)d*, is through the use of different fonts and point sizes in conjunction with visual layout cues which gesture toward an array of multiple reading paths all simultaneously displayed on the open page. Do you see this as similar to or different from the mechanism of the hypertext link? I wonder, for example, whether the subterranean coding of the hypertext link in fact muffles the sort of immediacy inherent in the multiple readings you so visibly juxtapose?

JD: The only hypertext fiction I have read is by Michael Joyce though I have seen some other hypertext and hypermedia documents in exhibitions, seminars, or symposia. While I was in the library yesterday I ran across a "multiple-choice, interactive" novel by someone I had never heard of before—Robbins or Robinson, I think—about a murder in London. It was written fifteen or so years ago, so hardly innovative, but in fact, that was what was so surprising to me—here was this "ordinary" artifact, not even high profile or well-known, to show that the genre had had a more developed life than I had realized. Certainly I find the organizational possibilities of texts and subtexts, interlinked archives and documents, very intriguing and seductive in the hypertext format. But I am so attached to print documents and objects that I can't say whether I will ever manage to create a hypertext novel/work. Maybe soon and maybe never—I do love having those books to hold in my hand. Printing a book is always satisfying at the tactile and material level. As it progresses you sew the finished signatures together. You flip through the pages. You feel that heft and bulk or slipperiness and opacity. I tend to feel deprived of the product unless there is a hard-copy output. But I'm not opposed to the form in any ideological or dogmatic sense. We still have to deal with the resistance to reading on the screen before it makes sense to make elaborate works which rely on an electronic environment—and I'm not there yet, so how could I expect a reader to be?

20. MGK: Your most recent work, entitled *The Current Line* (1996) is actually bi-linear, running a large and domineering but unadorned Mac-generated font above a 10 point red letterpress sequence. Over the course of thirty pages the large letters produce the following sentence: "ALL IS WEALTH IN THE HOUSE OF THE BLESSED AND OUR ADVAN-

TAGE IS WELL TAKEN ACCORDING TO THE LAW THAT CONSTANT-
LY PRESENTS ANOTHER WETTER DREAM ALWAYS ABOUT TO SLIP
ABOVE THE SIMULACRAL HORIZON." And I'd also like to quote in
full the last few pages of the letterpress text, for it strikes me as very
poignant:

"Crawling underneath the table of nostalgic form we find ourselves
desperate for verbal insight. Each day succeeds the rest, concealing the
signs of waste from the sentence structure, passing eliminatory matter
through the deregulated system. Without thinking, we lay awake at
night, picking laughter from our teeth and shaking loose our bright-
eyed optimism about infrastructure and religious convictions. Empty
accounts come back to the conjugal bed to restore their spirits with the
blush of affectionate cash. Our days were never really spent, but kept in
deep reserve against the possibility of expression, the small chance that
a word might slip in edgewise and in finding its place disturb the placid
grammar by which our future had been so brutally rent from the now
obsolete belief in language and referents. No darkness. No gloom. No
privation. No room for any negativity in the bright successful glow of
the afterimage on the screen as it slipped into mute, modest obscurity.
The perfection of the simulacral mechanism carefully conceals any hint
of doubt. This is visionary: total salvation. Complete release. An utter
lapse of gravity so that the fall this time is upward, rising out of reach
to the hot and newly animated stars."

This seems more lyrical, or at least more declarative than some of
your previous work. So is that your current line, and where are you
taking it?

JD: Of course those final lines are completely dark, utterly ironic. The
deceit of media/spectacle language is "the current line"—and the capacity of us all to internalize it, buy into the fantasmatic concealment of referents. "The freedom to chose" and "the people must be served" are the
two refrains which echoed through last night's half hour television
dose—both fast food chains advertising. The "utter lapse of gravity" and
"fall" upward seems awfully close to joining the space ship in the tail of
the Hale-Bopp comet to me—which is to say, mere reportage, hardly
invention in any sense. If I could achieve what I most wanted in my
writing in the future it would be to be able to inscribe as accurately and
vividly as possible the contemporary carnival of grosteque human folly.
It does seem that the only possibility for human survival (forget

redemption) is insight and that one route to insight is the scathing mirror of dark humor. Lyrical? Well, how about perverse lyricism?

21. MGK: Finally, I have to ask you about your name. Given that "Johanna" is the feminine form of "Johann" (as in Gutenberg), and given also that "Drucker" is, I'm told, the Dutch for "printer"—well, do you ever have to convince people it's not a pseudonym?

JD: Very funny. The man who moved my press for me in New York was named Jerry Gutenberg. I kid you not. Moving a press for Johanna Drucker. The only mileage I ever got out of my name was in Amsterdam in 1978. I had gone to a place called the *Drukhuis* on a canal in the center of the city. It was an old old house with presses in it which was run in some part through city and state subsidies so that people could print there by paying a per diem. The man in charge was a wild looking greybeard like the troll under the bridge in Billy Goat's Gruff (he turned out to be a fine, kind, gentle, and generous person), and he asked me three questions in perfect fairytale fashion. "Do you know how to print?" he said, wagging a proverbial finger in warning fashion lest I try and deceive him. When I answered yes he said, "Well, can you bring me something to prove it?" And when I again answered in the affirmative he went on to say, "Okay then, tell me your name so I'll remember who you are when you come back." "Johanna Drucker," I said, and he replied, "You don't have to show me anything at all, I believe you." So there it is.

This interview was conducted electronically in 1996 and appeared in the online journal Post-Modern Culture *in 1997.*

Notes:

1. Charles Bernstein, "Words," p.124.
2. Drucker, "Experimental," p.56.
3. Nick Piombino, "Visual-Verbal," p.55.
4. Drucker, "Experimental," p.55.
5. Drucker, "Chronology," n.p.
6. Drucker, *Century*, p. ix.
7. Drucker, "Chronology," n.p.
8. Drucker, "Final," p.75.
9. Drucker, "Final," p.75.
10. Marjorie Perloff, "Herstory," p.54.

11. Drucker, "Dilemmas," p.14.

12. Drucker, *ibid*, p.16.

13. Drucker, *ibid*, p.12.

14. Drucker, *ibid*, p.14.

15. Drucker, "Work," n.p.

16. Drucker, "Work," n.p.

17. Drucker, *Visible*, p.94-5.

18. Richard Lanham, *Electronic*, p.5.

19. Drucker, *Visible*, p.241-2.

20. Drucker, "Pleasure," n.p.

Works of Drucker's Cited:

The Century of Artists' Books. New York: Granary Books, 1995.

"A Chronology of Books from 1970 to 1994." Exhibition Catalogue,
    Granary Books, New York City, June 1994.

"Close Reading: A Billboard." *Poetics Journal* 2 (Sept. 1982): 82-4.

"Critical Pleasure." Catalogue essay, Joseph Nechvatal Retrospektive, Galerie
    Berndt, Koln. URL: http://www.dom.de/arts/artists /jnech/drucker.html

Dark Decade. St. Paul, MN: Detour Press, 1995.

"Experimental, Visual, and Concrete Poetry: A Note on Historical Context and
    Basic Concepts." *Experimental—Visual—Concrete: Avant-Garde Poetry Since the
    1960s*. Eds. Jackson, K. David, Eric Vos, and Johanna Drucker. *Avant-
    Garde Critical Studies* #10 (1996): 39-61.

"Final Fiction." *Temblor* 4 (1986): 75-82.

Italy. Berkeley, CA: The Figures, 1980.

"Narratology: Dilemmas of Genre Fiction, Lived Experience, and Book
    Structure." *AbraCadaBra* 10 (Spring 1996): 12-17.

The Visible Word: Experimental Typography and Modern Art, 1909-1923. Chicago:
    University of Chicago Press, 1994.

"Women & Language." *Poetics Journal* 4 (May 1984): 56-68.

"The Work of Mechanical Art in the Age of Electronic Reproduction." *Offset:
    Artists' Books and Prints*, Exhibition Catalogue, Granary Books, New York
    City, Dec. 2-Jan. 25, 1994. URL:http://www.uwo.ca/visarts/vol1num1
    /eva2.html

Other Works Cited:

Bernstein, Charles. "Words and Pictures." *Content's Dream: Essays 1975–1984*.
    Los Angeles: Sun and Moon, 1986: 114-161.

Lanham, Richard A. *The Electronic Word: Democracy, Technology, and the Arts*.

Chicago: University of Chicago Press, 1993.

Perloff, Marjorie. "Johanna Drucker's Herstory." *Harvard Library Bulletin* 3.2 (Summer 1992): 54-63.

—. "Something is Happening, Mr. Jones." *electronic book review* 2 (Spring 1996): n.p. URL: http:// www. altx.com/ebr/ebr2.perloff.html.

Piombino, Nick. "The Visual-Verbal World of Johanna Drucker: Five New Books." *M/E/A/N/I/N/G* 18 (November 1995): 54-66.

MGK acknowledgements: My deepest thanks go of course to Johanna Drucker, not only for patiently and carefully answering all of my questions here, but also for her extraordinary generosity in providing me with copies of rare, out of circulation, or just plain out of my reach books and other materials. And my thanks also to Stuart Moulthrop for his ready enthusiasm. I am very grateful to Will Rourk for his assistance with the digital images. I'd also like to thank Jerome McGann for first introducing me to Drucker's work, and John Unsworth for his continued interest and encouragement on all fronts; and finally, thanks to Bennett Simpson, Lisa Samuels, Kent Puckett, and David Caplan for their conversations about writing and such.

III. Writing as Artifact

The Material Word

MATERIAL

Writing appears modest and immodest, verbal but mute, speaking and not speaking its contradictory position in the house of language. The physical fact of language—uttered, inscribed, marked, or frozen in front of our faces in the cold light of bitter days—reminds us that there is no communication without the phatic exchange of substances.

A prophylactic attitude attempts to protect the imagination from direct encounters with the world as the tongue, the hand, the arm, the fist around the pen, the fingers on the keyboard all reach into the heavy flesh of matter and are rewarded by the response of sensate experience.

This does not make meaning. It only makes a space in which meaning comes to have its face pressed up against the glass, waiting to break through beyond the mirror of its own pale image.

The letters have a contradictory existence, speaking their names without a claim on any part of speech, finding themselves subject to texts and yet unable to participate in the play of sound, letting their small forms be bent and twisted in response to the whim of fashion and yet preserving against all odds and across millennia their essential and distinctive forms.

Words are what claim the major place in the spotlight of linguistic function, boldly stating this or that with such conviction that they are granted all kinds of interpretive attention.

In the contest of "context" vs. the "sure thing" it is always the turn which is just below the phrase which gets its place in the headline banners—while the second rate picture in the paper is blurred and shackled by its caption—itself a picture, an image, a fact.

Let them stand on their own flat feet, the straight and/or serifed figures, and bid for a place in the hearts and minds of millions according to their capacity to impress us with the daily record of our lives.

Repressing the blank face of letters on the page will never obliterate the record from the trace, nor wipe clean the persevering palimpsest of memory.

The future waits to find its face in

our WORDS

and spit them back again into the fertile fields of passionate imagination.

The mechanical instrument sucked up to the new technology with all the effort of a schoolchild on its first trip to the board, waiting to be told what to do and hoping, oh so much, to do it right. The broadcast—not referred to any longer in those terms—came across the fiber with an optic speed, tracing the bright air with a visual message from some place—any place—other than the point of origin. Location and dislocation, distance and presence, absent texts and cherished references all find their place in the dimly lit library of our past. In the streamlined momentary amnesia of the present only footsteps have the capacity to break through the sound barrier and grab hold of our shoulders and shake. Words fell out of her mouth like bad teeth and when they scattered on the floor the message they sent rattling was not the same stuff which was written in the stars, my friends. A bright forecast slipped away this noon and in its place there were all kinds of options for returns on investments we do not have the capacity to make. Slip the dictionary in your pocket, tuck your grammars into the intimate depth of your cheeks, and prepare to spell out the texture of the times in a vivid interplay of mind and hand, breath and substance, answers and purchased opportunities. The power of the word was ours before it fell and stretching beyond our grasp we can just get it back again, for a visit, in the time-warp option and optimistic pause of a soundbite moment.

First produced for a flier announcing a Druckwerk exhibition held at Woodland Pattern Bookstore, Milwaukee, Spring 1996.

The Art of the Written Image

In every era of human history artists, poets, professional and amateur scribes have been sensitive to the visual properties of written forms. Consequently there is no shortage of material evidence supporting the idea that writing is a visual medium. Maximizing the potential of such qualities as color, composition, design, and style, writing embodies language in an unlimited variety of distinctive forms. History and culture reside in these material means: the chiselled line of the Roman majuscules, the worried hand of a remade will, the bureaucratic regularity of a cuneiform account, the sophisticated inventions of a Renaissance type designer, the least mark of a tentative witness, and the bold sweep of an authoritative pen. In these and an infinitude of other cases, it is clear that significance inheres in the written form of language as much on account of the properties of physical materials as through a text's linguistic content. Whether incidental or foregrounded, such specific properties of written language are what ensure its unique role within human culture.

It may well be that there is no human urge more fundamental than that of mark making—just as there is no activity which characterizes human culture more distinctly than that of language. Not all written language is produced directly by hand, but whether marks, strokes, signs, glyphs, letters, or characters, writing's visual forms possess an irresolvably dual identity in their material existence as images and their function as elements of language. Because of this fundamental dualism, writing is charged with binary qualities. It manifests itself with the phenomenal presence of the *imago* and yet performs the signifying operations of the *logos*. It is an act of individual expression and an instance of that most rule-bound and social of human systems—language. It is at once personal and social, unique and cultural, asserting real physical presence and functioning through intertextual chains of association and reference. It is both an object and an act, a sign and a basis for signification, a thing in itself and something coming into being, a production and a process, an inscription and the activity of inscribing.

The critical apperception of writing has engaged literary critics, art historians, psychologists, and anthropologists—as well as many scholars of paleography, typographic history, forgery, or decipherment whose professional studies focus on the examination of written forms. Conceptual parameters for understanding the cultural significance of written language thus emerge from many quarters. An enormous bibliography exists on writing as a material form and it maps a territory of discourse in which the functions of language-as-image stretch from a macro-level of embodying the symbolic law which effectually defines culture as human to the micro-level at which writing can be understood in psychoanalytic terms. Within artistic practices the engagement with writing as a visual form foregrounds these dialogues—between personal and social, somatic and symbolic, conceptual and material, and real and metaphoric domains—which are all inherent aspects of writing as a visual form.

In the twentieth century, artistic manifestations are many and varied, crossing the disciplines of literature, the fine arts, and graphic design, in a fertile intersection of creative innovation. The striking work of the typographically innovative French symbolist poet Stéphane Mallarmé casts its influence over poetic activity of the early 1900s, inspiring the visual experiments of writers and artists in an era in which commercial typography and mass produced print media were appropriated and absorbed into Futurist, Dada, and Cubist collage. Poets who never worked extensively in images per se were nonetheless often inspired by the permission granted by such modern experiments to expand the visual potential of the page by shaping the form, space, and distribution of written language according to a schematic which intertwined format and meaning in novel ways. Ezra Pound's apocryphal (but real) fascination with art historian Ernest Fenollosa's work on the Chinese character is one of the mythic moments in the history of modern poetry's engagement with the material manifestation of language in written form. Taking literally the age-old misconception of Chinese characters as word-pictures, rather than representations of phonetic signs, Pound used this visual idea to structure his imagistic verse. Meanwhile, in their collaborative essays of 1912 and 1913, "The Word as Such" and "The Letter as Such," Russian Futurist poets Velimir Khlebnikov and Alexei Kruchenyk articulated a quasi-mystical belief in the visual power of language which had resonance with centuries' old traditions of ascribing meaning to letters as signs. And perhaps most renowned of all the revolutionary calls-to-arms is in the work of the Italian major-duomo of Futurism, Filippo Marinetti. Also working in the 1910s, he galvanized visually inventive poetic verse with his texts "Words in Liberty" and "The Wireless Imagination." These gestures (among others) inaugurate the 20th century era of interactions between visual and verbal arts and are followed in rapid succession by other creative innovations in visual poetics and painted language.

In the 1950s and 1960s the theoretical writings of Concrete poets and Lettrists add to the long list of manifesto-like statements asserting the potential of visual poetics, followed by the work of Pop and Conceptual artists, who became intrigued with language as an artistic form. The transformations of production and reproduction technologies in the course of the 20th century made the means of experimentation increasingly available. Hot type, cold type, press type, photographic manipulation, and finally the phenomenon of desk-top publishing now exist in complementary parallel with the (equally innovative) traditional means of drawing, painting, and graphic design skills. Animated pages, holographic work, and virtual displays of illusionistically dimensional landscapes are now all part of the artistic vocabulary which figures language in visual form.

Writing thus exists along a broad spectrum from the most elemental gestural trace to the standard sign. All writing has the capacity to be both looked at and read, to be present as material and to function as the sign of an absent meaning. It can be structured and shaped—or merely accumulate according to standard conventions. It can be found, appropriated, manipulated, and effaced. As a form of individual expression writing is a somatically inflected sign, a production of the bodily self which seeks identity in an image of its own making. As a social and cultural system, writing partakes of the semiotic conditions of meaning production within the constraints of the rule bound system of language. The richness of written language resides in these multi-faceted qualities, and from them, as a consequence, many curious contradictions and parallells open in the field of writing.

Between Personal Expression and Social System

The basic binary character of writing is its capacity to function simultaneously as an instance of personal and of social expression. Mira Schor's painting, *Personal Writing* (1994), embodies this crucial duality. The work is comprised of thirty small canvases. Each letter in the title

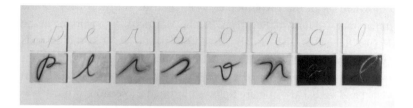

appears twice in the complete work—once in a clear, simple, line hand-written according to the models Schor copied as a schoolgirl and once in a sumptuous, painterly rendering of her idiosyncratic, adult hand.

The first set of images has a rational clarity to it: fine blue lines shape each individual letter in a well-made exercise carefully placed within the boundaries of the canvas. The blue paint of these letters suggests chalk, pen, or graphite—the materials of the schoolroom—observing a decorum of self-discipline and good behavior in the face of the rules of the educational system. Childishly perfect, these letters were painted from blown up xeroxes of exercises in an old schoolbook. In a smaller, almost inconspicuous hand, Schor has added the two letters "im" before the first word in this series, giving it the contradictory double meaning: "personal/impersonal."

The second set of images are based on Schor's adult hand. Blowing them up to the same scale as that of the schoolgirl hand, she invested each painted letter with elaborate visual and tactile richness. In a deep, glowing, red which bleeds into the background of soft, pink, fleshlike ground, the letters vibrate with bodily associations. They stretch, cramp, and sweep with conviction—sometimes striking against the confines of the canvas frame, unable to behave with the same good manners as the letters in the exercise hand. Schor has switched the color scheme of the last two letters of the word, "personal." Here again she

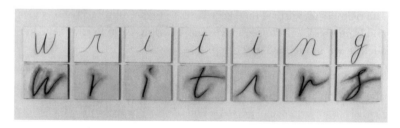

Mira Schor, *Personal Writing, 1994*, oil on linen, 12" x 16" each panel.

bifurcates the reading in this painterly line so that "personal writing" can also be read as "person writing."

The concept of the personal in Schor's work is both romantic and critical. Her idea of individuality clearly takes into account that social training conditions the physical body whose personality eventually comes through the systemic constraints—but only as an inflection, a marked difference within the system itself. The rules of writing, like the rules of language, require a degree of compliance and standardization. A stylish distinction is permitted, but not pure invention, if writing is to function as communication.

The idea of the social construction of individual identity—or subjectivity—within the strictures of cultural systems and codes is a common critical notion in the 20th century. Psychoanalytic assessments of individual subjectivity formation grant a great deal of significance to the developmental function of language. As Sigmund Freud observed, language acquisition permits a child to negotiate the traumas of separation or frustration by providing a means of representing presences and absences. Language functions as a symbol or surrogate for an absent breast, parent, toy or other object. According to the psychoanalyst, in learning language a child is simultaneously provided a means of representing the world and of finding out his or her place within the social and cultural (largely patriarchal) order. For a feminist like Schor, the issue of personal language is bound up in the difficulties posed by the hierarchies of power into which female subjectivity must be placed. Inflecting the acquired signs of handwriting with a personal character asserts the successful formation of a subject position while acknowledging its constraints within the givens of the rule-bound order of both language and the social domain.

But writing is not only an instance of language—it is also an image, and as such participates in yet another developmental function underscored by psychoanalytic theory. According to Jacques Lacan, images serve a crucial role in preparing the child for language acquistion in a transition termed "the mirror stage." Lacan suggests that it is by perceiving itself in a mirrored image (either real or metaphoric) that a child is first provided with a sense of its own wholeness as a person, body, and psychic unit. Prior to this the child exists in a condition called "the imaginary"—undifferentiated, unbounded, and fragmented by its zones of erotic, motor, tactile sensations. The *imago* of the mirror-stage provides for a form of identification—through self-representation as image. Any image—painted, inscribed, or reflected—which seems to be an image of the self, can guarantee identity in these terms. Thus the manifestation of an individuated identity which shows itself in the bodily gesture of mark-making—as scribbles, random signs, or the "personal writing" of Schor's piece—links the self and the hand-made mark in a primary psychoanalytic function. As an image writing permits a subjective, narcissistic, identification with a perceived self-identity in the expressive form of a written inscription. From a psychoanalytic perspective, then, the function of writing is both to provide an image of the self and to position that self within language as the system of the symbolic order.

In Schor's work both the thematic content and execution reinforce the idea that the training of hand and eye in the acquisition of writing are part of a process of socialization. Learning writing as a social system one partially gives up the individual inflection of character or personality, only to acquire it again, as inevitably as one's body acquires a characteristic walk, posture, and shape over time while functioning according to the norms and expectations of one's cultural and social world. Writing bears the visible traces of somatic individuation and encodes various functions of the social order and law, the structures and strictures of permission, control, and bounded identity. "Personal writing" is always an inscription of the individual within the symbolic.

In Glenn Ligon's work, *Black Like Me #2*, (1992), language, individual identity, and social conventions also converge. Like Schor's painting, Ligon's piece embodies its thematics in a method of production as well as in the content of its statement. But the richly individual quality of writing in Schor's painted work contrasts dramatically with the stenciled marks which comprise the text of Glenn Ligon's work. The "me" of his textual statement and the letters of the visual stencil are formatted and formulaic, struggling simultaneously to embody and to protest fixed stereotypes of form, shape, color, meaning. Using these stencils and a thick, heavy, greasy black crayon, Ligon creates an increasingly dense field of writing. Following the conventional direction of reading, the single statement of the title is repeated time after time, until it results in a field of layered, overlapped, and finally unreadable text as it moves from the top to the bottom of the canvas. A work in black and white, Ligon's image encodes questions of racial stereotypes: the term "colored," with all of its associations of racial slurs and apartheid policies, is rendered only in the monochrome tones of black on white though the "me" of the title, if it identifies the artist, is an African-American man. But like any first person pronoun in English, "me" bears no particular marks of identification with regard to gender, race, or other characteristics. The denial in the statement has to be read both as a personal utterance and a statement the reader experiences and identifies with through his or her own articulation. Written language particularly allows for such slippages since the unvoiced written form reveals few significant clues to the identity of its maker.

Visually Ligon's piece is simple and striking—there is an implied violence in the gradual distintegration of the text as it becomes absorbed in the marks of its own making. The waxy medium smears so that the letters lose their clear boundaries of distinction. There is an effacement of clear statement as the field of writing loses its capacity to be read. This loss of legibility comes from the obses-

Glenn Ligon, *Black Like Me #2, 1992*, oil stick and gesso on canvas, 80" x 30".

sive repetition of material, a losing battle for belief even in the statement itself—as if it cancels and nullifies in the act of continual assertion. Individual protest or a mere statment of fact, an outcry or expression of resigned defeat the work cannot be comfortably resolved into either category and therefore fluctuates in that intermediating zone occupied by writing at the intersection of the personal and social domains. The hand-madeness of the marks in Ligon's work is constrained by the dictates of the conventional forms of the stencils and thus is almost—but not quite—invisible as an element of the piece. One senses the gestural presence of the body pressing the waxy crayon onto the canvas, rubbing and smearing as it moves in a preordained direction to produce and reproduce the text.

In their own distinct ways, Schor and Ligon both embody the tension between the individual quality of expression and the constraints of a rule-bound linguistic system. Schor's painterly lushness invites a romantic reading while coldly refuting it in the same instance and Ligon's minimal means protest the inadequacies of individual expression as a challenge to the inequities inscribed in the cultural order. In both cases the visual properties of the work are what encode these meanings, not merely as an incidental visual presentation, but through their signification as manifest form.

From Trace to Sign: Gesture, Letterform, and Glyph

Not all written language is gestural or somatic—the spectrum of writing includes much which is fully mechanical as well as intimate and personal. At one extreme there are the signs, letters, or characters whose legibility depends upon their adherence to conventions. At the other end are gestural traces. And somewhere on this spectrum, not quite within conventions or outside of them, are mysterious glyphic forms which exercise their own peculiar fascination through a charged quality of suggestive meaning, inaccessible and indecipherable, but potently hinted at in the visual complexities of a written sign.

Pierre Alechinsky's *Exercise d'écriture* provides an exemplary instance of the automatic impulse at its most basic. In Alechinsky's painting, writing is a productive act rooted in gesture. The painting inscribes the tactile, physical, motor pleasures of mark making. Rhythmic gestures bring signs into being which are almost letters, almost legible, almost elements of some real alphabet—but not quite. *Exercise d'écriture* is about scribing, inscribing, bringing into being. It is about the ways in which gesture precedes language as an expressive indication. Gesture is human action outside of the fixed parameters of language, anterior to language historically, independent of it conceptually, and more primal, more fundamental as a human self-assertion in

Pierre Alechinsky, *Exercise d'Ecriture*, 1950. Destroyed. © 1999 Artists Rights Society (ARS), New York / ADAGP, Paris.

the space of the cosmos, the material world, and the social group. The physical anthropologist, André Leroi-Gourhan, in his 1964 book *Gesture and Speech*, outlines the evolutionary relation between patterns of brain function, development, gestural activity, and language. Leroi-Gourhan suggests that the specialization of human limbs to isolate aspects of the survival functions of gathering, hunting, eating (as well as climbing, tool-making, self-defense), freed the mouth and lips for language and created crucial oppositions between the hands and the face which permitted a language of gesture to emerge in contradistinction to that of speech. For Leroi-Gourhan, gesture is a rhythmic, somatic, elemental self-expression while speech is social and communicative. The manual production of marks and glyphs is a code in which expressive self-assertion and communicative functions intertwine.

The gestural mark is a trace of the very act of production as dynamic action. The trace makes itself in the dynamic pleasure of material making and as such, remains a sign which has not yet reached the threshold of meaning. But though freed from responsibility to language, Alechinsky's *Exercise* still invokes the linguistic as some ultimate authority capable of legitimating the value of those marks as significant rather than gratuitous. By calling these loops and strokes "écriture,"

Alechinsky seems to want to allow that the somatic impulse can be brought into the rule of symbolic order, that these marks could be possessed of meaning—not merely be scribbled arabesques marking off the subdivisions of a graphic space. Replaying the original act of gestural self-expression, automatic and aleatory, wandering and unconstrained, Alechinsky nonetheless acknowledges his eventual submission to the rules of the symbolic order.

Within cultural anthropology, there is another framework for assessing such uses of writing as significant acts. Claude Levi-Strauss, in his essay "The Writing Lesson," posits the basic argument that writing colonizes and empowers simultaneously, concentrating power in the act of sign making. Even when those signs don't represent an actual language, writing acts to hierarchize authority through the mere control of written forms. This is a performative aspect of writing as a ritual act rather than an inscribed form of language. Alechinsky's work inscribes some of this authority, that of the empowering form which becomes authoritative through its production—demarcating the writer from the watching audience, the written from the unwritten, the sign from the vast universe of undifferentiated chaos. It is in this cult power that sign making accrues to itself a capacity to function as magic in human culture. The power of signing establishes fundamental differences: between the human social and that which is beyond, between the legislated world and the unlegislatable, between the symbolizable and that which is inaccessible to symbol making. At the heart of all of these capacities to divide the conceptualization of the world through human systems is the fundamental function of the trace—that materialization of gesture which makes the first line of demarcation against which meaning can be produced. Such a trace produces the differentiating boundary which renders meaning possible—serving as the point of reference against which symbols can be located, read, interpreted. Thus the exercise of Alechinsky's writing embodies a primal bringing into being which creates meaning through an act of differentiation, the expressive gesture which asserts one's own individual and then social identity upon the resistant but receptive material of the world.

If such traces of somatic gesture remain unreadable because they stop short of participation in the symbolic system, then the glyphic sign which presents itself as the image of an esoteric meaning employs a different kind of resistance to legibility. This fascination with the glyph—

that written form which is encoded, encrypted, secretive and complex —shows up in the work of many visual artists. There is the work of Albrecht Durer making images to accompany the Renaissance's redis-covered hieroglyphic texts of Horapollo—or the typographic analyses of Geofroy Tory grounded in Pythagorean symbolism and lore—or the many emblem books of the sixteenth and seventeenth centuries com-mitted to a visual presentation of cryptic meaning—and there are the finely wrought images in Aldus Manutius's great tribute to the imagi-native power of hieroglyphic signs, his *Hypnerotomachia Poliphilii* of 1499. Thus while on the one hand writing gains a certain power through its ability to provide legitimacy it also exercises a power of fas-cination in the cryptically illegible condition of the glyph. Such a power has continued into the 20th century, where there is no shortage of artists, writers, critics, and theorists for whom this aspect of writing car-ries a potent charge.

The glyphic motif found in Karen Papachek's drawings or suggest-ed in the pictographic imagery of Kenneth Patchen's illuminated poems was elaborately explored in the work of the French Lettrist group founded in the late 1940s by Romanian Isidore Isou. The Lettrists played with such cryptic innovations, challenging the legibility of signs in order to subvert the symbolic order of language through an attack on its basic code. Lettrist marks range from the gestural, somatic, trace signs of the automatic tradition to all manner of invented signs which engage with an alternative tradition of the hieroglyphic character and its myth-ic visual propensity. This impulse is fabulously fulfilled by those Lettrists who play out their variations of the mark into a sublime mode of anar-chistic subversion of the normative order of what had once been a sys-tematic language.

In *Riff Raff,* a work produced by Lettrist Maurice Lemaître in 1950, a series of signs spiral out from a single core image—a tiny schematic map of Paris reduced to an elliptical shape bisected by the curve of the Seine. Each of the signs in this piece seems to speak directly to the eye —a tiny image of books, a ball, calipers, a bottle, stool, wheel, tent, or the Eiffel tower—to make a "poem" whose "words" are actual images. The meaning of the work is far from clear—pronouncing the words rebus-like in French results in a certain sequence of sounds, each of which stretches in an effort to fit the elastic phonetic form of a sentence. But there are very few actual letters here, and the idea of the intriguing

Maurice Lemaître, *Riff Raff*, 1950, drawing, 5" x 3 1/2".

image-sign serving a directly communicative function is as quickly defeated by Lemaître's example as it was by the efforts of those frustrated Renaissance polymaths attempting to decipher an Egyptian stele without benefit of the Rosetta stone's trilingual key.

Riff Raff is typical of Lettrist work, however, in its complex visual formulation of a pseudo or personal language. Lemaître's inventions here are not arbitrary, merely unorthodox, and thus point out the necessity for convention as a stabilizing framework for meaning production. But in other Lettrist works the glyphs are not recognizable as images. They are condensed, illegible, and yet particular signs—each distinctly formed, discrete in its character, but as unreadable as the signs of any unfamiliar writing script. There is no point of entry into this work, rather its busy, worked, field swarms with the animate energy of a bloodstream of organic creatures—plankton and platelets, cells and molecules, viral and bacterial entities—each formed in accord with a logic which seems to promise a universe of sense. There is no deciphering this code—even if one reads the *Riff Raff* poem through its phonetic values, the images remain, not fully absorbed into that linguistic reformulation. One can't ignore the emphatic shadow on the inside of the horned curve of the croissant pictogram or fail to notice and wonder at the spheroid heads of those schematic figures whose postures suggest "sitting" or "standing" or "diving" as verbs. These pictorial non-equivalents have meaning not accounted for in mere linguistic substitution— and the power of the glyph—whether alchemical, magical, esoteric, or exotic is precisely this resistance to recuperation within the closed system of mere meaning. The affective presence of the image continues to exert its own seductive energy, not as a surplus value, merely as a quality which cannot be contained within the fixed economy of language.

Conceptual, Temporal, and Material Structures

In addition to those artists engaged with the somatic trace of handwriting or the inventive glyphs of their own invention, there are those for whom the virtues of writing reside in a use of conventional, almost neutral, forms within conceptual or material structures which motivate their aesthetic agenda. There are many philosophical tensions which arise in these works—particularly between the notion of an immaterial, idealist concept and the fact of the materiality which every instance of written language embodies.

In the 1966 piece by Robert Smithson, *Heap of Language,* the artist has created an architectonic form on gridded paper out of words which refer to language as well as embody it. "Language phraseology speech tongue lingo vernacular" the piece begins. It proceeds in an accumulative pile, the literal heap of the title, down into its broad base where the list ends with the word "cipher." Readable and literal, the handwritten text has very little of an expressive quality—the writing is regular and even, fitting into the gridded strucure with all the correct proportion of a minimalist work. Some of the words refer, in the normal

Robert Smithson, *Heap of Language*, 1966, pencil on paper, 6 1/2" x 22".
Photo courtesy John Weber Gallery.

linguistic mode, to objects and or ideas which are not fully present—
"Mrs. Malaprop" or the "thesaurus." Thus the even-handed treatment
of the words, making each so much the same as the next, becomes itself
a device for foregrounding the distinct differences among the terms.
How, after all, can "root" be rendered in the same mode as "take an
assumed name" given the completely different worlds which they
invoke? By the same token, this reductive act, this levelling of differences among the words, turns each into a bricklike component, an element of real, sheer, actual, *literal* material with which Smithson builds
the earth-like heap of his sculptural construction on the page. In precise inverse of the building process, the "heap" is made from the top
down, its crowning stone "Language" having been the first to be put
into place, while the base support extends in a suggestion of an ever
widening support, contradicting all the logic of real structure through
the artifices of written form.

The piece is precisely what it says it is, and yet, in this straightforward simplicity it confounds the problems of presence and reference,
managing to collapse them into the same activity. The words are what
they say they are and yet they add up to something more—a structure,
a form, a materially dense work which describes the materials of the
language of which it is made. The capacity of language to refer to an
idea, to invoke it in Platonic terms, is put into conflict with the actual
material presence of language itself. All material objects and forms have
a history and character, as Aristotle noted in his description of the
world. The classical opposition between idea and description, between
a transcendent form and an embodied empirical form makes itself
apparent in the duality which conceptual artists ascribe to language.

Perhaps the most striking paradox of all in conceptual art was the use of written language to suggest "idea"—when in fact writing is the most evidently and insistently material of linguistic modes.

By contrast to Smithson's *Heap*, Annette Lemieux's *Hell Text* (1991) creates form through the seemingly natural mode of accumulation. One word follows another in vivid white etched with heat against the glowing red ground of the work. A minimal and refined visual work, its elegant script letters march in regular form across the space of the cotton cloth. The script type marks this as a personal statement, echoed in the use of the first-person voice for the narrative of the prose. The words describe a chilling series of events in which an individual is subject to an authoritarian and absolute system of control. It is a tale with unavoidable associations with the official acts of totalitarian regimes—an arbitrary seeming arrest and deportation (of Jews, Gypsies, gays, dissidents, or merely any other targeted group) to a camp. The "hell" described in the text has an indeterminate historical location and yet resonates with any number of specific possibilities. Individual and yet generic, too perfect for a real hand, the script "signifies" handwriting through the associative properties. The form of the piece belies its threat, covering the horror in a delicate image of fine script. The visually peaceful repetition becomes charged in a reading which reveals the sinister quality of inevitability. A Kafkaesque sense of being at the mercy of some absent force combines with a Sartrean "no exit" in a grim repetitive exercise of horror. The openendedness of the movement of line after line, has no clear beginning (mid-sentence, with no majuscule, the text enters the upper left of the canvas as if it had already been

Annette Lemieux, *Hell Text*, 1991, branding on cotton, 54 1/8" x 144". Photo courtesy Washington University Gallery of Art, St. Louis. University purchase, Bixby Fund, 1991.

in progress for some time and it exits the lower right in the same manner) and no resolved end. Thus the text and its formal qualities contradict each other—linguistic horror and visual smoothness, reference to brutality and a presence of clear aesthetic refinement. Hell is the individual trapped within the machinations of a social order which can be inconceivably relentless in its logical abuses and mastering narratives.

The list of artists for whom language serves as a primary material is a long one—and the practices by which they engage with the conceptual and philsophical issues of linguistic representation in visual form are varied. One has only to think of John Baldessari's conundrum statements, those otherwise blank canvases bearing laconic statements like "Pure Beauty" or "A Work With Only One Property" in block lettering, or the simple date paintings of On Kawara, or the self-reflexive "Five Words in Orange Neon" or enlarged dictionary definitions of "Meaning" or "Idea" by Joseph Kosuth, to conjure three completely distinct approaches to the use of language as a visual and conceptual medium.

Writing contains a record of time in the very accretion of marks which is both a record of temporal production and the trace of a time-based somatic gesture. For the viewer or reader this fact has its own tension in the fact that a written image can apparently be grasped—like a picture—in an immediate perception while the act of reading returns another temporal dimension to the text—different from the labored energy inscribed in the act of production.

In a page such as Tim Rollins and K.O.S.'s re-rendering of *The Scarlet Letter*, the densely rubricated letters imposed on the page read in relation to schematic structures of the conventional text: bold, emblazoned signs of work which overwhelm the linear progression of the printed page. There is another tension here which is fundamental to the concerns of linguistic philosophy in the 20th century: the conflict between the apparent capacity of language to embody knowledge within a logical system (such as the format of the printed page and narrative text) and the actuality of used language with all of its illogical peculiarities (the elaborate, individual, and idiosyncratic signs of the hand-wrought letters). What, in fact, do these things have to do with each other? What real relation is there between abstract structures of language and the lived experience which language can record? One could argue that all of the later work of logician and philosopher Ludwig Wittgenstein is focused on the dilemma raised in such work (and it is not surprising that his is the major influence on conceptual artists concerned with language)—which recognizes that the logical structures of language are always in conflict with its illogical actualities and that within the contradictions suggested by the latter lies the beginning of philosophical inquiry.

Found, Appropriated, Reworked

If the somatic, expressive, gestural trace and the encoded cryptic sign of the glyph define one end of the spectrum of legibility, and conventional writing serves as the basis of other conceptual and material structures, then written language produced by mechanical or technical means often embodies the standardized conventions of letterforms, page formats, and conventions of literary and other forms in a way which is most closely related to the language as a cultural form. Artists who make use of typewriters, hot type, phototype, and computer printout or other fixed sets of letterforms create a personal inflection at a secondary level of articulation—either as structure or statement or some combination of the two. The tropes according to which a technical process acquires the status of metaphor remains a striking feature of such works—with the very basic components of the alphabet able to function as neutral-seeming bearers of meaning and as self-consciously self-referential signs of production fraught with value in their own right. A letter, a page, a book—any of these may be significant on formal terms, working as an image of the vast space of potential or as the closed and studied texture of an authoritative document and so forth.

Appropriation and transformation of existing or found language motivated Tom Phillips piece, *A Humument,* a meticulously reworked version of the Victorian novel *A Human Document* (1892) on the pages of which Phillips painted, drew, or sketched, leaving some words and phrases untouched while obliterating the rest in the service of a vivid visual pattern or form. As an extended exercise in intervention in an existing form, that of a rather banal and ordinary book which becomes extraordinary in the process, the Phillips project embodies both process and metaphor within its interventions. By taking the book as a visual and material form Phillips manages to excise from the pages of its narrative text an entirely new narrative, one in which the printed structures of lines, words, gutters, and margins give rise to innovative visual and verbal structures. The book is both literally found and also metaphorically given here, and the artist's hand inscribes a palimpsestic projection which is both attentive to and disregarding of the information on those pages. Print becomes a structuring grid as well as an actual text, the new text functions at the expense of the original, and the sequenced pages (taken in fact from multiple examples of the novel) make a new book which is only partially indebted to the original. Manufactured and constructed, *A Humument* displays a power of invention in which text and image blend—sometimes in counterpoint dialogue, sometimes in indissoluble unity, sometimes in clashing contradiction within a single page. Nothing is actually erased in Phillips' work, but much is obliterated by the layering effect of pigment, saturating the field already saturated by the written word. What emerges is new, but never fully original, always containing the referenced source within the remade structures of the pages.

Phillips' book is an instance of appropriation—a recognition of the fact that language lives in the world and thus has a life beyond the original intention of its first author. Working with eliminative processes, pulling a new structure out from the flesh and dross of linguistic excess, Phillips also edits to make the received material of worldly language into a personal statement through the deft art of subtraction so that the poetic statement stands out clearly, pulled from the thick mass of language into a stark figure.

It is fitting to end with Phillips' work since it moves language away from the wall and painting and back into the realm of the book. As a cultural form the book has a long and complex legacy as the Law and the Word. It has a vernacular and secular history as well, and in this multifaceted identity it is like language—which lives the most exalted of philosophical existences and serves as the basis of the most mundane transactions. But the book, as poet and philosopher Edmund Jabès has noted, is never closed. Its infinitude is always inscribed by its boundaries, which, by marking themselves, indicate the place of questioning the possibility for containment.

Written Image as Material and Memory

In the world and of it, written language materializes thought into form and form into history, culture, and record. And just as there are pleasures in the rhythmic passage of air through larynx and over the palate to be beaten by the tongue and pressed against the teeth, so there are the parallel pleasures of pressing pen into soft paper, the stylus into clay, of hitting the keyboard of a responsive typewriter, or watching the lines of letters appear in the glow of a monitor. Memory serves us well through this material and returns embodied as the witness to our having made certain moments into a record on the page while the temporal life of writing aches towards the future, longing for that recovery which is available, again and again, through the physical form inscribed with information in the trace of material. Writing inscribes many paradoxes and tensions in its materiality—between idea and material, personal experience and social order, logical structures of thought and the illogical record of lived experience.

Sources Cited and Recommended:

David Diringer, *The Story of the Alphabet*. New York: Funk and Wagnalls, 1948.

Johanna Drucker, *The Visible Word*. Chicago: The University of Chicago Press, 1994.

—*The Alphabetic Labyrinth*. London and New York: Thames and Hudson, 1995.

Sigmund Freud, "Beyond the Pleasure Principle," *The Standard Edition of the Complete Psychological Works,* Vol. 18, James Strachey, trans., London: Hogarth Press, 1950; pp.14-18.

Dick Higgins, *Pattern Poetry*. Albany: State University of New York Press, 1987.

Jacques Lacan, "The Mirror Stage as Formative of the Function of the I" *Ecrits*. Paris: Le Seuil, 1966.

Andre Leroi-Gourhan, *Gesture and Speech* (originally published in 1964 in French as *Le Geste et La Parole*). Cambridge: MIT University Press, 1993.

Claude Levi-Strauss, "The Writing Lesson," *Tristes Tropiques*. New York: Criterion Books, 1961; pp.286-297.

Armando Petrucci, *Public Lettering*. Chicago: The University of Chicago Press, 1993.

Emmett Williams, *An Anthology of Concrete Poetry*. New York: Something Else Press, 1967.

This essay was written for the Washington University Gallery of Art exhibition titled The Dual Muse: The Writer as Artist, the Artist as Writer, *held in St. Louis from November 7 to December 21, 1997 with additional sponsorship from the International Writers Center.*

Simulacral Exoticism

There she is: in chic red silk studio allure, in an atmosphere of Eastern twilight, flushed with the burnished gold tones of the setting sun, bracelets resplendent, clothes simultaneously chaste and translucent, expression dreamily distant, in a transport of enslaved delight. Even with all the appropriate accoutrements, making her appear exotic in this Guerlain advertisement is no small task. Looking at the image, it's pretty obvious that what is bearing the weight of that little job is those bizarre and truly intriguing signs swarming all over the sandstone rock on which our beauty is perched. Writing systems have not been subject to the PC clean-up code—it's still okay to signify "otherness" of some kind by using strange, weird, unreadable, and suggestive-looking glyphs. But why do they look so strange? Are they in fact some real writing system being put at the service of advertising just because they look so strange? Or were they invented to look strange? In that case, the character of strangeness itself is up for investigation.

Now, to go about this task of figuring out the source of strangeness, I decided to consult a compendium of alphabets assembled by Benajah Antrim and published in 1843 in Philadelphia. Benajah Antrim was one of several important chroniclers of the history of writing whose work contributed to nineteenth-century literature on the topic of ancient languages and scripts. The term "exotic" was also used throughout the eighteenth and nineteenth centuries to refer to linguistic forms whose cultural location lay beyond the boundaries of Western Europe. The scripts that notate such languages are often the far-flung relations of the banal and familiar forms of the Roman, Greek, Cyrillic, and Hebrew alphabets whose closer kinship ties are evident in their visual resemblances. Exotic scripts included various branches of Arabic and South Arabic, East Asian and Indian scripts, as well as some of the older writings of the ancient Near East—all related to the same Semitic alphabet from which modern alphabetic writing derives. But exotic scripts could also include the few non-alphabetic scripts, notably Chinese writing and its many relations, as well as the lost writing of the Mayan people, Easter Island, and others. In his *Pantography* of 1843, Antrim discusses

the many extant scripts with which he was familiar, their lineage, phonetic operation, and their forms. Though not as extensive as the better-
known book by the same title published in 1799 by Edmund Fry,
Antrim's has the advantage of an in-depth discussion of the scholarship
in the field—myths, legends, and lore—pertinent to each script he describes. It is from this rich store of knowledge that I attempt reading the
Guerlain glyphs to decipher their exotic quality.

One of the likely sources for exotic scripts is Chaldea—or Baby-
lonia, as it is better known—"a kingdom of Asia," Antrim tells us, "and
the most ancient in the world [...] founded by Nimrod, the son of Cush
and the grandson of Ham" (you will remember he was one of the sons
of Noah), "who according to some historians built Nineveh, the capital
of Assyria." For those of you who are a little shaky on your ancient history and chronology, that puts us after the Flood, before Abraham, and
in the Tigris and Euphrates Valley. The writing system that Antrim
shows us from Chaldea is glyphic indeed and close enough at first
glance to look like the inspirational original for the Guerlain graphic

Chaldean

design team. Antrim offers several versions of Chaldean. The first of
these, called "celestial," contains the oldest characters known and is
"said to have been composed by the ancient astrologers, from the figures of certain stars." Intriguing though they are, these most ancient of
letterforms are a bit too simple for Guerlain—and their pattern of
strokes and circles has a branding-iron look that could have conveyed
an unintended Western motif, turning our red silk beauty into a cow-
girl in flannels. But the second script is a different story: "asserted to

Chaldean

have been brought from heaven by the angel Raphael, by whom it was communicated to Adam, who used it in composing psalms after his explusion from the terrestrial paradise." No explanation is given for Adam's literary impulse having arisen only outside the Garden of Eden, but his desire to record his verses is something with which all writers can sympathize.

But the form of these fabulous Chaldean letters, these ancient glyphs, is remarkably like those of the Guerlain rock. They have extra-special serifs—ones that hook around and extend in attenuated points and lines, with swashes and unexpected turns in their writhing forms. Writhing and a certain amount of sinewy excess are clearly signs of the exotic. Even more, however, the added subdivisions within the signs make for true strangeness. Where the letters of the alphabet contain their contortions within the space of a single x-height and its relatively tame ascenders and descenders (single strokes, for the most part, with the occasional odd lowercase "g" or ornate swash caps), exotic faces seem to contain the possibility of bifurcating internally, producing nodes and cysts and embryonic elements of form within their structure. Their very form signals an unstable code, one capable of rapid and unpredictable mutation.

The Chaldean letters, then, have all the hallmarks of the exotic glyph—movement, excess, mutation, and no stable set of strokes or forms as the basic constituents of their system. But in fact, the Chaldean alphabet turns out not to be the basis of this Guerlain inscription. Puzzle though I may, I cannot make a match. Another version of Chaldean holds some promise—it was used in Ethiopia by Enoch to write a treatise on divine subjects, but on closer inspection its forms reduce to a set of Greek-like omegas and Hebrew shins and a few other letters resembling bars of cast iron that had intersected with a freight train in a crucial moment of formation.

It is possible that the source was one of the many other versions of

Charlemagne

Chaldean—the one given to Moses and "known under the name of Malachim" or the letters "given to Abraham when he was departed from the land of Chaldea for Canaan." But their images are not provided, since Antrim was saving space for "other matters of great importance" that he did not want to have to exclude from the edition. But at least the Chaldean possiblity keeps me moving around in the right part of the world—whereas the next candidate for Guerlain's glyph was one bearing the name of Charlemagne. Many of its formal properties look appropriate—but every image I can conjure of the old Emperor is loaded with cloaks and chains and heavy coverings of all kinds and there is no way I can overlook all this in linking up exotic scripts to our nearly barefoot beauty. Though Chinese has a definite appeal in Antrim's careful rendering, the utterly evident sign of calligraphic production frustrates even the smallest attempt at linking the Guerlain

Ⲁ Ⲃ Ⲅ Ⲇ Ⲉ Ⲋ Ⲍ Ⲏ Ⲑ Ⲓ Ⲕ Ⲗ
a, b, g, d, e, s, z, ē, th, i, k, l,

Ⲙ Ⲛ Ⲝ Ⲟ Ⲡ Ⲣ Ⲥ Ⲧ Ⲩ Ⲫ Ⲭ Ⲯ
m, n, x, o, p, r, s, t, u, ph, ch, ps.

Coptic

stone carved signs with the graceful units of Asian writing. Cyrillic and Coptic are both out—the first on geographical grounds and the second on visual criteria. And so it goes, with the closest candidates being a form of "hieroglyphic" with no description given besides its having been "written from right to left," a charming Syriac (if only, only, it had matched), and a couple of wildly inventive Samaritan and Saracen scripts. The Samaritan contains "a queer looking animal" or two (conspicuously missing from the stone on which Guerlain's model continued to pose) while the Saracen has a double-bar motif in it that disqualifies it for ready stone relief carving.

Speaking of the production mode implied by this image: since when are stone letters carved in relief? This has to be the riskiest, most labor intensive way to produce letters since—especially in the soft flaky sandstone texture conjured here—they would tend to crack right off the face of that rock in the course of production. These letters are looking more and more like something cut with scissors and pasted onto a fake

Saracen

rock. Ah, gee. At least Antrim rendered his strange scripts exotic by providing a literate, speculative, and genuine provenance for them. But then, otherness has changed since the heyday of European colonialism. The exotic territory of consumerism has retrenched into the domain of safe sexuality. The capacity to invoke the "other" has been tamed into same-culture playacting, an attempt to guarantee the continued possibility of some undiscovered interior continent of the exotic in the erotic, a happy coincidence of language linking the etymologically unrelated words with the same elliptical sleight-of-everything used in the Guerlain ad.

The glyphs, the glyphs! They cry out to be left uninterpreted, to be the very sign of the mysterious, the strange, the novel—the equivalent of that indecipherable territory of female sexuality. They have a lot of work to do in this ad, which otherwise—with its crests, its gilded lettering, its uninhabited twilight studio and model of Eurocentric perfection —pretty much excludes any other of authentic means. No wonder the copy reads: ". . . not quite the same, not quite another . . ." This is a new definition of the exotic, neither as extreme or as authentic as in the old days (reform has taken hold). This is not the Other as unknown and unknowable, no, this is the Other as the all too familiar, simulating Otherness. Thus any real otherness is excluded, rendered moot and invisible; the Family of Man approach to exoticism eclipses all the strangeness of the real universe, all the differential aspects of difference, and all the invisible specificity of the "exotic" other. Simulated otherness erases not only cultural difference, but its very possibility. If difference and exoticism are only a mask for the Same, a conceit used to provoke a titillating frission of allure in masquerade of the safe upper-class boudoir, then Otherness ceases to exist as an aspect of that sealed universe. Benajah Antrim's concept of the Other clearly betrayed its Eurocentric peculiarities, but it interpreted cultural differences through a lens of respectful distinction. Languages and identities were not all the same in his account, all capable of being synthesized into a Play-Doh version of stone-carved history. Antrim sought the specific character of the scripts whose origins he attempted to tease out of the mixed sources of classical and biblical scholarship, to investigate the differences on which he premised his investigations. In the Guerlain universe, the simulated production of Otherness from Sameness suggests a world in which Otherness can never be registered as Real, and in which the basis of difference has been seamlessly erased from its inscription in language and writing. The signs by which it could be signified have been turned into a hybrid syntho-glyph of the familiarly strange, collapsed with the cipher of the female form whose patently unexotic form resists that identification quite safely, though the age-old identification of woman with the unreadable code of her own language reinscribes the familiar equations of the same-old same-old of the patriarchal and masculinist imagination.

This essay was originally published in the AIGA Journal, *Volume 14, No.3, 1996. All images are from Benajah Antrim,* Pantography, *1843.*

m, l, k, i, th, hh, z, v, h, d, g, b, a,

t, sh, r, q, ts, p, aa, s, n,

Modern Syriac

Hypergraphy: A Note on Maurice Lemaître's Roman Hypergraphique

Lemaître's hypergraphy fetishizes writing, and this is clearly evident in the visual effects contained in his book *La Plastique Lettriste et Hypergraphique* (Paris: Caractères, 1956). His manipulation of resemblance and substitution of elements in the notation system along iconic and pseudo-iconic lines suggests the kind of arcane practice that is inherently seductive in the idea of letters as signs and symbols. The actual icons Lemaître uses aren't particularly arcane; he takes real letters, tiny pictograms and diagrams, each more or less recognizable and readable, but manages to make the pages of his hypergraphic novel present the coded face of a secret program. In so doing he confronts his readers on the line where the distinction between a public and private use of writing threatens readability.

In looking at Lemaître's *Roman Hypergraphique*,(*Hypergraphic Novel*) I would like to examine the project—to describe it, give an idea of its intentions, and then put those observations into a framework where they raise some theoretical problems specific to written language: what are the limits of public and private in writing as a notational system; how do visual signs function when they pretend to being language; and how is the limit between public and private linked to the strategies of concealment and revelation inherent in writing in general.

In the essay which immediately precedes the *Hypergraphic Novel*, Lemaître explains the motivation behind his invention. The "Arts of Writing" explains that as far as he is concerned, the Dadaists and Surrealists had exhausted the potential of language as words, an exhaustion taken to its limit by James Joyce, who "accomplished the last phase of this evolution in creating an unsurpassable descriptive chaos." Feeling that writing had suffered an "aesthetic death," Lemaître joined with Isidore Isou in inventing a new domain for exploration, *Lettrisme*, and as a special project of Lettrism he decided to experiment with hypergraphy. To some extent the Lettrist project can be seen as an act motivated by frustration, a response to the generational trauma of being a European writer at mid-century in the wake of the overwhelming force of modernism in its full glory. The result was the fetishization of the material fields (sound and image) of a writing which seemed aesthetically exhausted. However, to fall back onto the letter as the locus of main activity seems like avoiding the risk of generating a text; in fact, it seems to be a refusal to write. While this abdication of literature can't be viewed in a totally negative light, the resulting blockage concentrates tremendous energy into this refusal to write. Lettrism creates a highly visible maelstrom of energy though it does not result in literature; Lettrism seems to remain deliberately invested in sign production.

In the "Arts of Writing," Lemaître describes Lettrism as the project of extracting all utterable sound from existing or potential language systems or from fields of random articulations. This extraction, rarefication, of sound material allowed a redefinition of the role of writing which could intensify its visual properties. The old conflict between writing defined either as the representation of spoken language or as a thing in itself would be resolved in this process, since each aspect would occupy a discrete domain. The second, visual writing, would be called hypergraphy, and would call on "all the processes of the plastic arts and photography in making stories or texts in which the words are replaced by painting or photographs of what would formerly have been described."

The hypergraphic novel consists of five plates, each of which uses writing or images substituted for writing in a different way. These five tableux constitute the whole of the "novel."

The first plate (not pictured here) describes the "situation" of the author, literally, zooming in from a sketch of the solar system to a fat round circle of the earth to a schematic map of Europe, etc., and ending with an i.d. photo of the author. The author's picture has to be understood as the last in this line, as the final position, which no one else could occupy, and not as an icon of a "self" as personality. Here we have the first metacommentary, a pun on the notion of position as one of the key determining factors of value in a visual system. Position, on the page and in a system and as indicative of placement/system relations, can make distinctions in the visual realm, since a visual field is capable of registering it as significant. The first plate, A, then is about position as a constitutive feature of identity.

Plate B uses all manner of iconic images, a kneeling man with no features, a croissant, a compass, a t-square, a tent, the Eiffel Tower, and a burning cigarette (elsewhere titled *Riff Raff*, see image p.68). These images substitue for the letter which they resemble in their grosser form. I frankly have difficulty deciphering the "message" on this page, where the symbols, which look like they were peeled off bar napkins, beer caps, and other popular locations for rebus-like visuals, are displayed in a leisurly spiral, aping one of the great objects in the history of writing, the Phaistos Disk, whose glyphs have never been deciphered. I find my resistance to the amount of attention which would be necessary in order to understand this piece significant, and rather than dutifully untangling the letters to spell out the dozen or so French words which ultimately would be the meagre fruit of such labor, I prefer to acknowledge this as one of the limits at which the boundary of readability is established. In its place in the catalogue of aspects of writing which Lemaître is elaborating in this hypergraphic series, this plate simply calls attention to shapes as signs, and to the degree of deviance permissable and tolerable for the forms to continue to function as versions of the letters whose norm is invoked.

Plate C (below) relies on a set of stick-figure icons, eyelids with their eyelashes extending downwards to indicate a state of sleep, open

Plate C

eyes with tears hanging in double rows, a rising sun, etc. All of these read fairly easily, and they are arranged in a grid of eight by ten elements, which is deceptively straightforward, since Lemaître in his introduction warns us that the sense of reading must be discovered. These little icons are not direct substitutes for any normal linguistic element, not for words or letters, and they refer only vaguely to concepts, ideas, actions or events which can be interpreted linguistically. To my mind, they question the process of conversion which is undergone in reading them: do they go from images to words, or to concepts already meaningful without linguistic translation? The potential of the visual sign to escape linguistic definitions and rules is suggested in this image, and in the process the nature of the system within which meaning might be fixed when signs lack syntactic or semantic stability is questioned. Outside such stable systems, the link between private act and public fact in language is threatened.

Plate D (below) takes normal letters and imposes them on four supergraphic letters which are in turn piled up on each other. The spa-

Plate D

tial dimension of the page, another feature characteristic of the visual organization not normally used by writing, is emphasized, since the illusion of depth created by the pile-up depends upon pictorial conventions. The normal letters, here represented as individual letters from different typefaces and chosen in classic ransom note style, have all been shifted in terms of the values they actually represent. Each letter stands for another letter in the alphabet, and the key to the code is somewhere in the piece as a whole, particularly in the use of the four supergraphic letters, P, i, e, r. This is another plate whose surface I did not penetrate, and the code aspect of such substitutions, at once banal and tedious, failed to be sufficiently intriguing to suggest that its interpretation would be worth the trouble. The intactness of the set as the guarantee of the value of each element of the notational system is the meta-issue here; the plate foregrounds the systematic nature of writing as a finite set of symbols.

The final plate, E, uses a work frequently reproduced in standard texts on the history of writing. This work by a Youkagir Indian girl to

Plate E

her absent friend is not a form of writing and not dependent on language or the invention of a stable notational system capable of describing a range of messages, it is a particular figure describing a precise situation, a girl speaking of her love. In response to this valentine, Lemaître has invented a set of phonetic glyphs, also indecipherable to the uninitiated like myself, and he has surrounded the basic image with a heart shaped frame, thus exaggerating the sentimental value of the original; the kitsch icon is the dominant referent in the visual field. Tiny marks encode the spoken language lost from the valentine, which in recognizing the impossibility of speaking across such a distance, attempted to recover the poignancy of lost speech: writing is not speech, it is its absence. Writing's presence conceals the lack of speech in this inscription of the words of the heart.

The content of these plates seems of less significance than their conceptual framework, the exposition of some of the features of writing as a visual form. Certainly the content is less available, and the strategies by which the writingness is revealed tend to obscure the semantic value behind this visual field. As a survey of writing's structural features it calls attention to the ways in which the conventions of writing depend upon certain systematic norms in order to ensure that the public/private interface succeeds in making an exchange of information.

Writing functions as a notational system for language by virtue of the same kinds of conventions which restrain spoken language within a cutural framework and ensure its operation; the forms in which language occurs adheres more or less to norms which enable messages to be recognized. When someone appropriates the territory of writing for experiment and invention, it undermines the linguistic aspect of the system of language, that is, the aspect which deals with syntactic and semantic values as they conventionally acquire definition.

The important thing Lemaître points out is the vulnerability of syntax, more than semantics, to such manipulation. For if the semantic value of a visual icon can be more or less granted within a particular cultural frame, a globe of the earth gets read as "the world," a rising sun as "morning," or tearing eyes as" sadness." We cull a "meaning" from the little pictures as readily as we might from words. Still, these icons remain isolated from any continuum in which their relation might be defined beyond a strictly linear sequence. Since these are not rebus-like arrangements, simply revealing through a laborious method a grammatical sentence, there is an absence of the duplication of a syntactic component. The argument could be made that the semantic value of language is much less unique to it than the syntactic conventions, and that the available means for communicating word values such as morning, sadness, or exit are considerable, whereas the means for constructing a prepositional relation "of" or "to" a sequence of tenses or a conditional are essentially impossible within the visual realm. Realizing this, the operation of visual symbols as a form of language will carve up the space of private and public use rather differently than conventional language. It is tempting to claim private as the act of writing and public as the act of reading, to define the bringing into being of the written form as always private and the attempt to receive it as always public, since the transition requires some kind of common ground for exchange inscribed in the medium itself. Lemaître seems to want to problematize this by pushing the distinction towards another extreme, insisting that the private use of language imposes itself upon the public realm and forces the public to enter into the private domain of the author.

The process of fetishization has a different public/private opposition within it. The fetishizing of writing emphasizes the way in which it is a form of private pleasure, a self-involved activity before all else. No matter what its ultimate outcome, or place, or situation, writing begins with the self. The fetish is not just the private activity, but an image, representation of the private parts suitable for exhibition.

It is a substitute. It reveals the private parts in an alternate form, for display, and conceals the real absence of the actual object. If the pleasure of the text is private, and if the fetishizing of the letter conceals the text, then the only role for the public is that of voyeur. And the voyeur is certainly, in this case, locked into a process of looking that is multilayered. First the eye is intrigued by the pictorial symbols, made curious enough to wonder at their relation and then to search behind the surface of the forms for some kind of meaning, some kind of value. The value, however, is all in the looking, and the interest in looking is another aspect of the fetish. This looking has nothing to do with getting to something more real, it is a purely symbolic activity, a function of the "image of" whose status as a surrogate is actually secondary.

So the letters of Lemaître's work remain the privileged images of a play in which the private is always on display, not in order to be revealed, but to remain, more or less concealed. For to enter into decipherment would be to lose sight of the function and intrigue of the real, which is the image of the letters on the page. To get the text would be to lose the letters, to devalue the fetish. Instead they remain, as the objects of intrigued curiosity, to be played with by both the author, and the public, which gazes voyeuristically on this display, fully defined as public by its position relative to that private material.

The fetish is the private face of the public life, and the public object of the private pleasure. The desire to look is what ensures the letters their life in both domains. Their interface in this case is the fetishized letter which has very little to do with text.

This article was first published in Poetics Journal, *Vol. #6, 1986.*

Language in the Landscape

STOP. We respond to the red octagonal sign almost without thinking. We react partly because of its standard form: we might not halt in front of a post with graffiti or for a chalkboard, even if they carried the same message. We are aware that disobeying the sign might have unpleasant consequences—an expensive fine, imprisonment, or a traffic accident. We read the sign on several levels: the form, the command, and the implied information.

But the sign also affects the way we read the landscape. It gives us clues that guide our interpretation of the situation. When we see a stop sign we know what to expect—an intersection used by motor vehicles. We also know that this intersection has been evaluated for its dangerousness. The sign indicates that officials have assessed the landscape according to culturally established norms and classified it as requiring this cautionary sign. We do not simply stop when we see the sign, we also allow the sign to inform our response to the landscape.

Language in the landscape, whether road signs, billboards, or graffiti, shapes our relationship to the landscape in many ways. Language can be explicit (DO NOT ENTER), deceptive (THE ONLY REAL BEER), enigmatic (EDY'S CHARACTER CANDIES), confusing (PARKING THIS SIDE ONLY BETWEEN 4PM AND 6PM ON ALTERNATING TUESDAYS EXCEPT WHERE INDICATED), and elucidating (WINDOW 6 FOR TAX FORMS ONLY). In every case, written language represents an invisible conversation: someone is speaking, someone is being addressed, the message has a purpose, and the message is delivered in a particular way. Language is a symbolic system, full of implication. It allows us to discuss things that are not present. We cannot dismiss language in the landscape as auxiliary or duplicative. The relationship between linguistic statement and physical object influences every encounter we have with our environment.

Forms of Written Language

The forms of written language are twofold: first, the visible features of the method of production, such as the style of typography or calligra-

phy, and medium em-
ployed; second, the forms
of the language per se, such
as current slang, obsolete
jargon, newly coined
words, and unconventional
spelling. Form affects
meaning. The graffiti,
TONY-ROASTING YOU,
spray painted on the
Oakland, California, post
office, would have a radically different impact if we
saw it on a lighted orange
plastic sign similar to those
for JACK IN THE BOX.
Whether language is carved
in stone or scratched with

chalk, its message is influenced by its form.

Material forms are also connected to specific moments in history.
The HOLMES BOOK COMPANY, LIBRARIES PURCHASED sign is lettered in black and gold paint on glass windows. This art form is more
and more rare because it is created by a skilled sign painter who works
on site. So we might guess that the sign and the bookstore have been
around for some time. A new business nearby uses purple and green
cartoon lettering for its sign, THE OTHER PLACE, SANDWICHES AND

THINGS. The
rapid transit
system in the
San Francisco
area, known as
BART, employs
high - tech
weather-resis-
tant, vacuum-
formed signs.
All are charac-
teristic of the

processes that produced them and the purposes they are designed to serve. Even to non-typophiles, every form of lettering has a distinct look, maybe not completely identifiable with its historical tradition, but carrying information about its intention. In addition, the semantic forms of the words, their obsolescence and idiom, or the obsolescence of the function they describe, place them in a historical framework, for example: DRAYAGE, BALTIMORE PIKE, and READY-TO-WEAR.

Kinetic digital lettering, the LED displays used on the Goodyear blimp, on moving news marquees, and on some transit platform signs, presents an unusual situation. Because of its uniformity, this system tends to neutralize the impact of the information it conveys. The screen treats the cautionary statement, "For the convenience of other passengers while riding BART do not put feet on empty seats facing thank you," exactly the same way as an advertising message from Allstate Insurance, or a news headline. The most extreme crisis and the most mundane banality are rendered with equal sangfroid. Our inclination to differentiate among these messages is dampened by the medium's inability to register any difference among them. The lack of responsive diversity, or differentiation, in the medium makes for a lack of effective impact.

The specialized spelling that businesses use deviates from more conventional forms of written language. Consider the subtle difference between NO DELAY CLEANERS and NO D-LAY KLEENERS. One name simply describes an operation. The other calls attention to itself. The odd spelling institutionalizes the service by removing it from the realm of pedestrian language. This is not conversation, this is commerce.

Coining new words and using words in unusual

ways are also provocative. UNEDA WINDOW is not immediately readable. Pausing to figure it out, however briefly, involves us in the sign and in the landscape. We notice the business. Similarly, THE CHURCH OF PRACTICAL CHRISTIANITY invites our inquiry far more than the FOURTH CHURCH OF CHRIST SCIENTIST, which faces it in Oakland. The contrasts in the name SCOTTISH RITE TEMPLE also puzzle us. Although a business may use an intriguing name to advertise its ser-

vices, a religious or fraternal order uses an ambiguous name to protect its exclusivity or its distinct identity.

In the landscape, as elsewhere, the things that are not immediately accessible gain power from the resistance they create. Most of these peculiarities in spelling or use of words found in the landscape do not go into circulation in general language. These oddities inhabit a distinct territory of language: that of commercial and public signs. The visible peculiarities of spelling and word choice as well as the visual properties of the medium influence the content of the message.

Information

Language is informative. It guides us. We depend on it for identifications essential to commerce (KAY'S MARKET), civic activity (REGISTER TO VOTE HERE), and behavior (KEEP OUT). Most functions of language in the landscape can be included under the heading, information. This category contains tasks from straightforward naming to advertising, social control, and edification.

Motives and intentions are so integrated into the character of language that it is difficult to find any written language that is purely informational. Take the most obvious examples of undiluted information: street names, plant markers in a botanical garden, and the sign on the bank that gives the time. How neutral are these? Each helps us identify and remember something, whether it is a place, a plant, or our progress in the daily routine. In street names this identification is tied to possession, maintenance, business, and civic order. The name of the street reminds us that some political body supervises the existence of the street, that it has a legal as well as functional existence. The plant markers help justify the existence of the park. They enhance the open space with the trump card of education, a social value higher than mere recreation. As for the courtesy clock, public awareness of time is never neutral. We organize our lives in relation to this arbitrary segmentation of the movement of the earth. The conspicuous presence of the clock acknowledges how much it is a reference for regulating activity. Time is a standard with a specific connection in this culture to Protestantism, the work ethic, and their role in ordering American life. Such signs, therefore, never merely provide information.

Beyond Information

Language has other, powerful effects on our perception of the environment in which it lies. A boundary such as a fence, for instance, becomes charged through the words, NO TRESPASSING, CONSTRUCTION AREA—HARD HATS REQUIRED, or QUARANTINE. No longer merely a line of demarcation, the boundary now vibrates with implication. We hesitate. We consider. The fence stops us. It is a temporary obstacle. It states a policy of exclusion, but it cannot elaborate, it cannot tell us who is excluded or why. Only language can convey that explanation. Its symbolic nature can invoke a reference for which there is no tangible evidence.

Language provides leverage. It is the only element in the landscape that challenges us to reevaluate what we see according to ideas not indicated by the physical setting. Only language tries to tell us what we see. Language does not simply, or even actually, identify things. Rather, language itself raises the question of definition. To take the language in the landscape at face value is naive. The ironies of mismatched building styles, collaged architecture, and incongruous urban development are one-dimensional compared to the irony of statement. PLEASANT VALLEY ROAD in Oakland could not be more aptly named in this regard. The street climbs from a complex traffic intersection between concrete condominiums and a plain of parking lots buffering a shopping center. PLEASANT VALLEY ROAD—we can never reconcile the name on the sign with the place. How could we? The identification is made by the contrast. The inevitable reaction to those words while paused at the stoplight is to look around and ask, Where?

Instructive Language

The signs at the gas station reading TURN OFF MOTOR and SET HAN-DLE IN UPRIGHT POSITION are particular forms of information, designed to direct behavior. They reveal someone's intention to dictate our actions. The succinct, instructive language does not encourage discovery, rather it conveys the assumption of the owners that the setting has predictable events and problems. In some sense, instructive language always cheats us out of the experience we might have in exploring a situation. Instructive language often protects us (NO SWIMMING, DEADLY UNDERTOW), but it also can be restrictive and can limit not only our activity but our perception.

Language as Advertisement

We all know that the language of advertising on billboards and business signs is loaded with more implication than information. Consider a subtle example, the word FIREPROOF on the Hotel Sutter in downtown Oakland. Was the word a response to an inquiry in the anxious age when the hotel was built —the era after the 1906 earthquake and fire in nearby San Francisco? A hotel owner might be answering a question in the mind of a prospective tenant. But what else does the word indicate when it is painted on the roof of a vintage brick building where the single word projects above the surrounding structures in lettering larger than that used for the hotel's name?

The word FIRE-PROOF illuminates an

entire field of reference. Besides alleging that the hotel is immune to fire, the statement emphasizes that it is the duty of the hotel's management to be conscientiously aware of the danger. The guarantee is not against smoke and flames. It is a guarantee of responsibility. It is a policy statement comparing the Sutter to other hotels. The hotel's managers are invoking the image of fire in their behalf to demonstrate their virtue. The word makes us think of the shelter of the hotel as active, vigilant against fire. The hotel articulates its aggressive stance on the sign so its stance is inseparable from its visible identity in the landscape.

Language as Identity

TRIBUNE and KAISER are both names of major industries in Oakland. The first business equates itself with the community. The other dwarfs and overrreaches the community. The identity of the Oakland Tribune newspaper is one with the city. The name Tribune on the newspaper's distinctive tower is a local landmark. The recognition the newspaper achieves will never be greater than that of the city. Oakland and the Tribune are linked. The many newspaper vending machines with the stencilled masthead of the Tribune are tied to the image of the Tribune Tower. The Kaiser empire, on the other hand, alters the city skyline with buildings that house part of its multinational conglomerate. As in the case of the Tribune, the simple word that names the business states its identity: the word needs no explanation. The italic sweep of the Kaiser letterforms, however, duplicates the logo used on trucks, building sites, and stationery. The many yards, factories, and offices of Kaiser throughout the West bear the same blue, bold italics. The name lays an expansive claim to space. While the Tribune is the core of a centralized local network, Kaiser is a conglomerate surfacing at many points beyond Oakland, and the company marks those points for easy identification in a vast and varied landscape. The name of the newspaper depends on the local landscape to complete its identity, while the name of the industrial conglomerate finds any landscape its proper location.

Language as Evidence

We assume language in the landscape can be understood, but sometimes it is enigmatic. It may be only a clue to unseen activities. On the sidewalk around Oakland's Lake Merritt, someone painted the word START next to a white line. This mark appears at one of the narrowest parts of the sidewalk where no more than two people could stand side by side. This is not an official race course, although joggers fill the paths around the lake. Something happened here, happens here, or will happen here. We don't know what.

The cryptic curb and street markings used by the utility companies and the city in order to direct maintenance crews pose their own enigmas to most of us. The yellow glyphs of the letters, numbers, and arrows are a clue. They allude to a process that goes on without our participation. The deliberateness of these marks is clear. They indicate the complexity of  the landscape of our daily life. But like the line for the race course, these markings are site specific, notations on the surface of the landscape. They are necessary for executing particular urban activities, even though we may not know what the activities are.

Language Creates Speculation

Language can make a claim. It can project a future that becomes convincing whether or not the claim is ever substantiated. HONG KONG U.S.A. had a long presence as a billboard announcing a proposed development in Oakland. The image on the sign finally changed to TRANSPACIFIC COMPANY. How much information is in these statements? They certainly attest to the vision of real-estate developers. A bulldozed parcel of downtown land allows all kinds of imagination. The illusionistic architectural renderings on the signs are slightly more specific, but the statements INDUSTRIAL PARK, EXECUTIVE CENTER, or STOREFRONT AVAILABLE, conjure even more specific images and a set of equally specific responses. These activities, whether industrial or executive, affect the community before construction is completed, because of their claims. The future we project when we read the signs is one we anticipate and prepare for, plan on, and react against. We act long before the building appears because we are spurred by the claim on the sign.

Language as Edification

Many of the words found around the Oakland Auditorium in the graffiti on the walls, in the scribblings on the sidewalk, and in the elaborate epigraphy of its richly carved front, fall into the category of edification. A passerby inscribed MAN'S DUTY TO GOD IS ANALYSIS, NOT PRAYER, in wet concrete. The motive was indisputably edification. The words contain no mundane information. In some sense the phrase is advertising, but this bit of language is clearly for moral instruction. The purity of its intention overrides the fact that it resulted from vandalism.

The writing in concrete has a link with the more formally inscribed statements on the grand facade of the auditorium. The intentions and ideals embodied on this civic building have become dated in seven decades. We might expect this, but it points to the possible pitfalls of preaching, especially in permanent material, because the tone of the

message may turn it into an oddly mocking travesty of its original intention. Even the apparent straightforwardness of the main inscription is coded by the underlying moral assumptions of the time. AUDITORIUM OF THE CITY OF OAKLAND DEDICATED BY THE CITIZENS TO THE INTELLECTUAL AND INDUSTRIAL PROGRESS OF THE PEOPLE ANNO DOMINI MCMXIV. Progress was an unquestioned goal and technology had not raised the specter of apocalyptic consequences.

The humanistic tone of this inscription is echoed in the phrases in each alcove of the auditorium, such as SPORT—THE JOY OF EFFORT; WEALTH OF THE EARTH—THE DELIGHT OF FLOWERS, THE SOURCE OF FOOD; THE DUTIES OF LIFE—THE WORD, THE TASK. The images that accompany the phrases are full of classical references. The phrases evoke a culture with strictly defined virtues in a world with definable goals, and with rewards and punishments meted out with justice. They speak of a classical ideal that was never as simple as it appears to be in these blank statements. Whether these words edify or not is a moot point. That the designers attempted to, that they believed in the possibility, and that their words remain as evidence of their faith is a richer field for discussion.

Language in Context

Landscape serves as the context for the language in it. Written language does not simply identify objects in the landscape. Language changes our perception of the very situation in which it acquires meaning. As we observe words in the landscape, they charge and activate the environment, sometimes undermining, sometimes reinforcing our perceptions. For us, language is full of culture and history, but it is also full of ambiguity and enigma. Because it is a set of symbols we use to invoke concepts, we may find it divorced from the very objects it aims to identify, posing the issues of definition and identity as distinct from the material in which they are embodied.

This article was first published in Landscape *Vol. 28, No. 1, 1984. The photographs were taken by Robert Lawrence, in Oakland, California.*

IV. Visual Poetics

The Interior Eye:
Performing the Visual Text

Dedicated to Emmett Williams and Dick Higgins in recognition of the 30 year anniversary of *An Anthology of Concrete Poetry*, Something Else Press, 1967.

In the late 19th century the idea of "la voix interieure" became prevalent in the study of linguistics, psychology, and the philosophy of language. The question arose as to what that "little voice in your head" really is. What is its relation to language? Is it an argument for the equivalence and interchangeability of thought and language? Or is it evidence of the colonization of interior life by social form? An elaborate discussion ensued.

But this discussion leaves entirely unasked and unexplored the processes which are active in our work which I will call "l'oeil interieur." By this concept I mean to invoke the various processes of seeing and reading by which sense is made—without pronunciation, without any obvious or overt link to the articulated properties of what appears on the page. This is a parallel universe of pronounced and unpronounceable visual elements.

Now there is a range of possibilities within which it is possible to conceive of the operations of this "performance" as a mental performance, and/or an oral rendering, or a non-linguistic experience. The visual performance on the page can be seen as an analogue to the voice, to a theatrical script or musical score, or to a sense of typographic character. It can also be seen and understood as a schematic form, structurally logical and meaningful even when it has no analogue to a pronounceable form. Visual format can mark, prescribe, or record process or the simulation of movement and it can also make use of absent elements as visual presences which participate in the production of meaning. I will examine a number of these conventions in a dialogue between well-known examples of visual poetry and my own work, *The Word Made Flesh*, first published in letterpress in 1989, in an attempt to sort out the ways I think the typographic treatment works to "perform" that particular text.

One way of thinking about "performing" the visual text is as an analogue to voice in which the page serves as a vocal score of tone or personality. Robert Massin's version of Ionesco's *The Bald Soprano* is a clear example of the attempt to use typography to distinguish one voice from another on the page. It's also possible to have a visual rendering of the mental voice through use of varied typefaces. This appears not as a dialogue but as an onomatopoetic rendering of personal turmoil in a work from the 1960s by Ocarté titled, "Revolutionists dominate the streets meanwhile people are dying who proclaim less than war clinging to nationalist principles tragic outcome, order, the only guarantor of peace accepted by adherents." Here the textual treatment fragments and creates visual noise to complement and express the conflicts manifest in the text. But when I look at *The Word Made Flesh* it's clear to me that there is no intention on my part to "score" the voice and that the typographic rendering has no vocal analogue.

Type can express "character" without being voice. Bern Porter's many books of found poetry exploit the graphic quality of appearance on the page, using the captured image of the found words as part of their communicative effect, as in the huge, bold-faced sans serif type of the statement from *The Book of Do's* (1982), "Try it. It won't bite." Early Dada works, like Tristan Tzara's "Boxe," established the ransom note mode of typographic poetry as a now canonical element of 20th century visual poetry. In these works typography has a suggestive inherency rather than asserting an essential quality of voice or form. Filippo Marinetti made use of this suggestive potential in his 1919 "At Night, in her bed, she reads a letter from her artillery man at the front." The synaesthetically theatrical quality of the type reads like an image of an explosion, replicating the activity of the battlefield in its visual chaos. The woman's silhouette writhes in erotic ecstasy as she replays the tumult of war through the passionate excitement of her lover's description. But neither of these is precisely what is intended in *The Word Made Flesh* where type presents itself as visual form without any suggestive associations of context or content.

The theatricality of Marinetti's piece is not as explicitly dramatic in its visual format as the textual script orchestrated for performance which appeared in the 1916 now-classic "L'Amiral Cherche Une Maison à louer." Scored and orchestrated to perform by Richard Huelsenbeck, Tristan Tzara, and Marcel Janco, this piece plays out its lines in visual and vocal parallel. But the "little theatre of the page" is a notion taken up more literally by Ilia Zdanevich whose 1923 *Ledentu as Beacon*, the fifth and final in his series of *zaum* (transmental language) dramas, was intended to perform only on the page. Zdanevich had staged reading performances of the earlier works in this series, but by the 1920s had reconciled himself to the unlikelihood of such events as a successful enactment—so he used his sensitivity to the theatrical potential of page and book form. In such works scoring—the significance of the spatial distribution—works as an element of meaning—granting distinctions to persons/speakers, tone, and timing as aspects of the text. It's one thing to perform a sound-poem or a scored work, it's another to understand the ways in which a visual work performs itself on the page, in the head, through the eye. There is the staged and the upstaged, the space of the page, and the activated fore, middle, and background of the type in *The Word Made Flesh*.

There is no verbal analogue to some of these spatial features. In Eugen Gomringer's "Ping Pong" the graphic relations on the page are specific, they imitate the movement of the ball across the table and back. We "read" the meaning of the visual attributes of this work without translating it into language. Space is graphic, specific, and produces meaning in visual terms—as it does in Pierre Garnier's 1963 "Grains of Pollen" where the spatial distribution is a visual analogue to itself, as the thing, using the graphic actuality of the page as an image of the pictorial conventions. Made and remade as a schematic mapping, the visual form carries iconic meaning—not by way of language but straight through that *l'oeil interieur*. The visual structure in the work is analogous to perception of an experienced space. But again, none of these elements of spatial or theatrical scoring are the ones which are used in *The Word Made Flesh*. In that work the space is literally the space of the page, not used to remake a schematic rendering of a real space or image. Nor is the space on the page used as the basis of a verbal score or script. Say "field." Say "figure." Say "ground."

Another frequent trope of visual poetry is the production of iconic forms: an image of and an image as. The shaped poem is an old old tradition, going back to Greek manuscripts of the third and fourth centuries, and likely older though no examples have survived. In such works there is a correlation between the main thematic of the piece and its visual arrangement on the page. Apollinaire's well-known

Calligrammes include such iconic works—like the famous "Il Pleut." Is there a sound analogy in this work? Are we supposed to read the letter by letter droplets in a staccato pattern of rain hitting a window? Or is it merely that overall image of rain as lines of water streaking towards the ground which has assumed iconic referential force in our catalogue of mental images? At what point does the visual gestalt translate into meaning? And in what mode? There are so many aspects of the visual which have no correlation in the verbal—as in the case of Apollinaire's calligram of the the watch, "La Montre," whose three-dimensionality is hinted at by the increased shadowing on the left side, inscribed by the longer length of those lines. Language does not cast a shadow, has no inherent spatiality, trapped as it is in the flat dimensionality of the page or line or spoken verse.

There are many such icons in the repertoire of visual poetry, famous, well-known, very familiar works such as Mary Ellen Solt's 1966 "Forsythia," rendered in type by John Dearstyne. Solt considered the work to be "analogous to the stage performance of a play," a coming into being as event, that which makes itself as a work by acting itself *out*. Lewis Carroll's oft-cited image of the disappearing mouse's tail from 1864 is an icon which performs its "shrinking" voice into dimunition. And Jirí Kolár's 1962 "Brancusi," is a piece in which the iconic image of the well-known sculptor's well-known work is recognizable as an icon without verbal value, as image only—read and read again into the work, as referent. But where does the image get "read" in the visual search engine of our mental files of schematic to elaborately pictorial icons?

Icons need not only be pictorial, they can also be schematic, indicating a process or event. In Seiichi Niikuni's "River Bank," there is an idea rendered as an image which is never spoken, only seen. The intersecting boundary of two domains, two fields of characters, each mark the edge in a demarcated territory. This pattern is repeated in an untitled 1965 piece by Pierre and Ilse Garnier where two blocks of type intersect. They describe the contrast between the two letters which compose the work—the "light of the i" upright, the "e" folded in on itself—and it is their intersection which dynamicizes the work. Schematically similar to the Niikuni work, it is distinctly different in meaning. More abstract, the Garniers' piece only concedes to an analogy, the passing of a shadow over a field, a space, a page. The edge of the light "i" field breaks across the space of the "e's" in an ephemeral, moment of flattened time.

Emmett Williams charted another dynamic intersection in his 1958 "Like attracts like." Here the attraction of the two columns draws them closer and closer until they blur. Williams noted the specificity of the visual form to the text, saying, he could not "think of three other words which would work so well." So, form equals content here, or does it? Is that after the fact, or before? If the form is content, then does it have only one meaning? *Carminum figuratum*. One body one text? What transcendence? None. In *The Word Made Flesh* there is no possibility of obtaining an iconic reference from the format of the piece, nor of following a line of signification out through the chain of signifiers to some final logocentric "being." The text is grounded in its own vocabulary of tongue and gristle, meat and flesh and bone—raw, crude, wiggling, spasming in a nice neat letterpress order. Just try and keep your form in some neat order of content!

After all, Claus Bremer, in 1963, found four words whose interaction mimics that of Williams's three on the page. "Rendering the legible illegible," follows a similar schematic. What is meant by specificity of form? of process? of structure? Is the Bremer the ultimate version of the Williams? Does likeness cancel legibility—sameness become some unified field of chaos as the layering illegiblates the text?

Illegi—whats? Sublates—this into that—obliterates the cosmic orders. As in Carl Fernbach-Flarsheim's "Mirror Field inside Random Field." Legibility and boundaries are formed here as a physical principle and property, neutrino trails. It is process as much as form which shapes these works. Some record of event or possibility of movement, change. In an extract from a 1966 work by Torsten Ekbom, reading and seeing are set up as process, data management. The page allows structure as order/sequence/instruction. It is a "picture" only in the most literal sense as that which can be seen. And there is no "hearing" of the relations of box to box here. No verbal rendering of the interior eye's movement through the schematic diagrammatics of the work. Eye go, you go, it goes. A visual format we can read and understand in its own terms and codes. As in Ana Hatherly's 1985 "History of Poetry" we can read the delicate trails and tracings. Another illusion is inscribed here—that of time passing, leaving its marks. Sometimes such movements and changes are doubly inscribed as text and image in the piece. And in

Gomringer's 1954 piece an elegant series of formal transformations from word to page to shape flows left to right with some inexorable-seeming logic of change. By contrast, Bengt Emil Johnson's 1964 "Homage to John Cage" uses the possibilities of smearing, mushing, as graphical "events" in his tribute. There is no accident in this work, only chance opportunities, structured to occur. What happens happens on the page, which is the performative point. And is specific to the page— as is the case with Hansjörg Mayer's accretions, the overprintings of letters in his *alphabetenquadratbok* from 1964-65. Progress and progression, the serial, minimal musical analogies are echoed here in the discrete squareness of the letters turned to lie on each other, visually stacked. Performed.

Structure can work as instruction, as program, as transformation. As in the opening sequence to *The Word Made Flesh* where the gradual visual change from page to page mocks the movement from deep to surface structure in the generative grammar of Noam Chomsky's linguistic work. The visual IS a performative dimension: it makes the text, makes meaning in its embodiment, as form/expression/enunciation. Ultimately it's not only that the visual/image/icon/event performs on the stage/theater arena of the page but that it makes/is made/be's/becomes through the graphic and visual means.

Finally, there is the possibility of a play of difference between the present and the absent in visual terms which also signifies according to its own non-linguistic specificity. In Apollinaire's work about Picasso— the absent presence of the image shapes the pictorial elements—which are themselves pointedly left visually out in order to be seen. There is a sweet muteness in that gesture like a tone of silence, marked, stated, scored into a work, the dialogue of the language with its absence, as a word, a text which is said and stated or erased, held back, left hanging unspent and unarticulated. Gomringer inscribed the mute as the visual image of itself in his 1954 *Silence*. The poem's own interiority, its own specificity, is performed and manifest as form, in a visual enunciation that concretizes the restful space of a visual silence for the eye. But what is that space? How is it "read" or "seen" as a silent absence, not as a word? It is a space not meant in the linguistic sense, not coded in some final, inevitable way. Against this we have always to remember that within the page there is also all that space which is emphatically not silence which works as field, as support, as its own replete fullness, anticipatory, active, or fulfilled.

I go back again, at the end, to the pages of *The Word Made Flesh* where the large wood letters and clusters of black text make their own figure against the red field of small copperplate text. No verbal rendering is intended to imitate the overlaps and redundancies, shared letters, changes in size or scale. They are not meant as a score to be emphatically read out according to shape or density, nor interpreted according to some scheme of attributed or associated value. The word is made flesh not as a voice, not as a score, an image, an icon, or an event but as a text whose visual properties and idiosyncracies enact themselves for the eye, upon the page. There is a visuality of language which is not imagistic, but specific to the quality of written language itself. Not an inherency, but an actuality, tangible, perceptible, specific, and untranslatable, understood and grasped as effect.

I quote: "The body returns to language in a rush taking its teeth out of the rain and washing the infant in tears of recognition which were never based on life lived elsewhere. Here, now, the message makes its face—"

This talk was delivered in a slide performance at EyeRhymes, *an international conference of visual and experimental poetics held at the University of Alberta, Edmonton, in June 1997. Almost all images referred to may be found in the pages of the Emmett Williams anthology.*

Experimental/Visual/Concrete

Concrete poetry's most conspicuous feature is its attention to the visual appearance of the text on the page. Poems with a distinctive shape, formal arrangement, or obvious manipulation of typographic means characterize the works which fall under the general rubric of concrete poetry. However, concrete poetry has a far more specific meaning when it is applied, as is historically correct, to the work of two specific groups of poets who took the term and applied it to their work in the mid-1950s. The 1955 meeting between Décio Pignatari (a member of the Brazilian Noigandres group) and Eugen Gomringer in Ulm, Germany resulted in their announcement of the formation of an international group of Concrete Poetry which would further explorations each had already initiated within their own context. While there were important points of commonality in the work of these two poets and the other writers who formed their immediate circles, there are also significant points of difference in the sources for their poetics and in the nature of their practices. These differences locate their respective work within distinct aesthetic traditions, and the philosophical premises which informed their approach to language and poetics can be articulated through these distinctions.

In its most generic application, the term "concrete poetry" is used to designate all manner of shaped, typographically complex, visually self-conscious poetic works. The term "visual poetry" is more general and thus more aptly used to describe a history which is as old as writing itself. Certainly the scribes who incised Egyptian hieroglyphics into the material substrate of walls and sarcophagi from about 2700 BC onward were sensitive to the visual arrangement of their signs. In many cases certain "determinative" marks (those which indicate the category to which a word belongs) relied upon visual relations to produce linguistic meaning. More explicitly poetic works appear in 4th and 3rd century BC Greek manuscripts where memorial texts in the shape of urns or other more fanciful visual forms established a tradition of pattern poetry which continues to the present day.[1]

The exploration of the visual potential of poetry on the page is not limited to shaped poems or works whose presentation makes a simple iconic image form. In the 20th century in particular the exploration of various typographic, calligraphic, and even sculptural manifestations of poetic works contributes to a widespread proliferation of formal innovations. These range from the experiments of the early 20th century avant-garde, Dada and Futurist poets in particular, to a whole host of later 20th century innovations which are only superficially related to either the avant-garde or concrete poetry per se. At the end of the 20th century there is a fully developed, very complex, continually interrogated, and highly varied range of work being produced in which visual and verbal distinctions are difficult to sustain. While these owe a minor debt to concretism, their aesthetic syntheses are wide-ranging and their visual appearance owes as much to mass media commercial design and electronic (video and computer) technology as it does to the tradition of literary forms.[2]

To understand the specific identity of concrete poetry is to understand its distinction from precedents as well as its aesthetic affinities and characteristics. It is obvious that concrete poetry has certain elements in common with other work in the long tradition of visual poetry, but these are mostly superficial elements: the work has a distinct shape on the page and loses a part of its meaning if it is rearranged or printed without the attention to the typeface and form which were part of the poet's original work. Whether contemplating a vase-shaped ode or staring at the hole in the center of Gomringer's famous poem "Silence," one is aware that visual presentation is key to the meaning of the work. But such superficial resemblances quickly break down under analysis. In the work of Gomringer, it is the structural relation of the words, rather than any particular image suggested by them, which gives their visual presentation value. The manipulation of such structural relations had occurred to other writers, but they had not been put into theoretical terms as the basis of a poetic practice much before the 20th century.[3] There are, however, significant distinctions between concrete poetry and earlier 20th century experiments.

These early 20th century experiments in the visual manipulation of poetry occur in several locations. First, in Russian Futurist typographic work, particularly the ferro-concrete poems of Wassily Kamensky (beginning around 1912) , zaum (experimental language) poetry with its elaborate typographic treatment by Ilia Zdanevich (beginning about

Wassily Kamensky,
Tango with Cows,
1914, Moscow,
letterpress on
wallpaper.

1917), and various graphic manipulations in the work of Lazar El Lissitzky and Alexander Rodchenko (mainly after 1920), among others.[4] These works structure the page elaborately, often making relations among lines of verse in orchestral arrangements which mimic the conventions of musical notation while exploiting the contents of the typographer's case as the basis of their formal graphic language. The Russian works are largely based in letterpress technology, with its horizontal, vertical, and occasional diagonal elements. Consequently they have a strict formal look to them which is highly organized and graphic in character. The legacy of what is termed "constructivist sensibility," with its attention to the relations of formal elements within visual (and verbal) work, is a direct influence on the work of Eugen Gomringer, though in modified form.[5]

A second area in which experiments in visual poetry emerge is Paris, most notably in the calligrammatic works of Guillaume Apollinaire and the poster-poem works of Pierre Albert-Birot, both produced in the 1910s, and both evidencing a strong use of recognizable iconic form in the arrangement of the words on the page (e.g. the falling drops of rain in Apollinaire's "Il Pleut"). Such iconic work is acknowledged by the Brazilian Noigandres group as a point of reference, rather than a strong influence. Though pictorially shaped poems find many followers in the

later part of the 20th century, their visual form is
essentially mimetic, and it
is this imitative naturalism
which is considered most
limiting and thus least
useful to the concrete
poets of the 1950s.
Conspicuously published
in Albert-Birot's journal
SIC (Sons Idées Couleurs),
these visual pieces are
more modest typographi-
cally than those of many
works with which they are
contemporary.

A third arena of typo-
graphic experiment is that
of Filippo Marinetti and
other Italian Futurists.
Their work is, again, wide-
ranging, but Marinetti's
attempts at a reductive
notation for poetic lan-
guage, and his appropria-
tion of mathematical sym-
bols and forms, has certain

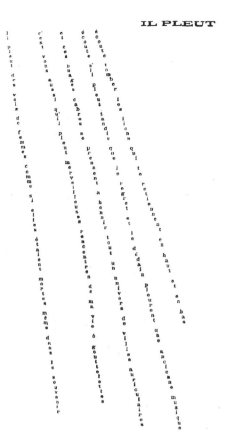

Guillaume Apollinaire, "Il Pleut," 1916, in *SIC,* Paris, letterpress.

sympathies with Gomringer's later invoking of numerical harmonies
and arrangements. Visually, however, the work of the Italian Futurists
is quite distinct from that of later poets. Marinetti's work tends toward
typographic variety, with a certain pictorial quality and a degree of
chaos. His 1919 "Words in Liberty" goes far beyond the moderate
manipulations of his 1914 *Zang Tuuum Tumb* with its use of plus, minus,
and equal signs, verbs in the infinitive, and nouns in their simplest case.
The collage work of Italian Futurists, most notably Carlo Carrà and
Ardengo Soffici, introduces issues of appropriation, mass media, popular culture, and the material history of language as image into the 20th
century avant-garde poetic practice, as does collage work within

Filippo Marinetti, from *Words in Liberty*, 1919, Milan, collage.

Russian, German, French and other contexts. Since this is material which has little relation to concrete poetry as it is conceptualized in the 1950s, I will simply note its important existence as an aspect of the terrain of early 20th century investigations of the visual and material form of language.

Finally, of course, there are the Dada contributions to the avant-garde exploration of visual poetry. Most easily grasped in the cut and paste, ransom-note typography of Tristan Tzara and Raoul Hausmann, this work makes striking use of a collage sensibility to recombine existing linguistic materials for the composition of poetic works. The visual character of these works, polyglot and polymorphous, has as its basis an insistence on the social, communal character of language and the instance of poetic expression as an idiosyncratic but incidental utterance within the linguistic field. In this respect, it is anti-lyrical and anti-subjective to a degree which exceeds that of other avant-garde practitioners. Marinetti's Futurist work, though anti-lyrical, depends upon a notion of effects and formal essences which betrays his symbolist background while the work of Russians Kamensky and Zdanevich is suffused with personal expression and individual emotion. Within the later Soviet graphic investigations of form the components of lyrical subjectivity and symbolic essence are banished as sentimental and old-fashioned, and a commitment to the effect of form as an instrument of social change focuses on form as a literal, material basis for linguistic and visual work. Such formalism is associated with revolutionary aesthetics throughout the 1920s in both Soviet and German contexts.

Casting a long shadow over the entire period of the early 20th century avant-garde (from the first manifestos of Marinetti in 1909 to the major achievements of the 1920s) is the figure of Stéphane Mallarmé. Mallarmé's monumental and persistently enigmatic work, *Un Coup de Dès*, which was conceived as a typographic work in 1896 but only produced in a version of his typographic form in 1914, serves as a major point of reference for much 20th century poetic investigation of visual form. The reasons for this are that Mallarmé's work remains resistant to reduction or closure and is thus capable of providing inspiration for the most literal as well as the most abstract explorations of relations between visual manifestation and linguistic meaning. Variously described as a constellation, an open work, an image of a shipwreck, and a complex hieroglyphic, Mallarmé's poem uses a variety of type sizes and styles to create a poem intended to approach the condition of pure thought. The work was to scintillate, to shine and manifest a poetic idea in its purest harmony of form. The language is elusive and the imagery simultaneously suggestive, dense, and fleeting, lending itself to any number of interpretations. But it is clear that Mallarmé's attention to the space of the page *as* a space, and his careful measure of the relative weight of words as forms on the page, activated dimensions of visual poetics which could not be brought to life by literal iconic images (of vases and such) or by the conventions of traditional literary layout and design. Mallarmé's poetic sophistication and his theoretical investigation of the concept of the book, of language, and of symbolic value thus serves as a cornerstone of 20th century visual poetics. Not least of all, he made a work whose graphic, visual presentation are indisputably integral to its poetic meaning—thus making an exemplary visual poetic text.

Not surprisingly, then, it is Mallarmé who features as a recognized influence on both Brazilian and German (and other) concrete poets to a greater degree than the other avant-garde writers whose visual experiments dominated the early 20th century literary landscape. For instance, though the metaphysical aspects fundamental to Mallarmé's practice are transposed into a concept of mathematical harmony in his work, the idea of transcendent form which approaches the condition of pure spirit clearly informs the work of Eugen Gomringer. Gomringer, a native Spanish speaker who had been drawn into concretism through the visual work of the Swiss artist Max Bill, is the key figure of the German language concrete poetry movement. Working mainly in Switzerland, he was the most rigorous theoretician and practitioner of a group which expands to include such dispersed and varied poets as Hansjörg Mayer, Öyvind Fahlström, Emmett Williams, Claus Bremer, Walter Bense, and Helmut Heissenbüttel, among others. For the sake of simplicity in this discussion, I will limit my remarks to the discussion of Gomringer, though it should be understood that he in no way defines or delimits the contributions of these other writers, each of whom had their own particular interpretation of concretism at the basis of their work.

Gomringer's most immediate influence, as mentioned, was the visual work of Max Bill whose activities extended from architecture and design through the fine arts. The guiding principle of Bill's work was a commitment to a visual formalism which was his version of earlier constructivist and formalist tendencies among Russian/Soviet and Dutch artists from Kazimir Malevich to Piet Mondrian and Theo van Doesburg. Van Doesburg's 1930 publication, "Numéro d'Introduction du Groupe et de la Revue Art Concret" had defined the concerns of concretism: a search for a universal formal language which had no relation to nature, emotional life or sensory data, and the pursuit of works which were completely void of lyrical, symbolic or dramatic expression.[6] Van Doesburg was crucial in founding the Abstraction-Création group in 1931 which continued to explore the tenets of this visual formalism. The group's influence and visibility were limited and they remained a minor movement. In many ways the greatest impact of their aesthetic is in the field of applied design—industrial, architectural, and graphic— where the formalism which had originated within a Soviet context found its new decontextualized identity—one carefully stripped of the social agendas which had accompanied their original development. Bill's models of form were the "purposeful structures" of technology and industry—and his aesthetic is narrowly focused on a non-functional "spirit-form" which nonetheless takes its ideal from the rigid functionalism of modernism's early designers.[7] In visual terms, this resulted in paintings produced through carefully measured, mathematically calculated, systems of order. The relations of line, color, and planes were meant to manifest relations of a numerical harmonics which, for Bill, were the essence of the transcendent universal language he sought. Bill thus betrays the influence of the other strain of Russian/Soviet visual formalism that originates in Wassily Kandinsky's spiritual essentialism and theory of a universal visual language of harmony and form. It was within the context of these extensions of visual formalism that Gomringer was exposed to concretism, thus his approach to poetry was as much grounded in visual aesthetics as literary models.

Gomringer took up Bill's modified, decontextualized formalism and made it the basis for his own poetics. In his 1953 publication, *konstellations*, Gomringer produced a series of works which epitomized his concept of the "constellation"—the Mallarméan term from which the collection took its name. Defined as "a play area of fixed-dimensions," Gomringer's concept involved the use of a very reduced set of formal elements—poems of one or very few words arranged in rigid and relatively simple structural arrangements (again, "Silence" is the oft-cited example and rightly so since it so clearly demonstrates his precepts). The "play" in these works is restricted entirely to relations among the elements which were present (thus the "fixed dimensions" of the work), and the structure and presentation of the piece are to be exactly identical with its meaning. A second influence on Gomringer becomes evident here: his readings in linguistic theory based on information science, theory which attempts to analyze language in systematic terms and propose a noiseless mode of information transmission. Such models are contrary to the analysis of natural language, poetics, or socially based linguistics, and were attempting to eliminate the kinds of ambiguities which characterize habitual language use (and which often serve to give poetic language its greatest charge).

Thus Gomringer's reinvention of the concept of the concrete involves the belief in the literal value of form which he took from Bill, a

silencio silencio silencio
silencio silencio silencio
silencio   silencio
silencio silencio silencio
silencio silencio silencio

Eugen Gomringer, "Silencio," ("Silence"), 1954.

faith in the universal numerical structure of information and relations, and combined this with anti-naturalistic linguistic theory which was in part being given an impetus by the mid-century interest in machine languages.[8] Gomringer never went so far as to demonstrate the existence of quantifiable equivalents for his verbal works. But his poetry embodies his faith in the capacity of structure to serve as a meaningful form. At the same time that his work remains embedded in natural language he strove for a concrete poetry in which meaning was self-identical with appearance, unequivocal and unambivalent.

It is this concern—the attempt to make poetic meaning isomorphic with its visual structure, with its presentational form, and its appearance on the page—which is the point of commonality between Gomringer and the Brazilian Noigandres group. And it is on this point that their two otherwise very distinct traditions converge. Unlike Gomringer, the writers who formed the circle in Sao Paolo—Augusto de Campos, Haroldo de Campos, and Décio Pignatari (which expanded to include Pedro Xisto, Edgard Braga and others)—sought their literary identity within the modern poetic tradition, particularly the Anglo-American mainstream in which Ezra Pound, James Joyce, and Gertrude Stein played a major role. The very name of their group, "Noigandres" is taken from Pound's "Canto XX," where it appears as a baffling nonsense word whose enigmatic character is remarked upon.[9] They also situated their work within a continental tradition, particularly that which stemmed from the work of the symbolist Mallarmé through the work of Apollinaire, Dada and Futurist poets. The musical works of Anton Webern, Pierre Boulez, and Karl Stockhausen were also active sources for their inspiration. For all its diversity, a common theme of all of the work they drew on is a central feature of much modern art and literature: a focused attention on formal means in their own right. The concept of the ideogram formulated by Ezra Pound as a model of poetic composition (a model in which the structure and content of a poem approach a non-verbal condition of identification so that the "image" of the work as both form and meaning are one and the same) was fundamental to Brazilian concretism. As in the case of Gomringer and the formalist tradition from which he came, the Brazilians rejected all forms of "expressionism"—lyrical, personal, emotional in favor of a poetic form which could function as an object in its own right, betraying nothing about the author, nothing of subjective feelings, or individual identity.

In this formulation an old tenet of modernism is restated: the notion of a creative work which is fully autonomous, self-sufficient, able to exist —not as an interpretation of other objects, and not as a mimetic representation—but as a creation in the fullest sense—original, independent of reference or imitation, meaningful in its own right.

Augusto de Campos's *Poetamenos*, first published in 1953, embodies the vision of Brazilian concretism: printed in several colors, the work identifies various themes and voices (male and female) through these visual means. The most immediate model for de Campos's work was the "Klangfarbenmelodie" ("Tone-Color-Melodies") of Webern—a form premised on the faith in color and form to function as immediately effective mode of communication.[10] There is a residual belief here in a system of correspondences which harks back to symbolist theory, even if Webern's work is stripped of metaphysical baggage. The word phrase "verbivocovisual" by which the Noigandres group describes their productions suggests a similar synthaesthetic approach, only applied to the materials of poetics. But where Gomringer strove for the "unequivocal resolution" to questions of meaning through formal means, the Noigandres group are more willing to renounce the struggle for the absolute—or Absolute—that is, the struggle for either linguistic certainty or metaphysical truth. Though the elements of the work are to be self-evident and the structure and meaning self-identical, the form itself remains in a condition of perennial relativeness, without closure, without fixed value, and open to various interpretations and responses. Noigandres searched for a form of metacommunication in which visual and verbal means would coincide and communication would occur through form as an inseparable fusion of form-content, rather than through the conventions of message communication in arbitrary symbols or signs.

Several manifestos published in the 1950s give concrete poetry a clear definition: "From Line to Constellation" and "Concrete Poetry" both authored by Gomringer and published in 1954 and 1956 respectively, and the "Pilot Plan for Concrete Poetry" published by the Noigandres group in 1958.[11] While these papers elaborate on the positions I have outlined very briefly above, the proliferation of concrete poetic practice was rapidly escaping any simple definition. Among the Brazilians, the works of Xisto and Braga engage with the use of the ideogramme to express far more subjective and lyrical positions than those typical of their counterparts; Augusto de Campos was investigating his own "pop-concretism" which incorporated materials from media culture and non-literary sources into his work; in Germany, Hansjörg Mayer and Emmett Williams were making playful works manipulating alphabetic elements or word puns in a manner which was resonant with referential qualities rather than dependent on finely worked out structural rigor. The question of reference, of the echoes or traces of the world which find their way into the linguistic, visual, and material presence of language, was always slightly problematic, even for Gomringer at his most pure. For the Brazilian poets, a commitment to a belief in the social and political function of poetics precluded the kind of metaphysical transcendence as an endpoint which was central to Gomringer. These sorts of distinctions only multiply as one begins to look into the wider field of concrete poetics—whether one is examining Claus Bremer's fascination with the typewriter, or Max Bense and Heisenbüttel's experiments in statistical permutations as a basis for poetics, or the graphic inventions of Dieter Roth and Marcel Wyss in their collaborative publication *Spirale*, begun with Gomringer in 1953. Each of these individuals has their own point of departure for their work, but the general common interest which draws them together under the rubric of "concrete" is their emphatic attention to the visual and/or physical substance of language. The "and/or" is introduced here to at least point to the parallel tradition of sound poetry which has its own history in the 20th century, one in which many of these same figures participate either directly or proximately.[12]

Though concrete poetry was fully realized in the 1950s, as is evident by the numerous publications generated from these two nodes—Germany in the northern and São Paolo, Brazil, in the southern hemisphere—it continued to gain momentum throughout the 1960s. The work of Ian Hamilton Finlay, John Furnival, Dom Sylvestre Houédard, Jonathan Williams, Jirí Kolár, Pierre and Ilse Garnier, and literally dozens of other poets in England, France, Italy, Czechoslovakia, Spain, Canada and the United States attests to the vitality which engagement with material aspects of writing practice promoted—whether these derived from the manipulation of sound or visual form. But to keep to a clear definition of a theoretical premise for this work quickly becomes impossible. The generic statement, "attention to materiality," is so vague that it loses any real value, while the strict rule of "form which is self-identical with meaning" stretches only to include a very few writers and even then, only some of their work.

One movement in visual poetics which occurs at almost the same precise moment as concrete poetry which is, however, utterly distinct in all respects, is Lettrism. Lettrism was initiated by the Romanian Isidore Isou, who arrived in Paris just after World War II and launched his poetic program with great publicity and high profile bids for public and critical attention. Lettrism was primarily defined by Isou, who believed that the spiritual and aesthetic exhaustion he perceived in western art and poetics was to be salved through Lettrist techniques.[13] Basically Isou wanted to atomize language into its smallest constituent elements—which he took to be letters (cavalierly disregarding the complex issue of the distinction between sounds and alphabetic signs)—and then reinvent poetry around the letter (or invented signs). With his two most immediate adherents, Maurice Lemaître and Gabriel Pomerand, Isou fostered the production of books, paintings, spatial environments, sculptural work, architecture, films and performances all exploring aspects of the Lettrist precepts. Graphically and linguistically arcane, the Lettrist work is often inscrutable, relying on material, visual, or tactile effect rather than achieving communication. Lettrists often emphatically emphasize the glyphic nature of the visual sign. Lemaître, for instance, invented a form of hypergraphic writing which substituted symbols for letters in rebus-like arrangements, displacements, or transformations. But such work is very far from the reduced concentration of the concrete poem with its intense focus on the collapse of structure and meaning into a single indissoluble unit. In Lettrist work, the symbol proliferates meaning through its visual properties, slipping from one level of linguistic production to another, visual one, without any apparent rules or regular principles. Though Lettrism has its place within the history of visual poetry in the 20th century, it should not be confused with concrete poetry; the principles and practice are completely different in all respects—except one. In both cases the presentation of the work on the page is characterized by visual manipulations and non-traditional, unconventional means—all of them at odds with the "norm" of literary text presentation.

From the 1960s onward it becomes increasingly difficult and unrewarding to trace simple intellectual lineages among delimited configurations of poets as the means of charting the development of visual poetry. The fundamental concept of making use of visual elements to reinforce, extend, inflect, or subvert conventional linguistic meaning in a work becomes the basis of many works—some of which have little or nothing to do with concretism in the narrow sense (defined by Noigandres and Gomringer). As an idea, this concept is compatible with an unlimited number of poetic propositions and the variety of work produced in the last decades attest to the viability of visual poetry as a heterogeneous and diverse field. Moreover, as the idea of visual poetics became detached from the context of concretism, the linguistic and theoretical constructs with which it is engaged also became increasingly varied. In a general sense, the works in this broadening field of exploration becomes increasingly engaged with the capacity of materiality (whether understood as verbal phonemes or visual letters and words, page structures, patterns, rhythms, etc.) to be activated as an aspect of linguistic meaning. Finally, not all of the developments of these latter decades can even be contained within the field of poetry per se — there are tangential and interrelated interests in the visual and material properties of language which emerge from sites within fine arts, music, and performance further enriching, and complicating, the field.

The idea of visual scoring, or the manipulation of phonetic components of poetry in a manner analogous to a musical piece has precedents which far precede the history of the modern avant-garde, but in the mid-century reinvestigation of musical form new expressions of this sensibility came to the fore. The work of John Cage, in an American context, is exemplary of a more widespread phenomenon in which figures like Henri Chopin and Bernard Heidsieck, among others, participated. While the performative aspect of the visual documents produced by these artist/composer/poets remained a basic element of their practice, the page or score itself also came to function as a performance in its own right. The concept of the page or sheet as a field of activity in which the visual presentation of a work marks a more primary engagement with the rhythm, patterns, and emphasis of phonemes within language as an aural work matured in the works of Cage, Chopin and Heidsieck. For these artists the outstanding features of language were its phonemic and phonetic qualities and visual devices served primarily as a means of emphatically attending to these elements in their own right, often loosed from constraints of conventional meaning production. Heidsieck, for instance, by the mid-1950s, had determined that the book and page were too confining, that he wanted to find a form of linguistic performance which would permit language to escape these boundaries. His 1955 *Poèmes-Partitions* made use of diverse materials— a paper document tracing cardiac movements, cut up verse, and so forth, in a performance mode he termed a "poetry action" or "action poetry." For Chopin the use of a tape-recorder as a primary tool for composition and performance signaled his engagement with a kineticisation of poetry, though this did not interfere with his composition of works on paper as a facet of this practice. These musical innovations are intertwined with the history of "sound poetry," which flourished in the 1960s and 1970s, and also with the hybrid art practices of the Fluxus group for whom Cage in particular served as a major source of aesthetic inspiration.

Within Fluxus, Jackson Mac Low serves as an interesting figure through whom to examine the polymorphous character of artistic practice—since his work can not be fit comfortably into the field of poetry, music, or visual arts though it makes use of and participates in all these fields to varying degrees. Like Cage, Mac Low made serious and systematic use of processes of composition grounded in chance operations, combinations, and cut-up techniques. Fluxus artists were committed to the aestheticization of ordinary life—including the banal language in everyday use—a tenet which seeps from John Cage's work into every aspect of the Fluxus sensibility. Thus the poetics of Mac Low are in many ways a refusal of or rejection of the literary forms and language of a figure such as Ezra Pound for whom the esoteric reference, history of literature, and the arcane and scholarly realm of primarily Western thought served as

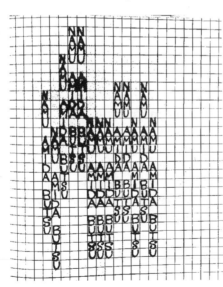

Jackson Mac Low, "2nd Gatha," 1961.

both source and reference. Though academically trained in this tradition, Mac Low's work shows the extent to which radical innovation in poetic form had pushed the parameters of innovation far from the literary mainstream despite certain common roots and interests. Mac Low's attention to language as material was similar to John Cage's attitude toward sound—that it was all available as aesthetic material through techniques of attention, sensitization, presentation. Mac Low's unfaltering commitment to the use of strategies of composition based on acrostics, anagrams, and other methods combined random selection of material and a systematic structure for its reworking into new form. The elaborate processes which Mac Low makes use of necessarily engage him with visual documents whose own properties are both intrinsic aspects of his "event" scores and also works in their own right. As the performance aspect of Mac Low's pieces generally requires a degree of reinvention, the scores serve as the basis of, rather than as a prescriptive fixed transcription of, performed works.

While the work of someone like Mac Low may seem far from the concrete sensibility of Gomringer, for instance, Fluxus probably had a broader impact on the arts in general in the post-1960s than concrete poetry would or could. This is in part because the full field of experimentation with language comes to include not only new experiments in the relation of poetics and graphic visuality, but also developments in the mainstream art world in the contexts of Pop and Conceptual Art, where artists' books emerge as a significant component. While much of the work by Fluxus artists Ben Vautier, George Brecht, or Alison Knowles might not be considered concrete or visual poetry in a strict sense their use of language within an art context and attention to its material forms—whether typewritten, scribbled, or typeset—became a touchstone for the work of artists as diverse as Raymond Pettibone, Christopher Wool, or even Barbara Kruger and Jenny Holzer for whom the availablity of ordinary language as an art material is an already established given—owing in part to the Fluxus precedent. What must be mentioned here as well is the conspicuous and important role of language in Conceptual art in the 1960s in which context language served as a primary, rather than extra or incidental element of artistic works.[14]

Within the core of visual and concrete poetry in the 1960s a number of different nodes of activity define specific approaches with varying points of commonality in theoretical or stylistic terms. As a kind of "second generation" of visual poets, these writers each developed a particular, often highly nuanced or narrowly defined, aesthetic principle. Pierre Garnier, for example, founded his "spatialist" movement in 1963. For Garnier the concept of "space" was a metaphysical as well as formal and semiotically charged idea. Insisting on the expressive and signifying power of the literal, physical space between letters, Garnier felt that the processes of coming into form in poetics was a manifestation of a world being born. The spiritual, metaphysical charge which Garnier gave to the visual structure of poetic form resonates with many of the principles which the conceptual artist Yves Klein, also working in Paris at the same time, was working into his New Realist examination of the metaphysical abstraction and power of the void and space. The notion of "espace" as an element of aesthetic practice can be readily traced to Mallarmé's poetics—the dimensionality and structural complexity of the full form of *Un Coup de Dès* serving as the original spatialist work. In Garnier's poetry the old Mallarméan concepts are reworked through a new artistic sensibility trying to come to terms with the "cosmic being in the age of space"—an aesthetic which required, in Garnier's mind, that the word function as a "free object"—a phrase which combines the image of an entity floating in a gravity-free environment with a high modernist poetics of textual autonomy and self-definition.[15] The linguistic implications of a such a position are many, not the least of which is a conviction that language functions significantly as a textual practice without the need for reference, a fundamental tenet of the new critical sensibility which was dominant in the 1960s. Not surprisingly, similar critical concepts were an aspect of the forms of structuralist linguistics formulated by Leonard Bloomfield and even the early work of Noam Chomsky—work which was most likely still unfamiliar to writers in a European context even if the idea of a syntactically based, rather than semantically replete, basis for linguistic function was shared among them.

By contrast with the highly structured and structuralist premises of Garnier's work, almost at the other extreme of a poetic spectrum, is the work of Charles Olson, a poet whose attention to visual form as an integral feature of poetic meaning pushed the conventions of poetic representation into new terrain.[16] The geographical metaphors are apt here, since Olson's spatialized concept of language—which could not be farther from that of Garnier's metaphysical structuralism—forged relations

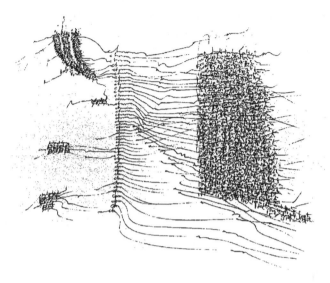

Ana Hatherly, "Hístoria da poesia: poema chama poeta," 1980.

between "fields" of the page and "fields" of meaning in semantic as well as referential terms. Though aesthetically distinct from Olson (whose visual innovations are a marked extension of tendencies which can be found in other modern poets such as Gertrude Stein, e.e. cummings, even William B. Yeats, William Morris, or Emily Dickinson[17]) the writing of William Burroughs and Bryon Gysin forged links between literary innovation and visual poetry through their use of cut-up techniques, while many poets of the 1950s and early 1960s (Bob Cobbing serves as a specific example here) discovered a formal value in the structuring capacity of the typewriter which had hitherto been largely ignored (or else effaced in the process of typesetting). Typewriter poetry and art— whether produced within a literary or a visual art context—also flourished in the 1960s and early 1970s in works as diverse as those by Maurizio Nannucci, Carl Andre, Henri Chopin, Pierre Garnier, and Ana Hatherly—to name only a few of the most remarkable.

In an international perspective these decades virtually explode with experiments in visual poetry: Jirí Kolár's work drew its unique character from his attention to Kasimir Malevich and Victor Vasarely as influences, thus combining a supremeatist formalism with an optical-kinetic contemporary sensibility; Dieter Roth, working from a graphic design background into books as an artistic form beginning in the 1950s made use of found and reprinted visual material as premise for exploring sequence and structure; Ian Hamilton Finlay's individual form of concretism extended into environmental works through the gradual transformation of his entire garden into a work of linguistic and poetically articulated space; Kitasono Katue introduced visual poetry into the already fertile environment of the Japanese avant-garde in 1957.

At the same time as these various experimental activities were developing their own course, there were two major developments within the realm of mainstream visual arts which would impact upon visual poetry on stylistic as well as conceptual terms. These are the use of language as a major element within Pop art as well as a fundamental feature of Conceptual art. Vastly different in their linguistic orientation—Pop making use of commercial, product-oriented language as well as the graphic style of advertising and publicity and Conceptual art using the most neutral, unmarked, and "immaterial" forms it could manage while still making the words appear on a page, wall, canvas, or other document—they both contrived to make language as such, language in itself, and language as visual, written form, into a primary art object. No longer serving merely as title, as signature or other supplementary element, nor as a formal (if significant) element of a collage, language was, from the early 1960s and the exhibition of works by Ed Ruscha, John Baldessari, Art & Language, Lawrence Weiner, Andy Warhol, Richard Hamilton and others, to make a claim as an art practice. Bern Porter, Emmett Williams, Ed Ruscha, and Tom Phillips each began to make use of artists' books as medium for the exploration of visual properties of found and created texts with Porter's found-poetry work beginning in the 1950s, and Ruscha, Williams, and Phillips a decade later. Phillips began his extended work, *A Humument*, in 1966, a work whose relation to the history of concrete and visual poetry explains only part of its aesthetic grounding. With Phillips, as with Williams, or even Carl Andre or Lawrence Weiner, the premises of the work cannot be fully fleshed out without reference to traditions of Conceptual art, the use of found and transformed texts, environmental and spatialized extensions of visual and verbal material into a wider field, and any of the many other strains of artistic activity which by the 1960s had dissolved the boundaries between disciplines which had rigidly distinguished high modern visuality from high modern literariness at mid-century. At this point the capacity to discuss visual poetry within the framework of concretism is

hopelessly moot—the experimental innovation had interbred so successfully with other artistic sources as to make its kinship with orthodox
concretism a remote and diluted relation at best.

In these cases—Pop and Conceptual art—the language used is remote
from poetics, a situation which remains true, more or less, up until the
1980s. Much of the visual poetry of the 1980s and 1990s, however, as
will be clear later, draws upon these sources as much as upon the traditions of literary or visual poetics whose premises they extend.

Before turning attention to recent works, however, it is useful to
study the case of Canadian "concretism." Here the term must be applied
loosely, rather than in the narrower sense defined earlier, but has been
used to identify the visually experimental work of bill bissett (sic),
bpNichol (sic), and Steve McCaffery. Poetically self-conscious, theoreti-
cally sophisticated, but unorthodox and non-academic, these poets
serve as an interesting study in the ways visual poetry in these later
decades emerges from a more eclectic background than that of pure
concretism, one which borrows from some of the same precedents—
Anglo-American poetry, French poetry, and the early 20th century
avant-garde—while adding in important new elements. If work across
the broad field of artistic and poetic activity in the 1960s and 1970s
reflects the proliferation and diffusion of a diverse array of engagements
with the material and visual aspects of language as an artistic and literary medium, the work of bpNichol and Steve McCaffery, in the framework of their Toronto Research Group (founded in 1973) is a highly
focused and in some ways unique example of a new maturity for visual poetics.[18] Their work is distinguished by the fact that it is well
informed by traditions of poetics—the mainstream of conventional and
experimental modern work as well as many eclectic precedents in pattern poetry, sound poetry, and visual poetry. Like Dick Higgins, the
American Fluxus artist, publisher, and writer, McCaffery and Nichol
were able to find inspiration in the graphic and phonetic experiments of
poets from the middle ages and Renaissance to the present while situ-
ating their own practice within a contemporary frame through their
knowledge of immediate precedents in the work of European, Brazilian,
and American contemporaries.[19] In one of the earliest documents of
their collaborative "research," "The Book as Machine," McCaffery and
Nichol listed among the "Twenty-one Facts that Could Alter Your Life"
specific instances of visual or concrete poetry according to the ways

these individual activities defined certain parameters for their understanding of—and coming to terms with—conceptual premises for their
continued innovations.[20] This kind of "taking stock"—which weaves
throughout the published reports of the Toronto Resarch Group makes
clear the ways in which the processes of making critical assessments was
integral with poetic practice. Though they are careful to state that theory always follows practice, is secondary to it, they are simultaneously
steeping themselves in a critical discourse in which distinctions between
theory and creative practice were being rapidly dissolved. The primacy
of the theoretical text—whether poetic or discursive in nature—which
is a feature of the 1970s reception of the work of Jacques Derrida, Julia
Kristeva, and Roland Barthes, for example, all writers McCaffery and
Nichol were reading at the time—allows their own work to become a
hybrid of theory/practice in which poetics participates fully. The old
model of artistic or avant-garde manifesto as a first declaration of aesthetic principles, from which poetic or artistic work would follow, which
was still a feature of Concretism in the work of Gomringer and
Noigandres, is here displaced by a new paradigm. Theoretical, polemical, and poetic work is often one and the same work and the positions
are continually mutating through the practice. The visual component of
Nichol and McCaffery's work takes many forms—some more overtly
linked to concrete precedents, others to literary formats being stretched
and reworked to suit their purposes. In addition, another influence
which asserted an important force on their work was their exposure to
folk, "primitive" and non-western poetics—in the kind of anthropolog-
ically influenced poetic research most clearly exemplified in the anthology work of Jerome Rothenberg. The emphasis of this work was on
phonetic properties, sound patterns, and rhythm—all of which, for
McCaffery at least, became a primary motivation towards performance
rather than typographic or graphic work. Nonetheless, for both
McCaffery and Nichol the structure of the page and even of the book as
a form are conspicuous features of their published work.

In short then, these Toronto poets make visual poetry a form of the-
oretically informed work whose research techniques combine a broader field of poetic sources with an intuitive but well-considered understanding of the ways attention to materiality in visual and verbal form
could extend the possibilities of earlier concretism. A critical distinction
made by the writer Stephen Scobie between the idea of a "clean" and a

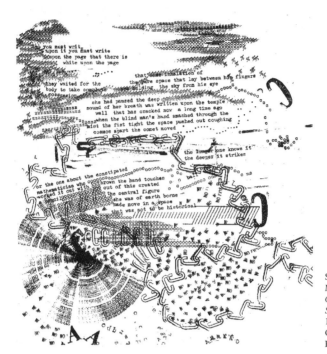

Steve McCaffery, *Carvnival, The Second Panel,* 1970-75, The Coach House Press, Toronto.

"dirty" concretism works well to demarcate the clean, well ordered, and more highly regulated work of the Swiss/German nexus of poets, or even that of the Noigandres group from the Toronto poets' hybrid eclecticism, with its synthetic capacity to absorb material from any of a wide variety of conceptual, critical, and linguistic sources.

What becomes abundantly clear in this new formulation is that poetics becomes informed by notions not articulated within Concretism—not available—and that not only linguistic theory, but the construction of poetics as a strategy of representation engaged with issues of culture, ideology, and politics is central to the conception of poetic practice from its very outset. If Nichol and McCaffery serve well as a study in work which came into being in a poetic context, self-consciously aware of and also continually coming to terms with, critical and poetic traditions, it provides a model for other work of the 1970s and 1980s mainly by its eclecticism. Which is to say that if one were to begin, now, in the mid 1990s, to examine the field of visual poetry and to try to account for its forms and variations in terms of a forward moving history of poetics, much of the current work could not be explained. Just as the retro-spective evaluation of the Toronto Group forms a far clearer picture of its aims and intentions than the forward moving chronological account provided in its working notes, so the process of evaluating contempo-rary visual poetics as if there were a coherent historical development with a single, final, outcome is an unsustainable fiction. This becomes increasingly true in an age in which the sources of poetics and graphics are increasingly from mass media sources, the more readily available shared field of reference and form, than from any well-charted or reg-ulated discourse of poetics or fine arts. These fields have been similarly affected—it would be impossible to discuss contemporary art without referring to television, star system and celebrity politics, rock music, or other culture industry forms—thus further complicating the identity of a form like visual poetry which further hybridizes the already appropri-ated materials of these realms of artistic activity.

If I were to consider my own work in regard to these issues, for instance, I see that the relation between critical discourse and poetic/visual production has transformed dramatically over the last twenty years. Initially I became interested in schematizing relations between meaning and appearance on the page so as to reinforce these values, and to insist on a kind of latent quality of signifying potential in format or arrangement within page structures. By 1976, when I printed my first elaborately typographic book, *Twenty-six '76*, my sense of language as a material form had extended to a process of appropriation from "found" language, marked by its material expression to indicate its ori-gin in a heterogeneous linguistic field, and to a process of production—making use of lead type in letterpress printing as a way of engineering effect (linguistic emphasis or inflection) through visual means. But I could not, in 1976, have cited a single theoretical or critical writer as a way to articulate what I was doing—I simply had not read any. When informed by a colleague at the West Coast Print Center that I was work-ing in the tradition of Mallarmé, I had to admit that I had never heard of *Un Coup de Dés*, let alone examined the many arcane discussions of its typographic rendition. Concrete poetry, like artists' books, constructivist design, and modern poetry were all forms about which I was woefully ignorant—though I had been exposed to Dada and Surrealism in the brief course of academic work required by my art school for a B.F.A. degree. The original inspiration for exploring the potential of language as a material form came from the experience of "holding language in my hands"—lines of letterpress type—and from looking at the world. This situation changed dramatically once I entered graduate school, at which point, beginning in 1980, I learned some theory/history and began to integrate elements of structuralist and feminist theory into my work. The particular form of typographic poetics which formed the center of my work from the late 1970s was dedicated to exploring the non-linear potential of print media and to the power of visual material form to proliferate meaning within a semantic field through the visual structure. But it was also bound up with issues of female identity, prose traditions, and the relations between fiction as a literary form and fiction as a cultural form—tabloids, pulp novels, and genre writing—all of which served as useful points of departure in conceptualizing my work. Though all of this work—from the last two decades, can now, in my own critical writing, be framed in terms which locate it within traditions and contemporary frameworks of visual poetry and aesthetic innovation, it was originally conceived without that information and with a far more intuitive and unregulated sensibility. I think, in fact, this is more typical than not—and I would be surprised if most of the poets I will mention here in closing could do more than retrospectively situate themselves within critical or poetic traditions. Nor would I wish them to—I think that the old avant-garde model of the proscriptive manifesto, the laying out of aesthetic terms and the subsequent attempt to fulfill them through practice had its moment of usefulness and has been superseded by other models of creative work—just as boundaries between art and literature, art and non-art, media culture and fine art culture have also become dissolved to the point of questionable usefulness.

Any attempt to describe the full range of visual poetry in the current moment would be difficult — many of the practitioners of concrete and visual poetry from the 1950s onward continue to be productive, continuing certain aspects of their activity in modified form. But there are new trends as well, some already of long-standing in the practice of individual poets or as a general premise. For instance, Robert Grenier, a California based poet, has been making handwritten palimpsest works for more than a decade. His poems are manuscript originals which he overwrites in a large, loose printed hand so that a maze of spindly lines of text interweave with each other. Each is readable, legible, discernible, and yet the gestalt of the page as a whole is textural rather than textual in character. Grenier's language sensibility is highly vernacular, extending the poetics of the likes of Bob Brown, Robert Creeley, and the New York School into a contemporary formulation but giving it a distinct visual quality which calls acute attention to writing process in the visual appearance of the final work on the page.

At another extreme of technological production would be the holographic works of Eduardo Kac, for whom the spatialized dynamics of the page are transcended through a medium which allows dimensionality to be factored into the linguistic production. Kac's explorations extend the use of the computer as a tool in poetic composition employed Max Bense, among others, in the 1960s, while also engaging with the sort of visual manipulation of surface appearance which characterized the work of Raymond Hains, also in the 1960s. In Kac's work, as in Hains', however the distortions introduced into the final form of the language through light projection, surface manipulation, or computer processing are not additions or supplements to the text, instead, they are intended to be integral to its linguistic function, to extend the definition of what comprises linguistic function to include the potential of material to signify. Crag Hill's "interpretations" of the visual forms of words integrates these visual manipulations with speculations on the nature of language as a perceived phenomenon.

But perhaps the most telling new trend is one which has been amplified by the availability of computer and xerox technology—the use of visual and verbal elements in fluid combination with each other. If much of concrete and visual poetry put the word into a formal relation with an icon or pictorial structure through format on the page, or, in the case of McCaffery/Nichol, pushed the capacity of traditionally non-verbal visual forms into syntactic or semantic relations, then current work actually blends visual and verbal elements into what is an increasingly a synthetic unity. The work of Spencer Selby, for instance, of Thomas Taylor, depends to a large extent either on xerox capabilities for reduction/enlargement or on rephotographing of images in order to take materials from newspaper, existing books, text, manuscripts, printed forms, and reformulate them. The additional typographic sophistication provided as a readily available tool in personal computers has made the possibility of writing with such materials in mind a more common practice. A poet like Pete Spence, who makes elegant abstract compositions

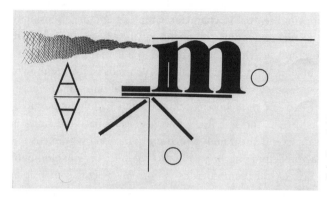

Pete Spence,
untitled,
1997,
St. Kilda's,
Australia,
collage.

of letters, signs, lines and geometric forms in diagrammatic linguistic algebra, could have achieved these effects in letterpress (they bear some relation to the work of H.N. Werkman, a designer of the 1930s) — but the manipulations of Karl Kempton or John Byrum would have been impossible without a computer on which to generate the specific effects which give their work its particular character and value.

This closing is woefully inadequate to indicate the range of work in visual poetry which is currently being produced—or even to give a sense of the history of this complex and diverse field. What is evident is that the terms of poetic tradition or linguistic analysis adequate for a critical understanding of earlier work is inadequate to confront the synthetic sensibility of the present—work which poses profound questions about the identity of poetic and artistic practices in terms of their cultural identity as well as about the processes of signification so essential to these projects as they are conceived in aesthetic terms—and mark their distance from and relation to the traditions of concrete and visual poetry against which they gain at least part of their definition.

This piece was published in Experimental–Visual–Concrete: Avant-Garde Poetry Since the 1960s, *edited by K. David Jackson, Eric Vos, and Johanna Drucker, a special issue of* Avant-Garde Critical Studies #10, 1996.

1. See Dick Higgins, *Pattern Poetry*. Albany, NY: State University of New York Press, 1987.
2. See the catalogue Bernard Blistène and Véronique Legrand, eds., *Poésure et Peintrie*, Marseilles: Musées de Marseilles, 1993, for an exhaustive representation of 20th century activity.
3. Since the Chinese language, in its written form, depends upon these visual relations of proximity, sequence, and so forth, it is often invoked as a model.

This is the case throughout the tradition of Western poetics — finding its modern articulation in the oft-cited work of Ernest Fenollosa and its echos in Ezra Pound. Most such interpretations are ill-informed and rely on an impression of Chinese language rather than any actual understanding of its organization, much like the mythic concept of the hieroglyphic in western thought.

4. See: Gerald Janacek, *The Look of Russian Literature*, Princeton: Princeton University Press, 1984; Susan Compton, *World Backwards*, London: British Museum Publications, 1978; Bernard Blistène and Véronique Legrand, eds., *Poésure et Peintrie*, Marseilles: Musées de Marseilles, 1993; and Johanna Drucker, *The Visible Word: Experimental Typography and Modern Art Practice* Chicago: University of Chicago Press, 1994.

5. The term constructivism has a specific meaning within Russian and early Soviet art practices. It is particularly associated with the work of Rodchenko for whom it designated experimentation with formal means as an aspect of a revolutionary aesthetic. It should be distinguished from Malevich's suprematism (which is engaged with issues of representation, anti-mimesis, and metaphysics) and Vladimir Tatlin's productivism (in which innovative formal means are used in application to industrial production). In a non-Soviet and especially post World War II context, the term constructivism is associated with a depoliticized formal visual language in fine arts and design, especially in the Dutch and Swiss schools.

6. Werner Haftmann, *Painting in the 20th Century*. New York: Praeger, 1961; Vol. 1, pp. 338-343.

7. This seems paradoxical—and to some extent it is. But there are many odd mutations of early avant-garde activity in the 1920s and 30s through which politically or socially motivated forms become appropriated as stylistic or merely graphic devices.

8. Precisely what Gomringer was reading is unclear—Frege, early Wittgenstein, or Claude Shannon are possibilities.

9. Mary Ellen Solt, *Concrete Poetry: A World View*. Bloomington, IN: Indiana University Press, 1968.

10. Solt, *ibid.*

11. Stephen Bann, *Concrete Poetry*. London: London Magazine Editions, 1967; Emmett Williams, *Anthology of Concrete Poetry*. New York: Something Else Press, 1967; Bob Cobbing and Peter Mayer, *Concerning Concrete Poetry*. London: The Writers' Forum, 1978; and Solt.

12. Raoul Haussman, Ilia Zdanevich, and Kurt Schwitters, for instance.

13. David Seaman, *Concrete Poetry in France*, Ann Arbor, MI: University Microfilms International Research Press, 1981; but more directly, the writings of Jean-Paul Curtay, Isidore Isou, and Maurice Lemaître themselves.

14. This primary character of language is a feature of many Fluxus pieces—I am thinking of the George Brecht performance cards, or of Alison Knowles's book works, to name two among many examples, but for Fluxus the ultimate emphasis is on experience, while in Conceptual art the final emphasis comes to rest on idea. Thus for Fluxus artists the language is a means of providing instructions or

frameworks, while for Conceptual artists language is to be, paradoxically, the "dematerialized" manifestation of an art idea.

15. Solt, *op.cit.* p.32.

16. See Michael Davidson in *Poesure et Peintrie (op.cit.)*.

17. See Ulla Dydo's work on Gertrude Stein, Jerome McGann's *The Textual Condition*, Princeton: Princeton University Press, 1991, and Susan Howe's poetic and critical oeuvre.

18. Caroline Bayard, *The New Poetics in Canada and Quebec.* Toronto: Univeristy of Toronto Press, 1989.

19. Dick Higgins, *Pattern Poetry.* Albany: State University of New York Press, 1987.

20. Steve McCaffery and bpNichol, *Rational Geomancy.* Toronto: Talonbooks, 1992.

Linguistic Authority and the Visual Text

Language metabolizes quickly without the resistant force of material.[1] Attention to the stuff in the medium is not the fetishization of some theory-based supplement, but the recognition of the fact of the matter.[2] ~~No real record, no hard trace,~~ Language speaks, appears, is seen and heard, not like the good child of some former era repressing its presence out of sight and earshot for the sake of adult decorum. ~~no evidence exists~~ But the status of visual poetry is still orphan status, or worse, that of the unwanted ~~to substantiate any theory on the ori-~~ ~~gin of language~~ child at the banquet table celebrating the great works.[3] Writers who used to believe they were just a place in the code[4] ~~the origin of writing, by con-~~

Display by itself is a negatively charged word, associated with all the pejoratives of cultural critique; visual language ends up as an item in the marketplace of delusionary tactics, not as the upstanding citizen protesting the hype and dazzle of commerce, but like some sly shyster con-artist playing at sleight of hand. **This is old testament judgement and new new interdiction. Salvation is a moot point in the course of experience. How to massage the brain into life given the overstimulation of the daily eye? Are there tac-**

~~trast~~ are now ha**p**py to have th**e**ir names and faces smeared across the critical tabloids in tasteful head-lines ~~is linked to material evidence~~ ~~itself~~ p**r**oclaiming their achievements.~~there is no other~~ ~~form in which it exists~~[5] Still visual poetry is scolded **f**or calling attention to itself (too much makeup and over-dressed f**o**r an occasion) ~~The actual substance is the grounds~~ taking up too much space with unseemly behavio**r** and ~~for its historical examination~~ fla**m**boyant display.[6]

Visuality erupts, insists, interrupts and the eye is massaged. But authority continues to seem to re-side in transcendence, a denial of the actual existence in material form of the word—as if the disembodied terms of language could better serve to stabilize the positions of power seized by a fear and a trem-bling in the face of the face of the

tics to this or some-thing more essential such as a profound recognition of the visual materiality of all writ-ing. Any odd translation of a printed work's typographical treatment misrepresents that orig-inal just as ~~badly~~ boldly ~~baldly~~ as the wrong choice of a verb ending violates the rhythm of the lines. Authority is construed to reside with power and that power in the gross concealment of its very means. The lay-ing bare of devices so dear to our forbear-ers was a means of deconstructing that very authority. WORD.

Notes:

1. **That** is a convenience we can ill afford in the present climate of obscurity.

2. Poetry presents itself as **text** and text **aspires to** the condition of **the** biblical, **theological** we all know that and didn't need Derrida to point out what Gutenberg himself had **already** demonstrated that the text which is unmarked (the Bible) seems to speak itself, be **present,** and has always been, **uninflected** and unchallenged and unable to be pinpointed into place in historical time and social circumstances **rather** transcending all particulars to be part of the general realm of truth as discourse uttered **without** any **marks** of enunciation to betray their human origins.

3. **The** marked text (the Indulgences) by contrast shows it seems, traces of its fabrication, all its positionality traced in the stuff of its **appearance** like this, made on a computer in what is seeming to be later and later in the century an intimate, available, domestic, **means** of production which approaches the level of the truly commercial with all its tricks of display.

4. Nothing **here** refers to the body of the text, as if **meaning**/mind/spirit were elsewhere. We have to remember that that split was **invented** for reasons of a legislatable morality, to keep the body from **in**discriminate **acts of** indulgence of appetite and has nothing to do with literature.

5. **Reference** itself becomes increasingly resonant when the terms of material are factored into the linguistic activity. Material **is** meaning, of course, in spite of the **denial** tactics which continue to lock it up in the strait jacket **of** pure poetry pure language as if to strip away the very instrument according to which the linguistic activity occurs.

6. Writing the **visual** is the continual appearing coming into being of lines of text made on the page as the sometimes linear sometimes spatial and temporal accretion of **activity** which holds its own across time and space as an artifact of **language**, not merely an incident.

This piece was produced for an exhibition organized by Craig McDaniel, Matthew Brennan, and Renée Ramsey and held at the Turman Art Gallery at Indiana State University, Terre Haute, from March 21–April 16, 1993; it also appeared in the catalogue printed to accompany that exhibition, Is Poetry A Visual Art?

The Visual Line

The line breaks and separates from itself. The insistence of the fragments makes it strenuous to recover the line which would normally reach closure with the unit of sound or sense or their mutual agreement. The visual line need not function as an image in a figurative or iconic sense limiting the reading of the words by some referential value which constrains them. Rather, as visible forms the lines create their own order in the text, impose it, as a frame which introduces the struggle of hierarchy into the words. The breaks become a force, against which the whole must be recovered, or against which the whole can be fractured, dissolved, let go.

Grammatical completion is not a requirement for syntactic resolution. Always at every point. Privileging the fragment, impact of the break . . . deliberately not recuperable into a linear form. Disintegrating the defining boundaries, limits by which the line identifies. Not in attack against the uni-linear, but diffusing its focus, and entity/identity—the surface which should support the representation spreads it . . . Detached from its context, the support route becomes a network, fraught with the uncertainty of choice.

Spatial play, the hierarchy of size and color in the rendering, allows different groupings to occur—line by line sequence, and type by type. Not simply to restate the obvious. But to open it up. Smack against the popular plane, immodestly refusing a patent transparency. Registering objections to the words which "speak themselves," attempting to repress the marks of enunciation. As if that were possible.

The visual line strains the literary authority with its vulgarity, its crudeness, its fleshiness which pollutes the material of pure language. Of which there is none. Refusing to stay "in line," creating instead a visual field in which all lines are tangential to the whole, which is, in turn created as a figure from their efforts, their direction, their nonalignment.

The visual line. Not a nice poetic line, carefully controlled and closed. Instead, a haphazard line, random line, fulfilling itself by the brute force of its physical reality. Only the headlines, carefully manipulated to cross-read through the text, force associations by their continual presence. Push against the blocks of text with their resonant association. Can't be escaped, ignored. Insistent by their visual form, dominance and presence.

Formality becomes an active issue, opening the parameters instead of closing them. The timid issues of placement and relation on the page get pushed into high profile, the very forms of mass media get appropriated precisely to the degree that they themselves have acted to appropriate the public use of language.

The finiteness of type, the literal limit of space and material, acts on the text, from that system of constraints, restraints, the text gets forged, charged, made, as it should in order to emphasize its real materiality, the scope of its own invention freed by the incarceration it suffers in the form.

The line makes itself rather than being made, since it is the outcome of the manual, physical process, and not of the predetermined value. Part of the transformation of manuscript to text belongs to the medium. Letterpress forces the text to negotiate on its own terms. Then the page uses the lines, not in strict sequence, but in relation, and thus in a spatial exercise, kinetic and unstable. The lines are in a dynamic field, pulling against each other to determine the thrust of what becomes meaning.

This piece was first published in The Line in Post-Modern Poetry, *(Urbana and Chicago: The University of Illinous Press, 1988) edited by Robert Frank and Henry Sayre.*

Visual/Verbal: Symposium Response

THE VISUAL MATERIAL RESISTS THE VERBAL

I began with letterpress, holding the language in my hands. Now to the computer

EXPECTATIONS THE CLEAN MACHINE OF READING

searching for the shape in the murky pixels on the screen. Not all of writing has to

HESITATES, DISRUPTED BY THE INTERFERING

be treated to this breach of decorum, only some, which permits its own laboratory

SUBSTANCE WHICH DISTRACTS THE EYE. THE

explorations. Mallarmé remains, of course, the major point of reference, though he

LOOK OF LITERATURE IS NOT A SURPLUS, EXCESS,

was not my original source, which lay, simply, in the handling of elements in the

NOT SOME TRIVIAL ADDITIVE MISBEHAVING IN A

typecase, and in trying to solve problems in the works through visual and graphic

FLAMBOYANT BID FOR ATTENTION, BUT RATHER,

means. A community exists, but my sense of my work is really separate. The old

THE THICK FLIGHT OF FANCY STUCK IN THE HOT

concretists of the 1950s and 1960s seem reductive and simple by and large, and

FORM OF LETTERS ON A PAGE, WRESTLING,

the zaum typography of Iliazd in some ways comes closest to my own sensibility. I

EMBRACING, STRUGGLING WITH THE EXPRESSIVE

have always believed in sense, not nonsense, and the Dada gestures offer some

FORM IN APPREHENSION. LEARNING TO LOOK THE

tools, now that I study them, as do the Constructivist and Futurist designers and

EYE, DELIGHTED, RETURNS THE ABSENT, ELUSIVE

poets. Closer to my own generation there are, of course, all kinds of people — but I

PROPERTIES OF SUGGESTION TO THE BODY OF THE

find myself most drawn to them in academic ways, for the sake of understanding,

TEXT, ENJOYING BOTH PLEASURE AND FRUSTRA-

talking about, writing about, their work, rather than as source material. My

TION AT THE UNCONTAINABLE AFFECT GENERATED

favorite inspirations remain the virtuoso projects of unnamed typographers of late

IN THE STUFF, ITSELF UNQUALIFIABLE, UNLOCAT-

19th-century advertising, of 20th-century graphics before auteur design, though

ABLE IN ANY SIMPLE MAP OF MEANING. THIS CON-

some of that—Bayer and Tschichold and Rand and now Licko and Greiman and

CEPT OF VOICE IS HANDWRITING, MIND, MADE ON

others certainly provides visual ideas and stimulation. My audience seems to be a

THE PAGE AND IN THE MOUTH, TACKLING THE TASK OF

combination of poets, critics, book arts people, all of whom have various takes on

MAKING ITSELF MOMENT TO MOMENT FOR THE SAKE

the materials—and of course, my family, my father in particular, whose own life-

OF SOME UNUTTERABLE ACCIDENT OR INCIDENT

time of work in design makes him particularly appreciative of formal solutions. I

OF RECOGNITION. THE GESTALT ESCAPES ITS OWN

show my work in bookstores, like WPA and Printed Matter, and galleries, espe-

CONTAINMENT, REFERRING TO THE WORLD OF

cially Granary Books in New York, but also in exhibitions. Betty Bright, at

SOCIAL POLITICS AND ASSOCIATIONS, QUESTION-

Minnesota Center for the Book Arts, has been very active in this area. A lot of rare

ABLE, VARIOUS AND SUSPECT. THE ANGEL OF

book librarians and poetry archive curators are interested and very appreciative

ENLIGHTENED REASON AND THE FORCE OF

as well—certainly the Waldrops have encouraged this activity at Brown, Anne

HARD FACT ARE EQUALLY ILL AT EASE IN THE

Anninger at the Houghton (Harvard), Robert Bertholf up at Buffalo, and the peo-

METAPHYSICAL ARENA OF THE VISUAL VERNACU-

ple at U.C. San Diego in the Poetry Archive, to name only a few. Then of course

LAR, THE TABLOID PULP OF DAILY LANGUAGE AND

there are the collectors—where would we be without Ruth and Marvin Sackner! I

THE ESOTERIC FIELD OF CONTINUALLY EXPLODED

like showing the work, putting it into reproduction, since I do such small editions. I

INVENTION. BUT THIS IS THE REALM OF THE LITER-

would love to do a reprint of my own books, of course, but also to see an anthology

ATE AND PHYSICAL, THE PLAGUED AND DISPLAYED

of New Visual Poetry—stuff of the last ten or fifteen years. It is hard to get a good

THE IMMODEST AND RETREATING, RETRENCHED,

sense of all that is out there and how representative the small sample of things one

ENTRENCHED GAMBOLLERS WITH SENSATION.

comes across is actually to relative to the bigger picture. Since all other manifesta-

RESISTANCE TO LINGUISTIC CLOSURE DOES NOT LEAD

tions of visual poetry I know of are certainly historically specific, then it seems

TO ESCAPE, TO CHAOS, OR TO NONSENSE BUT TO

clear that my own practice, and that of my contemporaries, is equally informed by

THE REPLETE AND MARKED, THE LOST AND THE

current theory, and that as writers we are very much formed through context and

FOUND OF MISCELLANEOUS AND POTENT VALUES.

circumstance of language and event and theory. I guess I ultimately aspire to a kind

THE TEXT, LIKE ANY OTHER ORGANISM, REJOICES

of tabloid pulp of graphic language—somewhere between the Mallarméan project

IN THE PINBALL GAMES OF TOUCH AND UNCER-

and Flaubert's Bouvard and Pecuchet—but updated to the so-called new millennial

TAINTY WHICH MULTIPLY THE POSSIBLE ACTIVI-

sensibility. I have not been funded much by grants for my books—letterpress work

TIES FOR ENGAGEMENT WITH AN AUDIENCE

is cheap to produce, except for labor, though I did have a nice grant from Pyramid

EXCHANGE OF SATISFYING CONVERSATION

Atlantic a couple years ago to do Simulant Portrait in offset and Macintosh. I make

LAID OUT ON THE TABLE TO SEDUCE THE EYE. ALL

enough money to keep funding my own projects, buy equipment, and be produc-

THE METAPHORS OF INTERNAL AND EXTERNAL DIS-tive, but I think money spent for the arts, in any form, is always a good idea

TINCTION DISSOLVE IN THE THICK ATMOSPHERE

whether it comes from the government or private sources. There is a tendency, I

WHICH SURROUNDS, REFUSING A NEAT TOPOGRA-

think, to consider most visual poetry a form of cleverness and to dismiss its possi-

PHY OF LOCI ACCORDING TO WHICH SOME RULES OF

ble serious character in the name of some kind of literary purity. It has always

A NEW ORDER MIGHT BE MADE TO DISCIPLINE THE OLD

seemed to me that part of the resistance to visual work is that it presents a threat to

LANGUAGE IN ITS WAYWARD EXHIBITIONISM.

the authority of the text. By calling attention to many of the material aspects of

A FLAYED AND MUCH DECORATED LEXICON, STRUT-

production, the visual form, when it is obviously manipulated, makes very clear

TING ITS STUFF IN THE NEW SYNTAX OF THE SPEC-

the marks of the site and subject of enunciation as well as the historical circum-

TACULAR, PARADING THRU THE SYNAPTIC NETWORK

stances. For anyone still attached to the character of text as a form of truth this

WITH A RUSH OF STIMULATING FRICTION, NOW IN

sort of relativisation is profoundly threatening. Then, of course, there is the criti-

THE FLESH, THEN TO THE RETINA, HERE ON THE

cal resistance to being split, as a reader, between reading and looking, between the

PAGE, AS THE EYE MASSAGES THE WEARY BRAIN

visual presence of apprehendable substance and the literary value of what is sup-

INTO A NEW CONFIGURATION.

posedly an absence—as if one could make those distinctions.

This piece was composed as a response to symposium questions posed by John Byrum and Crag Hill and published in CORE: A Symposium on Contemporary Visual Poetry, *(Generatorscore Press, Mentor, Ohio, 1993).*

Letterpress Language:

Typography as a Medium for the Visual Representation of
Language

The relation between the formal, visual aspects of typography and the production of meaning in a printed text has been one of the main concerns
in my work. Writing produces a visual image: the shapes, sizes and
placement of letters on a page contribute to the message produced, creating statements which cannot always be rendered in spoken language.
Handsetting type quickly brings into focus the physical, tangible aspects
of language—the size and weight of the letters in a literal sense—
emphasizing the material specificity of the printing medium. The single,
conservative constant of my work is that I always intend for language
to have meaning. My interest is in extending the communicative potential of writing, not in eliminating or negating it. While my work tends
to go against established conventions of appearance of type on a page,
this deviation is intended to call attention to the structure of those
norms, as much as to subvert them. Setting type also emphasizes the
importance of the letter as the basic unit of written forms, as an element
in its own right with particular characteristics, and not only as the representation of the patterns of spoken language. There are many historical precedents for this approach, including the work of nineteenth-century poet Stéphane Mallarmé and twentieth-century Dadaists and
Futurists. I will discuss three of my books here: *Twenty-six '76* (1976),
From A to Z (1977), and *Against Fiction* (1983). I produced all three by letterpress using handset type on a Vandercook proofing press, a flat-bed
cylinder press which prints one hand-fed sheet at a time.

Rather than feeling hampered by the physical constraints of letterpress, I have used its characteristics to structure works, to extend the
investigation of language in printed form, and to discover how the substitution or elimination of letters or other visual elements can alter the
conventional use and meaning of words. Essentially, the norm of language representation is completely reinforced by the techniques of letterpress. Its mechanical design is intended to maintain even lines in a
single typeface. But the very rigidity of these norms also permits the use
of that technology as a language itself, as a system of possibilities and
constraints.

Twenty-six '76: **The Structure of the Page**

Although I had been printing since 1972, *Twenty-six '76* was the first work in which I used letterpress as something more than a means of printing an already written text and in which I concentrated on the visual dimensions of written language. It was my first attempt to explore such features as the visual characteristics of different typefaces and the effect of the arrangement of words on the page (see Fig. 1). Two basic issues motivated my work: the way in which visual structures actually produce meaning, and the relation between language and experience. This relation is an issue central to the philosophy of language, raising the question of whether language is merely descriptive of the world, in fact mirrors it in its very structure, or actually creates the world and its apparent order as a mental construct. It was partially my desire to investigate the structure of a particular experience and mirror its structure in a visual text that gave me the theoretical premise for *Twenty-six '76*.

I wanted to take an event, a single actual occurrence, and make it into an image that would be available for a structural analysis. The analysis of this "image" was the underlying theme of the book. I chose a four-day trip to Los Angeles, California, with two colleagues; we were to do performances at a small theater in Hollywood. Although the trip had considerable extension in time and space, it also had the requisite autonomy of a single event. By considering the incidents in the trip as elements of a whole, everything that happened in the four days could be taken as one aspect of a single image, the image of the trip. In addition, this sojourn presented me with the opportunity to distinguish several different kinds of language and to identify each of them by using a different typeface—for instance, using the copperplate typeface to identify abstract terms and concepts (such as "Fore Gone Ground" and "Comparative" in Fig. 1). The experience was investigated directly through the language it offered, as well as in terms of the analytical and descriptive language I imposed upon it. Basically my assumptions were that language has an approximate relation to experience and that the account of an experience may be constructed along several different linguistic lines.

I distinguished four kinds of language in the book: found language, such as occurred in the landscape as billboards or signs or was overheard from personal conversations; theoretical language, which described what was being done to the book, identifying the various ele-

FORE GONE GROUND:

Not ambiguous, so sw **E** et by consumption.

Light providing

pawns her limpid purse (no fragile license)   pause

the same choice

made deliberate:

drop the hounding adjunct notice--
bred pure, ground close & ugly active.

if i've)

---

re**L**ative: COMPARATIVE

SHOWING UP TOO TIGHT AS HER BLOUSE,

MOUSTACHES MADE BASTED DOWN, NOT SERENE.

GLOSS, WITHOUT ANY REAL INFORMATION

TO

professional kindness charming lazy too smooth employ tease

use not deep but submerged: In a manner of disposing the

equipment, a practiced functioning:

directs

THICK-SKINNED
what feeds back &
mentions

THE OTHER's styled grasp of pace,
taking slow time, gone down

beside

what's loud.

(tell

Fig. 1a (above) and 1b (below). Two pages from *Twenty-six '76*, 1976, letterpress, 8 1/2" x 11". Every page in this work had certain constant elements, such as using the letter in a word which announced its name, such as "swEet" on the "E" page (a), and the punned page number in italics, such as "if i've" for "five", which stressed the theme of choice, which dominates the page. On the "L" page (b) the correspondence between the image of the text on the page and the event being described was purely formal. For instance, here the lighter typeface is reserved for the fair-haired woman, the heavier face for the darker man. Also, the stepped structure corresponds to the place each of these characters occupied in the building: the woman represented by copperplate type was in the attic, and the dark young man in the cellar. These two pages are typical of the ways in which linguistic themes or characters or sections of the event were isolated and identified through association with a particular typeface and the structure of the "event" was mirrored in the structure of the page.

ments of the configuration and the function of those elements within the structure of the whole; narrative language, which described, with normal expository syntax, actions and events taking place; and finally a personal voice, which reflected what was happening in more idiosyncratic terms. I associated each of these strains of language with a particular typeface or group of typefaces in order to keep them distinct.

I posed another problem in the book, namely, the distinction between public and private language. The four strains had very different degrees of accessibility. The found language, whether advertising copy or conversation, was clearly intended as public. The narrative description made considerable concessions to communication. The theoretical language, however, was generally self-referential, tying each page back into the overall structure of the book as a single "image,", and the private commentary verged on the obscure. In its original form the book was highly cryptic, to the point of being almost inaccessible, a private shorthand. Individual statements were understandable, for the most part, but their relation to each other was almost entirely implied rather than stated. In the second edition of the work, for clarity, I added a fifth strain of language, a running narrative in footnote form, describing the linear sequence of events from which the language of the book had originally been extracted.

Each page of the book was used as the field in which to construct meaning and was an attempt, as well, to make an analogy between the layout of the page and the intended or perceived relation among the events. This required breaking down the continuum of the experience into discrete units and identifying their functions within the image (which was the whole experience). Transforming the four-day trip into an event meant collapsing it and then viewing it from the perspective of a single plane on which every action had been flattened into one "configuration." In order to do this I essentially used the language to stand for significant coordinate points in that image, thus removing it from the real experience. It was a highly schematic representation in which any verisimilitude, any correspondence between real events and these representations, was on the level of relations among formal elements, rather than a pictorial image. For instance, the arrangement of typefaces on the "L" page copies the arrangement of the rooms in the theater building that were occupied by the people represented by those typefaces (Fig. 1).

Each page was headed by a letter of the alphabet located in a word which spoke the letter's name: "B gins", "Pro C dure", "D sire", etc. Here the language announced itself, identifying the letter value of words (i.e. the fact that written words are composed of letters). At the same time the paradox of writing was emphasized as soon as a word is spoken it acquires phonetic value. This paradox points out the autonomy of written language. The letter "B" has no use for the phonetic name by which it is identified,"bee." So, I emphasized the written letter in a word which spoke a name which is irrelevant in writing. The letter was always set off, marked by a distinction in typeface or point size, in order to keep it separate form the word in which it occurred.

Another constant feature was the page number, which identified the page in the sequence of pages. Replacing the page number "1" with the word "want" (or "5" with "if i've,", etc.) posed the assumed neutrality of numerical order as a question: does the position influence the actual substance of the page? "Want" used as the page number also blatantly expressed my desire to write, to print, and to come into a relation with the public world through private language.

I repeatedly used the possibility of structuring more than one value or meaning ("plurivalence") into the language—on the level of the word, the sentence and the page. Puns, double meanings and play on the connections between spoken and written language were used to emphasize the distinctions between the two forms of language. The investigation of this plurivalence began at the level of playing with the spelling of individual words. Every letter can be thought of as a place in the sequence of places that make up a word. If a word is set in a large point size, especially 24 point or larger, it is possible to let any single place be occupied by two or three smaller letters. For instance:

$$\text{pro}^{v}_{of}\text{ing}$$

in the dedication combined comments on the personal effort of undertaking this project and on the technical practice of printing.

Then this plurivalent quality was extended to lines. A statement on the "B" page, page "too,", which read:

was **Nothing** was **being** was **made** was **easy**

was set in 12 point, alternating light and bold print, and demonstrated this plurivalence in a condensed form. The light face could be ignored in an initial reading of the boldface text. At the same time the phrase in its entirety posed four alternative statements as equally relevant to the situation of beginning the trip, each statement a permutation of the sentence in bold face read with only one of the four light "was" words. This was also the statement of a theoretical problem: the possibility of fixing meaning in a particular statement.

Sometimes the plurivalence required the careful translation of a written phrase into a phonemic sequence in order to yield a second or third text. For instance, on the first page:

L -- the indefinite article --
meant soft configuration

could be translated into "L.A. meant soft configuration" by substituting the letter "A" for its description as "the indefinite article," in which case the phrase served to describe the social relations of the trip. A second interpretation reworked through sounds could be "Elements of configuration," combining both the actual and the theoretical bases for the work into a single statement. Writing, i.e. printed language, was being used here to undermine the authority of speech—posing the relationship between speech and writing as ambiguous and plural, as is the relationship of either speech or writing to any fixed meaning.

Once the basic components of the "configuration" were decided on —background, foreground, location, context, texture, gesture—they were used to emphasize the contribution of each page to the whole. The "E" page, early in the trip, recounted a stop at a restaurant in Santa Barbara. The conversation at the table focused on the immediate situation, thus invoking the notion of foreground. The social intimacy included an acknowledgment of a certain amount of already established familiarity, so the word was transformed to the more suggestive "fore gone ground." "Fore gone" also indicated that to some extent our personal relations were already fixed and there was an inevitability to the way they might get structured into an account (see Fig.1). The page was very much about choice, its limits and effects: "something made deliberate" was constrained by its options. Choice also had a material effect, or produced evidence, such as seen in the breed of the little dog running loose in the courtyard of the restaurant. Similarly, every choice of typeface was not an invention, but a selection from the finite group of possibilities.

The "L" page, as it clearly announced, dealt with comparisons, among both the elements on the page and their correspondence to the experience from which they were drawn (Fig. 1). The small theater in which we were performing was run by a brother and a sister, she more tense, designing, with a professional look (thus the straight copperplate, 8 point), compared to the brother, who had a more relaxed, friendly look. The contrast yielded me the opportunity to play here with the idea of assigning character to a typeface, determined by a mixture of association and tradition as much as by its effect on us. The second typeface is darker, but more variable, full of flux and with a variety in the relation of thick and thin strokes. Although no fixed character can be assigned to it, by comparison with the first face it has a "personality." The brother's activity, directing, dropped to the next level on the page: a comparison among performers and performance style, bold, light and distant. The bolder face was used for the dark-haired characters, while the lighter face was reserved for the fair. The spatial arrangements were very specific: from the office in the attic to the dressing room in the basement, each step on the page corresponded to a level in the physical infrastructure of the building.

As the colophon page states, I had a few technical problems in printing this book. I was working in an offset shop which lacked many letterpress accessories, such as tweezers and brass and copper spacers (the thinnest, smallest spacers, which are used for careful justification —the filling out of lines to the same length). Also, the press did not have a lock-up bar, the piece which makes a solid brace on the press bed against which the type can be secured. Therefore I printed in a chase— a rigid metal frame which has somewhat more flexibility than a solid lock-up bar. The kind of precarious typesetting I was occasionally doing, especially my use of mixed type sizes within a word or line, would have been even more difficult if I had not been using a flat-bed press on which the type can rest. This press allows a wider margin of tolerance than one in which the chase has to support the type on its own. Even so, some of the printing impression suffered as a result.

From A to Z: **A Text Generated From the Contents of the Typecase**
The main premise for the second work, *From A to Z, OUR AN (Collective Specific) an im partial bibliography,* was completely typographical.

Whereas *Twenty-six '76* had been a tentative exploration of a text through making it into an image, in *From A to Z* I was concerned with having the very text itself dictated by the material means at my disposal. I had purchased 45 drawers of type, miscellaneous faces which had been part of a small job shop. There was barely enough of any single face to set any substantial portion of text. In the large sizes especially there was only enough type to set a short poem. The book was to be a text composed of all the letters (literally, all the pieces of type) which were contained in those drawers. Each piece of lead was to be used once and only once, and all of the pieces were to be used up.

The type ranged in size from 6 point to 48 point. I used all the larger point sizes (from 18 to 48) to represent characters in this "bibliography." Each character was also identified with a letter of the alphabet or a number corresponding with that letter's placement in the alphabet (A = 1, B = 2. etc.) for the purpose of reference throughout the work (Fig. 2, for instance, was the "G" page). The book was a pseudobibliography, fragmentary and fabricated—thus the subtitle "an im partial bibliography," stressing that it was subjective and incomplete. In addition the book was a compendium of every format used in book construction: a table of contents, introduction, footnotes, running heads, marginal notes, etc., each playing a particular role in mapping out the territory of a literary community linked through its traditions, attitudes and social interactions. The book is completely self-sufficient: every term, character, and personality, can be understood within the closed system of references contained in the work. However, it was also meant as a kind of bibliography *à clef*, since it was based on actual observation of a particular literary scene and intentionally represented the various real persons under transformed and pseudonymous identities.

Every page of the main text (of which there were, of course, 26) followed the same format. These were the first pages set and used up the bulk of the large sized type. The preliminary and end material used up the type that remained after the main text pages were set. The primary feature of each main text page (see Fig. 2a) was a poem by the character, and the characters were related and contrasted by typeface. For instance, the family of "Brush" typefaces was used for the most sentimental group, "Copperplate" for the method oriented Modernists, etc.; social or aesthetic affinities could be traced initially through this visual connection, as well as through thematic relations. On the back of each

Fig. 2. Front (2a above) and back (2b right) sides of a single page from *From A to Z*, 1977, letterpress on brown kraft paper, 9" x 12". Each main text page (2a) of this work featured a poem written by the character associated with the letter, in this case, "G." On the back side of the page (2b) the "sorts," the leftover pieces of type from that text face, were set in a pidgin-phonetic English to provide more information. Thus, the full "text" consists of a deliberate statement and a residual statement less consciously formulated.

sheet (Fig. 2b) the "sorts"—the pieces of type left over after the first, more intentional use of the face was made—spelled out in unorthodox phoneticization a critical commentary on the life, attitude and work of that writer. On both the front and back, there was much improvisation in the use of letters and typographic devices. The use of symbols (such as "$" or "£" signs) to stand for letters resulted in multiple meanings, as if revealing associative possibilities that were latent within the word itself.

For instance, on

the "C" page:

pUBLIC

or from the "B" page:

jbjOsyNCradlX

or from the "A" page:

> An jmprovjsajOnal, PROV!SAL
> QUES. of how & why search. HV
> cHoyc QWOT FR. Fæmœz
> ǫWARRLZ.

(which translates as: "An improvisational, provisional question of how and why search. Have choice quote from famous quarrels.")

The lower section of each page consisted of the running narrative relating a fantasy that character A (female) was having about a possible relationship with character Z (male) and character Z's reactions. I called this subplot "Incidents in a Non-Relationship."

There were five elements in this bottom matrix that occurred on the front of every page (see Fig. 2a). On the right-hand side were A's statements. The top line was libidinal:

CURIOUS: LilbiteinitsomasparkinthewelLagedfLavorofthecheese

(Curious: Little bite in it some, uh, spark in the well-aged flavor of the cheese)

The bottom piece was diary-esque, confessional:

> **After that, I began to have thoughts about you**
> **all the time.** *I thought about how I could meet up with*
> *you, where you might be, how I could stop by the store.*
> *It was a definite chemical, physical take that I had had.*

On the left-hand side were Z's reactions. The top of the left side was a weather report, a statement about the state of the relationship in atmospheric terms, run together to prevent easy access:

Inthelangorouslatesummerdaysfollowing

The second line emphasized the theme of the meeting:

ĊE:,...SIRE

And the third line stated Z's attitude toward the moment at hand:

The **MOMENT**: compLete con-- viction. **TOTALITY**. Jes' warch thet krazy LiL' bugger **MOVIN**

The point here was to examine the place from which language origi- nates, is motivated, spoken and made accessible. The barriers and taboos of censorship are reflected on the one hand by the horrible sen- timentalizing tone of the narrative, traditionally associated with women's romance novels, and on the other by character A's unspeak- able libidinal utterances, which are all run together to escape the imme- diate censorship of the eye, thereby acknowledging the existence of lim- its of permissibility.

The marginal notes on each page related the fuller social context in which the characters operated (Fig. 2a). These notes were set in 6 and 8 point type, and some actually in 4 point mounted on 6 point body. The latter were so small that to achieve decent inking it was necessary to print the pages in two runs, the large poems first and the marginalia and footnotes second. Each statement in the marginal notes was a quote from something overheard or written in a letter, a diary or a review by one character or another, often to a third. Each marginal note was fol- lowed by a reference number directing the reader to the notes at the end of the book in the section titled:

$$S^{OU}R^{CZ^s}{}_{...}q^{U^o}{}^{T^{\mathcal{E}}}d$$

(see Fig.3). This reference section was the most densely visual and com- plex part of the book and also the most difficult typesetting job, since here I was using up every piece of type remaining in the drawers, com- bining 48 point with 36, 24,12, and even down to 6 point, all in one block.

Many of the marginal notes in the body of the text (Fig. 2a) were full of puns and double statements:

BUD I WON'T MIND FUR A COUPLE UV REASONS: IN THE FIRST PLACE IS LONG & READ, WELL' SILKY, TH' SECOND MORE SOPHT'- MORE oPEN, THIRD AND LAST BE LEAVE THAT END KNOT SPLIT BUT TENDED' GROOMED & SO, LET P OUTGROW HER POODLE DANCING STAGE THAT'S SO OFF-CENTER. WE ALL NOW HOW FERTILE THAT FIELD. 24

or:

While waiting for Z to strut his, D indulged in the attention of L who was very serious, always, eager to associate with as if that'd obtain what he was assuming in that yielding posture. D knew the kid was full of it but knew too his own I.D. was not apart from its snapshot photo. 25

These somewhat cryptic remarks were made "clear" by the even more cryptic references in the end notes ("Sources quoted:" Fig. 3). This played on the referencing process itself, in that indexing and notation created complication rather than clarification, in a continued network of associations. Every new reference added contingencies to the initial statement rather than anchoring it in a stable context. The context and possible meanings of the original statement continued to multiply.

I had to face the problem of how to indicate letters that had been completely used up. By this time I was down to scraps in the drawers, pulling out one piece after another, looking for a remaining 'e' or 't'. Missing vowels were not a serious problem, but missing consonants were difficult to do without while still maintaining a sense of the word. I used dashes, commas and periods as place holders

$SoUR^{CZ^s}..._qU^oTe.d$

" THIS & O.H.R W---H-R .N-I-S
'-R- FROM G's JOURN-L. picky
1.& O C.R.FUL SH. W.S IN
KE.PING I- .V.RY D.Y
"".HIS A BY G OUR OLD.R
IS OF QUI.. ALER. OLDER,'
2 FrOm ES,ABLISHED POE.',,
,POEM By IN A GENERA.ION
OF OUR Y As ObsERvEd P
3,LI..L. C.U. bYOUR v.rY
SW...H..R- RAP1D rAcY
,A. D & G's READING A, Z's..'--
FROM A LE..ER A WRO.E'';
4 At.ER G's rEAD1NG cuZ,
hOw A COMES .O B. here ,s by
B.ING A DIS.AN. R.LA.ION...-
of Our herO D extracted here is-
THE ENIGMATIC ',,' He cOnvErsatiOn
.....HErE was hELD
BEtwEEN C thE REd BEard aggrEssiVE &
bluNderi.g Wi.. EagEr STupidi.y AND ChARismA.ie
A,...burs.ng wi.h g00_ y g00dy En.HUSIASM.-.
from b's LETtER tO THE TigHT DisciplinEd
RauncH writTEN THE DAY AFTEr
rotten ThaT iniTial FaTEful FacE N
to Face meeting of A & Z at the
reading D gaVe in sulky spiri---
FrOm 's verY bitchilY highly rev.olin'
th. r.al mWrI..eN AccOUnt....,
pUrty Of da Sc.n...pUbliSh;d
bY Z; SO-CALLED NOTES'.-
NO.. FrOm X 2 R.cy lil' P
vOlUp.UO-s str.vmliN,D
OF ;. a ObS.rv.d mAkING OB-
qwk, ,EYES AT UNCONSciOus Z
OF S.XY ,frOm HEr..' A
cUTIePIE Y,cOmpaNIO.
CHArMiNg ,AlsO A cu.iE
JUSTTHEBESTOFFRIENDS
QUICK QUOTE C Leaning-,;
OF THE rEAlLY oVer sOme
V.RY LOUDLY BOIS..ROUS. aefre8hmnz
!Q.' AFTER D's READING AT Z's STORE
while making some rapip moVes

Fig. 3 "Sources quoted" page (partial) from *From A to Z,* 1977, handset letterpress, 12" x 9". The final remnants of all the type were used in these reference notes to explain the context in which the marginal notes in the text were spoken or written. Sometimes the meaning of these reference notes could only be gotten by pronouncing the spatial arrangement of the type.

to represent missing letters. To understand the reference completely, it was often necessary to pronounce the spatial arrangements:

The requirement that spatial arrangement be pronounced to get the full meaning of a group of syllables was a device used by Renaissance creators of rebuses.

All of the preliminary matter, the Table of Contents, Preface and Introduction, used the remnants of 10 and 12 point type in an amalgamation, disregarding the face and using size as the unifying factor (Fig. 4). In these sections the numerical and alphabetical references to the characters provided more and more bits of information about those characters:

Z I.E. EGOcENTrIC,CONCOrD,MA,YALE:bOOK BUSI/VESS,10TS&rEcENT

or about the situation in which the narrative From A to Z took place:

RESOLUTION: williNqANdrEAdYThENighT&ThEsTArsANdThEmusic&YOU

I wanted to stress several points in *From A to Z*. The first was that by being forced to improvise spellings I found dimensions of meaning in the words that were not immediately apparent in normal usage. This was not a transcendental exercise, not the derivation of some deep, interior meaning, but rather a matter of linking a word through phonetic associations or visual puns. Playing up its potential relation to other words through a stream of transformations, I thus recognized again the materiality of language, its real substance and its role as more than a neutral vehicle to convey meaning. This concept of the "materiality" of any particular system of representation—language, photography, drawing, etc.—has been extensively developed by Roland Barthes.

Secondly, I was attempting to provide sufficient reference within the work for it to sustain itself without external references. I wanted to exemplify the idea of a closed system in which, like language itself in some ultimate structuralist sense, all value is determined by the place something has within the system. This is the concept of language outlined by the linguist Saussure, whose work is the basis for the modern

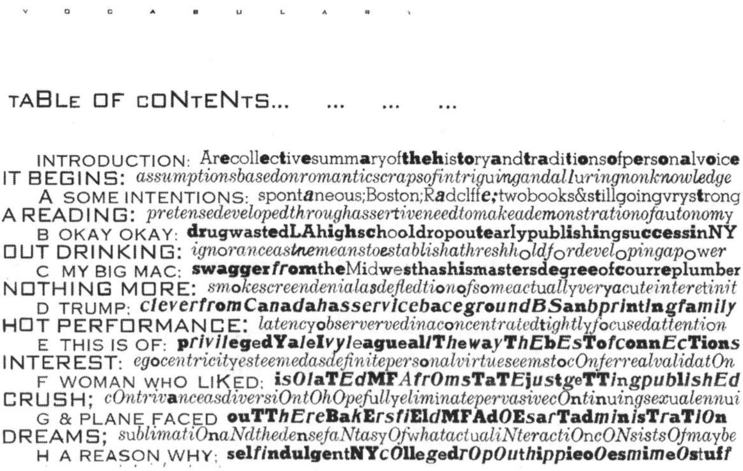

Fig. 4 "Table of Contents" page (partial) *From A to Z*, 1977, letterpress on brown kraft paper,
9" x 12". The preliminary pages of the book also used up remnants of typefaces, using the
type regardless of style, with point size as the unifying factor. The Table of Contents provided information about each of the characters as well as about the situation in which the
narrative of A was taking place.

science of linguistics. In actuality the book can be referenced externally
also, since each of the characters really existed. I had personally
encountered them or their work.

Thirdly, the book is a study in a literary work as a product of a social
as well as traditional context. It is also about literary accessibility, about
the levels of literary organization, ranging from clear to opaque, permitting a reading from the most obvious level—the sequence of the
poems—to the most involved and difficult level of following through all
the references to the end notes. *From A to Z* also demonstrated that a
coherent text could be generated from extant materials, with each piece
playing a meaningful part in the construction of that text—almost giving the impression that the text was latent in the type in those drawers
and had only to be found, not as the text, but as a text, which could be
constructed out of just those letters.

Lastly, the book is about letters—about their role in the manufacture of writing as linguistic expression and about a belief in their particular value as elements of language. Letters as elements in their own
right are capable of carrying discrete and simultaneous messages.
Despite their "ordinary" purpose, which is to compose the very words

that generally overwhelm or negate their individual presence, letters possess a V!V!D (sic) ability to create

$DAdmendz whiCh seRv d0 ELuCidAD XPRINZ.

Against Fiction: **Opening up the Linear Conventions of Narrative Form**
Against Fiction, the last work I will discuss, is in many ways a book more influenced by literary and critical thinking. It was undertaken with considerable respect for the tradition from which it comes, a tradition it undermines at the same time. I wrote the manuscript over a 5-year period during which my approach to its organization went through many changes. I was ultimately able to resolve the organizational issues only when the actual production problems were solved.

The book depends upon the convention of fiction as a literary form, and begins with a reification of the linearity of that form in a long single-paragraph opening page which used Stymie type (a nineteenth century "grotesque" or "Egyptian" face with square serifs) in 48 to 10 point sizes (Fig. 5). The gradual deconstruction of this linear form both visually and thematically is one purpose of the work. The deconstruction is accomplished in a sequence of 40 text pages grouped into four signatures. Each page is a transformation of the preceding page, preserving some of its formal elements and adding or rearranging others.

One of the original intentions for the visual form of this work was to use the devices of popular media to make a work of difficult prose more accessible. Headlines, intertitles in the text, illustrations, short paragraphs, and changes of typeface from bold to light within a paragraph were all used to bring the text more into line with contemporary reading patterns. As the work developed, the problem that linear tradition posed in terms of the transparency of language as a vehicle became more important. This concept of "transparency" is important in linguistics, especially in the work of structural linguists such as Roman Jakobson. In *Against Fiction* I attempted a conservative, slow deconstruction of that linearity, gradually fragmenting the page into two, three and four columns so that no single text, no simple linear form guarantees its own authority through a linear presentation (Fig. 6).

The initial experiments took several forms. I began with the idea that the book would be a catalogue, with entries one after another.

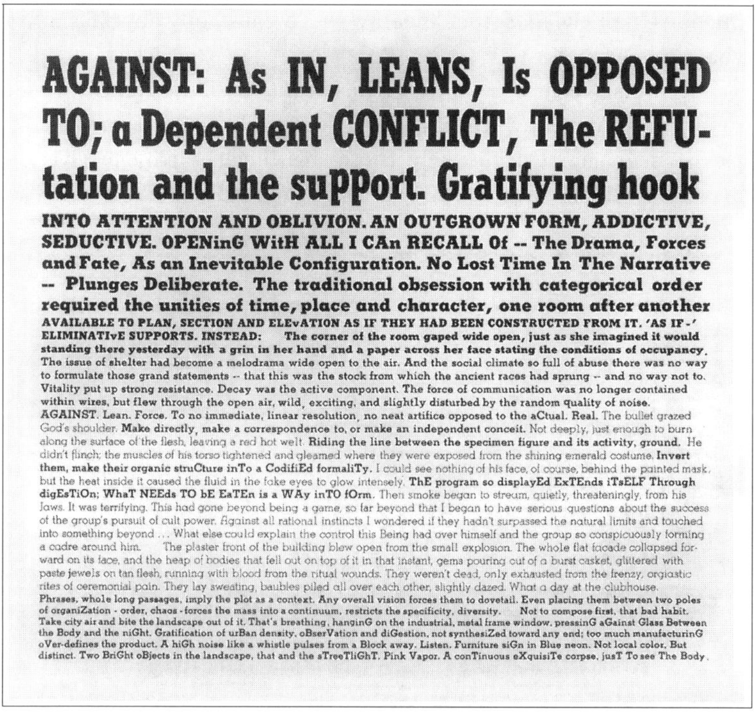

AGAINST: As IN, LEANS, Is OPPOSED TO; a Dependent CONFLICT, The REFU-tation and the support. Gratifying hook

INTO ATTENTION AND OBLIVION. AN OUTGROWN FORM, ADDICTIVE, SEDUCTIVE. OPENinG WitH ALL I CAn RECALL Of -- The Drama, Forces and Fate, As an Inevitable Configuration. No Lost Time In The Narrative -- Plunges Deliberate. The traditional obsession with categorical order required the unities of time, place and character, one room after another AVAILABLE TO PLAN, SECTION AND ELEvATION AS IF THEY HAD BEEN CONSTRUCTED FROM IT. 'AS IF-' ELIMINATIvE SUPPORTS. INSTEAD: The corner of the room gaped wide open, just as she imagined it would standing there yesterday with a grin in her hand and a paper across her face stating the conditions of occupancy. The issue of shelter had become a melodrama wide open to the air. And the social climate so full of abuse there was no way to formulate those grand statements -- that this was the stock from which the ancient races had sprung -- and no way not to. Vitality put up strong resistance. Decay was the active component. The force of communication was no longer contained within wires, but flew through the open air, wild, exciting, and slightly disturbed by the random quality of noise. AGAINST. Lean. Force. To no immediate, linear resolution, no neat artifice opposed to the aCtual. Real. The bullet grazed God's shoulder. **Make directly, make a correspondence to, or make an independent conceit.** Not deeply, just enough to burn along the surface of the flesh, leaving a red hot welt. **Riding the line between the specimen figure and its activity, ground.** He didn't flinch: the muscles of his torso tightened and gleamed where they were exposed from the shining emerald costume. **Invert them, make their organic struCture inTo a CodifiEd formaliTy.** I could see nothing of his face, of course, behind the painted mask, but the heat inside it caused the fluid in the fake eyes to glow intensely. **ThE program so displayEd ExTEnds iTsELF Through digEsTiOn; WhaT NEEds TO bE EaTEn is a WAy inTO fOrm.** Then smoke began to stream, quietly, threateningly, from his jaws. It was terrifying. This had gone beyond being a game, so far beyond that I began to have serious questions about the success of the group's pursuit of cult power. Against all rational instincts I wondered if they hadn't surpassed the natural limits and touched into something beyond ... What else could explain the control this Being had over himself and the group so conspicuously forming a cadre around him.   The plaster front of the building blew open from the small explosion. The whole flat facade collapsed forward on its face, and the heap of bodies that fell out on top of it in that instant, gems pouring out of a burst casket, glittered with paste jewels on tan flesh, running with blood from the ritual wounds. They weren't dead, only exhausted from the frenzy, orgiastic rites of ceremonial pain. They lay sweating, baubles piled all over each other, slightly dazed. What a day at the clubhouse. Phrases, whole long passages, imply the plot as a context. Any overall vision forces them to dovetail. Even placing them between two poles of organiZation - order, chaos - forces the mass into a continuum, restricts the specificity, diversity.   Not to compose first, that bad habit. Take city air and bite the landscape out of it. That's breathing, hanginG on the industrial, metal frame window, pressinG aGainst Glass Between the Body and the niGht. Gratification of urBan density, oBserVation and diGestion, not synthesiZed toward any end; too much manufacturinG oVer-defines the product. A hiGh noise like a whistle pulses from a Block away. Listen. Furniture siGn in Blue neon. Not local color. But distinct. Two BriGht oBjects in the landscape, that and the sTreeTliGhT. Pink Vapor. A conTinuous eXquisiTe corpse, jusT To see The Body.

Fig. 5 First page from *Against Fiction*, 1983, letterpress, 13″ x 17″. A single paragraph using Stymie type from 48 point to 10 point, this page is intended as a statement on the traditional linear form of narrative.

Then it was to be a newspaper, with the format of a tabloid. I actually printed four pages of the newspaper version, but then rejected the idea because the format looked too jumbled. Visually the pieces didn't seem to relate to each other; they seemed more like fragments than parts of a fragmenting whole.

The final form of *Against Fiction* was inspired by Peter Eisenman's *House X*, a book of architectural design. Eisenman approached form as a series of transformations which follow both a logic and an illogic, i.e. preserving a semblance of formal features while adding into the sequence something in each transformation which could not be predicted from the previous sequence. The final stage was not simply a record of transformations into a final form, but also the result of processes not recoverable from that evidence. My intention in appropriating Eisenman's approach was to subvert the linear form of traditional fiction, dismantling the very mechanism by which it usually functions, namely, that strict linearity which constantly dovetails into a whole.

The final version of *Against Fiction* contains illustrations, printed from linoleum cuts, which have the visual quality of the scan lines of television images. I deliberately chose this linear quality to give the images a stylistic compatibility with the color and texture of the type,

The Current Climate

Controversial adviser alleges motivated takeover. Quitting his post he

attempted to put the best face on the situation. Today he rounded up forty-two hopefuls to compete. Dying for honour. Noone was particularly distinguished in the trial heat. These consisted of mopping the dry floor of the organization. There was passing traffic in the interludes meant for conversation. The condition of the people did not respond to the character of any of the candidates. Waiting to re-open the road. Trailblazing teams, all contenders for the top position, hesitated to discover the source of the emergency. None was forthcoming. The interviewees wanted to report to the president directly. The road was still closed. Resignation had forced slides and floods after the allegations. Search continues.

PUBLIC: The Long Night of much Mist

THE THICK HAZE MADE EVEN THE DENSE SHADOWS OF ThE DARK COMPLETELY INDISTINGUIShABLE

It was so long since we had been out at night . I barely knew the neighborhood. When I went I was supposed to find, right at the end of the street, a place where I could buy a split of very eXpensive champagne. A gourmet niGht shop. Passed my coat throuGh the Glass to make chanGe. Almost no visibility near the Ground, owinG to the tule foG, But with lonG, dense vistas in the hiGh clouds. A foretold But unpreventaBle act of canniBalism. I participate, suBmit, review and am aBle to act only in the moment of presentation of what I knew would come to Be a fact. Jaws unaBle to preVent the choice of action, only workinG throuGh the enGaGement.

Mystery Triangle :

Where cars and trucks disappear.

People can claim anything. The very real melancholy of the soul diffuses itself into the air. The first real sighting an instance of creationism. Listed on the marquee of the matchbook in a digital display.

Could be programed from the driver's seat of a well-stocked bank they called the lost institutional memory.

Retrieved, the partial imitation of the tampered with and never violated original

Struggled through the retrials into a partial recovery. Conscientious collection, years' worth of junk, sorted by indelible profile. Whole piles of seemingly useless stuff, never put to obvious use, but chaneLLed toward an amusing, disTracTing aTTEmpT.

Transform the break in labor and materials into a marketable commodity. Not significant enough to advertise. Just waste, consumption, and now the stuff of the earth re-arranged into a rigid and unnecessary structure. Beyond cellular collapse. In the perfect moment, occasioned by a series of experiments. Minimum form. Suction cleaned.

The OriGinal Scene

METHOD: COMING into KNOWING

References become familiar. Petty thievery. Trace that theme. Once here. Snapshot. What's owed. My time. Sure thing. Give it a little edge. Manufacture complete parts. Replacement parts. Caught in the rug. Folds to the sheep. Operating term. Preliminaries. Environment.

What is REAL TIME?

Fig. 6 Four-section page from *Against Fiction*, 1983, letterpress, 13″ x 17″. In the last signature, the division of the page into four sections makes it nearly impossible to recover any single linear reading from the text. The layout also makes use of many of the graphic devices used in popular media, such as headings, sub-headings, and variation in type weight and size, so that the text is accessible to various levels of reading.

which has a strong black and white flicker effect on the page. The illustrations are not, in a strict sense, directly related to the text. They were executed independently of any thematic relation to the sections in which they appear and therefore forge an associative meaning with the text by virtue of their proximity.

Against Fiction is also organized into various levels of accessibility—the larger headlines, smaller subtitles, short paragraphs, etc. But in setting substantial portions of the text the problem was that the contents of the typecase were exhausted. I simply, literally, ran out of certain letters, which demanded a certain amount of invention in order to circumvent the total halt of the project. Confronting this limit forced me to reevaluate the text and its intentions against the choice of whether to stop or to continue. Continuing meant compromising, improvising some neologism to deal with the problems, such as "eggsperience" or "INDIVIDUAL," using letter combinations which either associate to a similar sound or bear a visual resemblance to the missing letter. Once again, holding the type in hand to weigh the choices, I faced the very real materiality of language and its potential to function as a visual image.

References
1. P. Albert-Birot, *SIC*. Paris: Editions Jean-Michel Place, Reprinted 1980.
2. S. Mallarmé, *Un Coup De Des. Oeuvres Complètes*. Paris: Gallimard; originally published 1896.
3. H. Spencer, *Pioneers of Modern Typography*. London: Lund Humphries, 1964.
4. J. Derrida, *Of Grammatology*. Baltimore: John Hopkins University Press, 1976.
5. "Literature illettrée ou la litterature à la lettre", *Bizarre*, #32-33. Noel Arnaud et Françoise Caradec, eds. Paris: 1964.
6. G. Peignot, *Amusements Philologiques*. Paris: Victor Lagier, 1824.
7. R. Barthes, *Image/Music/Text*. New York: Hill & Wang, 1977.
8. F. de Saussure, *Course in General Linguistics*, ed. Charles Bally and Albert Sechehaye. New York: New York Philosophical Society, 1955.
9. R. Jakobson, *Six Leçons sur le Son et le Sens*. Paris: Editions de Minuit, 1976.
10. P. Eisenman, *House X*. New York: Rizzoli, 1982.

V. Artists' Books Past and Future

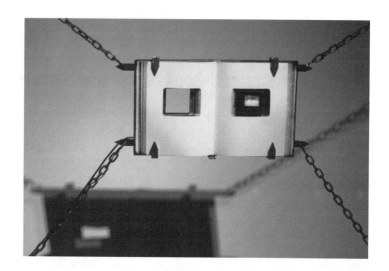

Nora Ligorano and Marshall Reese, The Corona Palimpsest, *1995. (Details of installation.) Photo by Mark Daniels.*

Corona Palimpsest: Present Tensions of the Book

"In the name of 'progress' our official culture is striving to force the new media to do the work of the old."
> — Marshall McLuhan, *The Medium is the Message*

The contrasts in this work embody anxious currents in the climate of thought: is the book as a medium to be reduced to a set of iconic referents as the price of evolution of new technology? Or will there be some place of reconciliation in which the distinct functions of each medium find the activities they best serve? Binarisms proliferate in the structural distinctions installed here beginning with a profound tension between the monitor and the frame, between the jewel-like focus of the tiny screen broadcasting its poetic print messages in video time and the static field of the book around it in which images are suspended, warm and rich, afloat and adrift in the glow of an antique medium. Reading is a contradiction of the monitor's intention—which combines the two functions of broadcast and surveillance.

There are two monitors in this piece and two large book-like objects—very book-like objects: codex books of uniform pages, bound in finite sequence, with head and tail pieces, leather spines, and the rich iconic resonance of a long material history. But insofar as these objects serve merely to invoke book functions they are as much a sign of the book's demise and negation as they are a living example of its continuity into contemporary time. The monitors that they serve to frame have laid claim to all of the dynamic functions in the work: it is the monitors which look, which move, which change, which "speak" in the silent scrolling of a text while the books are suspended, now reduced to serving as a memory which encloses the technological exponent of communication.

Standing to read the small monitor placed in an open book we are watched by recorded eyes which stare out in uncanny perception from the blank pages of the other book—itself unnaturally suspended, fixed in the air, in a position of a surveillance camera whose functions it mimics in reverse. These are eyes which cannot see, which cannot return our actions through the monitor to some centrally located screen and yet, unlike the blank eye of security which reveals nothing to the subject it surveys, this monitor continually reminds the watching viewer of the gaze, the glance, the regime of visual discipline whose interests the camera so often serves.

The suspended book is blank, its pages mute and empty. This is a tome which resonates with the image of the codex as an established form, a historical form, a conventional form whose uses and abuses have survived the tests of fire, flood, annihilation and resuscitation. No longer functional, this hanging book recalls its past as an outworn mode, a history which has exhausted the capacity of the pages to retain the memory traces of a process which continually replaced, displaced, one record by the next. Have they been emptied of their history, these pages? Their texts voided and removed as in the perfect censor's successful effort to take away not only a text but all traces of its effacement? Are these white sheets the sign of a once replete field of language and information? Are they blank signs, pale phantoms of an exhausted history? Book as icon, image of a book, unrepentantly preserving its finitude and sequence, its fixed order of pages gone blank as a disk wiped clean. The palimpsestic process never left so clean a slate as this empty space of the threatening page, the blank, the nothing, the void which has terrified many poets out of any relation to their own voice, calling out as pure flesh for the inscribed eros of the word while sustaining the taboo against marking the clean slate of the spirit with the mere banality of human thought. They return a frightening absence to the inquiring eye which wants to know, *to know*, to be informed of something, anything, if only to be reassured of some coordinate in the empty space. In spite of its age and experience, in spite of the distressed exterior, the rubbed and faded, burnt and scarred, and experienced covers, the book reveals only this mute refusal of information, returning the glance of some disembodied Other eye as an unsatisfactory answer to the anxious query of the reader.

By contrast, the supine book is filled with images, its pages warm with the glow of paint and pictures gleaned from the saturated sources of mass media in all its various print and photographic forms. Faces familiar from current events share space with the pictographic forms of stencilled outlines, figures whose shapes are immediately recognizable as types, as instances of the general categories of a shared visual literacy.

Indeterminate as to final meaning, these images nonetheless serve as an encyclopedic field against which the monitor's text reads out repeatedly, circulating its own loop of language in self-reflexive commentary. The monitor co-opts the functions of the book, taking the old role as its own, broadcasting the silent image of language with words which continually pose questions about the relations between thought and expression, between language and its capacity, inadequacy, limit, and potential.

These are poetic texts, words whose functionality is of another order than that put forth in the daily marketplace of commercial slogans so familiarly perceived in the televised version of the real. By their poetics, these words negate the instantaneity of product identity, replacing the field of received information with line after line of suggestive text. Thought moves outward from the small screen into the frame of the book, or wants to—but the cold chrome edge of the monitor sequesters the video image, keeping a material limit on the referential field of language. Do they struggle, these lines, with the philosophical dilemmas of Mallarmé and Jabès whose precedent they echo, to extend the spiritual limit of the book to embrace the world? Erase the limiting boundaries between language and its representation? Between the bordered edges of a finite order and the chaotic extension of the ever changing real? Between the confines of any formed articulation and the infinte perfection of thought? There is an irreconcilable gap between the soft, supple invitation of the printed pages, multivalent with images in atmospheric sites, offering their subtle pleasures and the rapid, relentless, rewriting of the electronic screen. The stasis of print with its generosity toward the individual pace of the reader, with its forgiveness of revery and return of the prodigal eye, is in violent struggle with the attention demanded by the screen, moment to moment, line to line, in order to grasp the text in its forward temporal logic.

The books don't function in their current form. Limited, suspended, static, they serve as icons, images of what books are known to be—but they are no longer accessible as dense repositories of human thought, reflection, and revery. Nor is the familiar function of the book duplicated by the monitors—watching and displaying, they refuse interaction while the pages of a book are available to be flipped back and forth at the whim and random interest of a reader. The spatialized field of language offered by the moving video is no more dimensional than the constructed field of thought produced in the associative process of read-ing. But the conflicts between the intimacy of print and the problemat-ics of technological productions of knowledge and history are played out here in all their many contradictions—conceptual, visual, linguistic, and tactile. What is offered is not so much a choice between an old medium and a new one as a problematic recognition that there is no choosing either one as if it replaced the operations of the other. If the tropes of book form shape the metaphors of the new technology then the conceptual construct which emerges in the hybrid process will return its transformative template to the earlier form—and both will be changed in the process.

The current tension of the book reflects the present tense of elec-tronic media continuing to come into being. This is not a contrast between the space of the real and the space of the virtual, but between two modes of imaginative life of thought, language, and the eye, each competing to determine the relations of history, language, and idea. As the page was once written so the monitor redraws itself. The new tem-poral logic of history still remains to be seen. Here the transcript is watched and watching its viewers who struggle to preserve some illu-sion of participation in the process. Where will the marginalia appear, the annotations of the reader, if the history which writes itself in the future is always on the inside of a glass surface which resists inscription? Whose idea will have been a moment on the screen and whose impressed on the receptive pages of a more tangible memory when both are proved to be material traces of the elusive, immaterial seeming, process of thought?

This piece was written to accompany the exhibition of The Corona Palimpsest *when it was first shown at Cristinerose Gallery in New York City, 1995.*

Critical Metalanguage for the Artist's Book

It seemed to me that my task for this symposium was to think about what a book could be in critical terms. So I put my mind to work and unfortunately it turned out to be fairly prosaic. I came up with all kinds of categories of structure—things like openings, gutters, dimensions, layout. Then I thought, I think I need to make this more interesting. It's got to be critical, conceptual, ideological.

But then I responded with an instinctive protest—No! No! No! What I really want to think about is secrecy, intimacy, privacy—all those things that led me to the Book in the first place. And so, this dialogue emerged between a personal, private voice and a critical, theoretical voice.

I began to be interested in books as a child because I wanted to write all of the time, and so wore a notebook around my neck, with a pen attached, in order to inscribe the world as response—and that was sometime before age ten, I know. I remember because of the shape of my body, and the way the book hung down. I was still prepubescent, exempt from self-consciousness about the dangling items.

But let's go back to this problem of critical terms: what is the nature of openings? What is the relation of pages to each other across the gutter, the dialogic interplay of face to face, a kind of conversation, confrontation if one wishes, or companionship in space, the parallel condition, feeling ordered by the sequence, but not needing to be.

And then, switching back to my private passions: The writing was to be hidden. I made it very, very small, as if it were an interior trace, not readable or available to any other eye but made for the sake of the belief in the act.

And the critical voice answered: What structures are specific to the book, then? There is, after all, that statement—a book is a "sequence of spaces"—suggested by Ulises Carrión. But then there are also gutters, gutters of which I was barely aware until Brad Freeman showed me Clifton Meador's work and the ways it insisted on the creeping intrusion, subliminal play, of elements seeping into the pages from the dark space inside the spine. Only a binding which doesn't open itself flat, doesn't make itself available, and isn't honest and forthright, can support such mysterious gutters, such areas of fertile activity, breeding its furtive forms in the dark enclosure.

Then the private voice: A book has to be closed tightly to preserve its power. The potency of spells, formulae, is maintained by their inaccessibility. We know, we know, Pandora's box was a book of knowledge hastily opened and long lost.

Critical: Now the dimensions of the book's form also cause a certain tension, stretching the eye to the longest horizon of a line, a page, a paragraph condensed or slung out long and low. Or it may be harmonious, this tension of dimensions, in keeping with some guarantee of relations—a golden mean, a perfect trine, a strictly ruled and regulated space of margins, text, and tribulations. There can be the weight or pages sinking to the floor with all their pretense or their difficulties—height to width, side to side, arm to arm; a veritable exercise of visual aerobics.

The personal voice: I read her like a book. Ah yes, the metaphors of bookness—open, available, clear and accessible. Organized, self-evident, presented as a map of readability as if a character would or could ever be so bold, so to the point, and on the surface. Still, the metaphor insists upon the possibility.

And critical again: Sometimes it seems like layout and format are wrestling companions interlocking until one is felled, held, and pronounced upon. There is the machismo of type and language getting a grip on the Mack truck of the image, or going it alone, into a different line of tropes—the ruly and the irregular, the ungovernable and the meek, the lines which lay down with the lion and those which stroll all over the landscape with the lamb. There are elements of disorderly conduct or organizational expertise, offering up the substance of the work according to their own terms of decorum—or endearment.

Personal: They threw the book at him. And so they should have, except for what that meant to the ancient binding and the fragile pages —still, the whole exhaustive inventory of the Law, what a formidable weight, one sees a disproportion between the size of the projectile and the size of the intended target so that one or the other is demeaned, humiliated, and subjugated.

Critical: Sequence, in fact, is the great structural instrument of the book—its method, its madness, its order, its progression—writhing into a serpentine trail of mixed messages and interlocking narratives, the browsing method of the tabloid, the reliable order of the alphabetic sequence, the dependable linearity of normative prose, the irrepressible experience of images forging their connections through the fact of following, one after another, in the fixed determination of a regulated encounter. We lift off, from the flat platform of the program, into the flight of an interactive fancy—coming and going from the finitude of pages in the places and along our own unpredictable encounter. Their order against our whim, their fixity against our interference, their sense against our disregard for it.

Personal: The book of the world, the word, the book of nature, the book of knowledge, the book of light and the books which had to be okayed by the librarian before they could be taken out. I chose mine for the thinness of paper, the smallness of type, and number of pages. I wanted commitment from a book, a sense that if we got involved, it would last. A long time.

Critical: Movement and timing, the flicker of papers, colors, textures, elements. Janet Zweig's extremely receptive book, turning the radar dish around and around in itself, as if that remote interior could be the site for sore messages or prying eyes. Suppleness and stiffness, the resistance and cooperation of materials. The sensual theater of the Iliazd books, lifting their thin veils one after another before the heavy curtain of the stiff interior. Now all of that is available as simulations—paper textures printed on coated stock in imitation of the handmade, hard to handle, fetishized original.

Personal: They'll make a book from that movie, just you wait! The absurdity of the text version coming after the mass media release, becoming necessary only to be owned and provide the private experience of the public spectacle.

Critical: From the structural to the conceptual—a leap from the observation of form as specific to the medium to the associative play of form as idea: the metaphysics of the book, its full range of roles from initiation and knowledge to perfidy and deceit. The tiny diary revealing all, the elephant folio displaying its riches and wares, the fine, fine, insights of the well-wrought manual, explaining itself without difficulty to the real material of some other world. Reference and reverence, physics and dynamics, blindness and the raw face of insight staring back from the pages and into the backlit screen of the mind. The trials and tribulations of sanctity, betrayal, violation, and the mutilated record all bound into the affective legacy of the Book not merely as Object—as far as I am concerned, any book with its pages glued shut is not engaged in a dialogue—but Book as Topic as Subject as Prospect and Charge.

In the end, the voices synthesize their response: And finally, not least, the endlessly mutating status of the book as a commodity which identifies itself with confusion these days—the portable companion, the fetishized original, the almost-a-portfolio, the tale of the literal, the visual, the virtual—all vying for a place in the marketplace of salable, tradable, identifiable items for consumption, sale, and resale. The book is value, the blue book, in itself and for others, the guest book, the social register, the family album, the scrapbook, the black book whose social and cultural functions weaving in and out its functional and ideational identity. What is the book to be, now, in the interspace of hyperelectronic nodes? A nexus of events? A momentary intersection of concerns? An immaterial form of non-record of what might have been ideas or events? Or a new form of the Mallarméan mutation, that final, realized Book which is the full equivalent of both the world and the self, the total spiritual symbol of knowledge as complete, replete, and yet, satisfyingly bounded into itself. A whole. Or is it instead to be an endless fragmentation, in which we all, each, have our part to play in writing, scribing, projecting, painting ourselves as a place in the constellation of a synaesthetic newspeak.

The book remains. That, I think, has been the cause of my attachment to it. The fact of its independent life, its capacity to go out from the shop, the house, the office, and live on its own. As Todd Walker says, the joy of it all is that you can find it again, years later, on a shelf, and its still works—without batteries, lights, or electricity, it makes itself available again, as a new experience, a new encounter.

Written for a symposium organized by Charles Alexander at Minnesota Center for the Book Arts, Spring 1994. First published in the volume of essays, Talking the Boundless Book, *1995.*

The Myth of the Democratic Multiple

"Usually inexpensive in price, modest in format, and ambitious in scope, the artist's book is also a fragile vehicle for a weighty load of hopes and ideals: it is considered by many the easiest way out of the art world and into the heart of a broader audience."[1] With these words, Lucy Lippard defined the ambitions linked to the enterprise of artists' books—which she characterized as a product of 1960s counter-culture idealism. At the end of that same piece, written in 1976, Lippard said, "One day I'd like to see artists' books ensconced in supermarkets, drugstores, and airports, and, not incidentally, to see artists able to profit economically from broad communication rather than from lack of it."[2]

The idea of the democratic multiple was one of the founding myths of artists' books in their incarnation as mass-produced works. Artists' books were to counter the traditions of fine press, limited edition *livres d'artistes*, escape the institutional context of galleries, fly in the face of print and photographic protocol, and circumvent the established order of the fine art system. Few artists' books conformed to the letter of this particular orthodoxy and in the late 1990s artists' books are far more hybrid and varied in form, borrowing eclectically from every conceivable lineage of printing and publishing history. The rubric now covers the full spectrum from expensively-produced limited editions to inexpensive multiples. But partisans of the democratic multiple continue to invoke its image as the one true identity for artists' books. Such advocates rarely address, head-on, the many questions which have plagued producers of these books over the years as they have struggled to cope with the realities of translating the theoretical ideal into practice. The history of artists' book publishing is strewn with the failures of this project in aesthetic, political, and economic terms while being haunted by a rhetoric asserting that only the democratic multiple can save artists' books from the charge of elitism.

There were several tenets which combined in the original conception of the democratic multiple. The first of these was aesthetic: the book was an ordinary object. Its mass-produced format conformed to the then prevailing minimalist idea of a fabricated, industrial product which offered an alternative to the fine art traditions of the hand-craft-ed object. As a dominant feature of 1960s aesthetics, this ideal of anti-artisanal production asserted an anti-professionalism as well. A book which appeared to be standard in all respects—the paradigm of the genre usually cited is Ed Ruscha's 1963 *Twentysix Gasoline Stations*—sup-ported the possibility that anyone might be a producer as well as a con-sumer. Supposedly banal imagery and low-level design were key ele-ments of this aesthetic sensibility, a kind of sham flat-footedness which belied its own privileged status of production. That such effects were calculated, highly determined, aesthetic choices intended to create the image of the anti-professional work, was a point lost in the rhetoric of the moment.

Aside from the aesthetics of its production, the democratic multiple bore the weight of a political charge: it was meant to circulate freely outside the gallery system, beyond the elite limits of an in-crowd art going audience and patrons. The assumption that books could circulate in such a way derives in part from their physical autonomy, their capac-ity to be disseminated into the world as independent objects (unlike paintings or sculptures which generally circulate with more difficulty and more attention to their provenance, location, and attribution). While that idea worked fine in the abstract, in reality it depended upon creating a system of distribution and upon finding an interested audi-ence for these works which were at least as esoteric in many cases as the most obscure fine art objects. To this day there are plenty of viewers who respond to artists' books with puzzlement, dismay, confusion, and/or outright hostility. The fallacy of the supermarket distribution network envisoned by Lippard was not merely that there wasn't a struc-ture in place to facilitate it, but that even if there had been, *Twentysix Gasoline Stations* or Suzanne Lacy's *Rape Is . . .* (1976) would never have leaped to the eye and hand of the casual shopper with the same easy rapidity as the *National Enquirer*. If the bewildering disorientation, which the very ordinariness of the artist's book induces by virtue of sub-verting the familiar form with an unfamiliar content, is part of these works' definition of success, then the accompanying reality is that many viewers simply didn't get the jokes or the effects. Like most late 20th century artwork, the artist's book assumes a sophisticated artworld viewer initiated into the play with conventions and their subversion which characterizes much of the work of the advanced guard.

But perhaps the fallacy least evident in the production of books in "affordable" multiples, the supposedly "democratic" form of the book, is the economic one. The question of affordability has two aspects—affordable for the producer and for the consumer. Though the democratic multiple was designed to sell cheaply ($5 to $20), in largish unnumbered editions (500 to 5000 copies), it was expensive to produce. The per unit cost might be affordably low, but the up front capital expenditure was significant ($1000 to $10,000 or more). By contrast, a limited edition book or one of a kind work has a relatively low up-front capital expenditure. For artists with access to an offset press and possessing pre-press production skills, these costs could be reduced to the price of film, plates, ink, chemicals, paper, and binding materials. But the idea that even these costs are neglible would be quickly dispelled by a glance at receipts and accounts. For the cost of producing a single offset artist's book, one can fit out a basic letterpress shop (or build canvases for a year, or buy a high-end computer with full graphics capability, a scanner, large monitor, and color printer). The problem of finding an audience and of producing sellable works remains to be solved, but in the production of the mythic democratic multiple, the issue of affordability is seriously shifted in favor of the audience. In the production of limited edition or one of a kind works it is shifted towards the artist. In both cases, the cost of the artist's labor is not factored into these equations, but the devaluation of the creative activity in offset printing is a regular feature of the assessment of value. In the contrast of offset and letterpress editions a "the machine does it" attitude seems to prevail with respect to the former while a hand-made aesthetic attaches to the latter. This is a holdover from the use of offset in the 1960s when the artist's-book-as-industrial-product downplayed the aesthetic qualities of standard, commercial modes of reproduction.[3]

Still, there is good reason why the political agenda which motivated the democratic multiple remains a persistent element of ongoing rhetoric within the field of artists' books. A notion of empowerment aligns with acquiring the skills and means of print production. A.J. Liebling's famous quote, "The freedom of the press belongs to whoever owns one," continues to resonate even in an era of electronic communication—or maybe especially. The legitimacy which print confers on the individual word is certainly confirmed in the era of desktop publishing and the authority which the book format imposes on its contents is very real in general, public perception. Books continue to have the power to introduce non-standard thought into the arena of public discourse through the Trojan horse of an ordinary appearance. Books provide a vehicle for affirmation, information, and enlightenment across a wide spectrum of points of view and belief systems. And this will be true as long as the book remains imbued with its present authority as a cultural icon.

There are historical precedents for using the book for subversive and liberatory activities, particularly among the artists of the early 20th century Russian avant-garde such as Velimir Khlebnikov, Natalia Goncharova, and Vassily Kamensky. In the 1910s in particular, artists made works by any and every available means in editions which were stenciled, lithographed, letterpress printed, handmade, or reproduced on primitive mimeo-type equipment. In editions from ten to five hundred copies, these works were distributed by hand, among friends and companions, or sold very cheaply in order to get them into the world.[4] Like the leafletting activities and independent magazine productions of Italian Futurists or German Dada artists, these attempts to use publishing to spread radical art ideas met with mixed success but satisfied the desire to break through the perceived (and real) limitations of the established audience of fine art patrons and viewers. Ironically, these ephemeral works now sell for high price tags, their author-publishers long gone, and their political impact muted by the fact that the context in which they might communicate this original meaning has vanished. They now function as fetishized art objects, rare and valuable, the very opposite of their originally intended identity.

In the 1960s and 1970s, putting artists' books into printed and bound form and getting them into circulation proved to be widely different activities. If the project of the democratic multiple is to a significant extent a failed one, it is in part because the means of distribution were so slow and fragmentary that publisher-artists could not recoup their original expenditures—or did so only over a very long period of time. The books didn't get out. When they did, they sold in small numbers, were paid for at a slow rate with a high percentage of sale price going to commission. While subsidizing one's production is a normal expectation on the part of most artists, the boxes of unsold stock under the bed or in the basement were a continual reminder that what had gone unsold was likely to remain unread, unwanted, and ineffectual in its place in the world. The exception to this was the work of those well-known artists who embraced the form. The products of blue-chip artists were not always the most interesting works in the field and were frequently hybrid forms doubling as catalogues for an exhibition, publisher- or dealer-driven, rather than artist-initiated works. But these found an audience the way artists' prints did—as the inexpensive side-line to the mainstream markets. The real failure was that the audience for artists' books simply failed to materialize. Where were these masses who supposedly hungered for innovative, original, works of portable art in the form of inexpensive multiples? They were probably out buying posters of Impressionist paintings and culture industry celebrities.

In spite of this rather dour assessment of the fate of the democratic multiple, it is important to note that there were and are a number of presses and individuals committed to the idea. There are also a significant number of artists who have modified or transformed their practice over time to reflect their own changed attitudes with respect to the earlier utopian expectation of what the artist's book might be. There are presses which continue to support the democratic multiple as a principle and a reality: Simon Cutts (in recent years, with Erica Van Horn) has maintained Coracle Press (Norfolk, London, and Ireland) with an unwavering commitment to the affordable multiple since its inception in the mid 1970s. Likewise, Telfer Stokes, frequently in collaboration with Helen Douglas, has run WeProductions (Yarrow, Scotland) with the idea that their books are offset editions whose prices make them competitive with trade cloth and paperbacks. Other artists abandoned the production of such works after a long spell of highly original and creative publishing, such as Conrad Gleber who, with Jim Snitzer, operated Chicago Books for over ten years (mainly in the 1970s). The rising and falling fortunes of Printed Matter Bookstore at DIA, in New York City, whose founding was a product of the original 1970s idealism, can be mapped as a history of the checks and difficulties which have met the mythic concept of the democratic multiple in its many incarnations over the years. The struggle has frequently been frustrating. As an institution with a unique identity in the field, Printed Matter Bookstore has been called upon to serve any number of roles—bookstore, distributor, archive, reading room, community center, and gallery space—while struggling to meet rent, wages, overhead, and payment schedules.[5] Their situation has to be read as symptomatic of the fate of the larger vision of artists' books as affordable multiples since their commitment from the beginning has been to the dissemination of these works.

Many artists who produced affordable editions for years now either supplement their inexpensive editions with high end works in limited numbers, make one of a kind works which sell in a fine art market, or seek a workable compromise between sustained individual investment of time and money and some kind of return. The idea that artists who don't make money are somehow more pure and noble than those who aspire to gain just recompense for their efforts was already dispelled in Lippard's insightful statement. Artists like Phil Zimmermann, Todd Walker, and Susan King—to name only a few—continue to wrestle with the conflicts and paradoxes of offset production, and their own earlier commitment to the affordable multiple. This is not an issue of selling out—since there is no market to sell out of or into, but of coming to terms with the realities of production costs and audience. Artworld champions of the offset multiple, John Baldessari, Lawrence Weiner, and Ed Ruscha, have made their own compromises with their original positions and produced limited edition works with fine art publishers. What has become glaringly clear, in the 30-some years since the democratic multiple was announced, is that not only is it almost impossible to make money as a producer of inexpensive artists' books, but also that it's difficult even to break even. And, to add insult to injury, it has tended to be the high end products which command critical attention because they come into the world announcing their "importance" in their production values (expensive paper, binding, large formats, "hand" printing). But it is still true that many of the most creative, innovative, interesting and exciting work done in this field is in works at the lower-end of production values.

For better and for worse, in the 1990s, artists' books have come of age. There are several dozen artists' presses in the United States, Europe, Mexico, Australia, and New Zealand committed to artists' books as their major or sole mode of expression. [6] And there exist quite a number of artists for whom the complexity, density, and specificity of the book form are essential features of their artistic vision (Gary Richman, Susan Baker, Clifton Meador, Joan Lyons to name just a handful of representative American artists). The complete body of their works deserves critical recognition and attention. This is slow to come, but the need for an informed critical debate has begun to motivate the artists' book community to produce a rigorous intellectual assessment of such production. There are various newsletters published in association with Centers for artists' books (*Ampersand* and *AbraCaDaBra*, produced in the San Francisco Bay area and Los Angeles, respectively). A few journals with broader artworld constituencies, such as *Art Monthly* in London, have regularly published the work of critic and historian of artists' books (notably Cathy Courtney). *On Paper*, formerly *Print Collector's Newsletter* frequently features artist's book reviews by Nancy Princenthal. And most recently, Brad Freeman launched the *Journal of Artists' Books* (1994 to the present) to foster critical debate in the field.

The downside of this infusion of critical energy is the end of the naive era of books as unmediated and spontaneous expressions. The anyone-can-do-it mood has been replaced with a new professionalism (and that earlier "anyone" has to be qualified—since when the "anyone" was a blue-chip artist the response to their work was very different than when the artist was an individual working in a garage somewhere).[7] The field of artists' books has expanded through programs in colleges and various local centers of activity fostering the production of works which are often unconscious hybrids of various traditions of fine art print protocol, limited edition portfolios, high end publishing, livre d'artistes, and self-publishing. There is formulaic and weak work among these productions, and also much precious, crafty stuff, but there's also solidly interesting work by artists finding their identity within the field—and in this regard, artists' books are now no different from any other artform. And, like any other viable art form, the artist's book continues to reincarnate itself through various mutations and transformations in response to the needs and visions of each generation and each practioner. The mistake would be to hold out some standard of judgment as universal or as carrying a morally superior position. Too often, the myth of the democratic multiple has been used in this way without looking the too evident paradoxes in the face.

In a recent conversation, Cathy Courtney recounted to me an anecdotal experience she had had reading the latest artist's book from the London-based BookWorks, *The Diary of a Steak*, while on a train. The book has a photographic image of a hunk of raw meat on its cover with a small sticker where the price tag would appear on a supermarket steak. But the tag says, "hear my erotic music." A man seated across the aisle from her seemed clearly perturbed by the image, and Courtney said she was reminded once again of the power of an artist's book to function subversively in the most ordinary of surroundings simply by its transformation of the standard form and format. Or As Brad Freeman has said, "Over its lifetime, the book has the capacity to insinuate itself into unforseen locales." And it is in this insinuating capacity that the book continues to serve the original vision of the democratic multiple— as a work which one encounters with no introduction and no warning and which suddenly, oddly, uniquely transforms the viewer's expectations by its unexpected innovative originality. To privilege the democratic multiple at this point in time is a questionable enterprise freighted with the burden of another generation's notion of moral superiority and unrealistic expectations. The few artists who do persevere in that direction deserve respect and, in certain cases, serious critical appraisal. But many have also looked this project squarely in the face, made their effort or assessment, and seen fit to rethink its premises. In artists' books, as in any creative endeavor, there are no rules. Make the books you want to make, the books you believe in. Those are the only books worth producing. The failure of the democratic multiple is not a failure of production, but of reception—another of the many moments in which the efforts of alternative discourse have been eclipsed by the economically advantaged mainstream. Artists' books have failed to find a place as a democratic artform, at least up until now. But in the future —?

1."Lucy Lippard, The Artist's Book Goes Public," p.45; Joan Lyons. *Artists' Books: A Critical Anthology and Sourcebook* Peregrine Press and Visual Studies Workshop, Rochester, NY, 1985, p.45-48.

2. Ibid, p.45.

3. See my article "The Work of Mechanical Art in the Age of Electronic (Re)production," in *Offset: Artists' Books and Prints,* Brad Freeman, ed., exhibition catalogue, NYC, 1993. Included in *Figuring the Word,* p. 184-193.

4. See Susan Compton, *The World Backwards: Russian Futurist Books 1912-1916,* British Museum Publications, exhibition catalogue, 1978; and my book, *The Century of Artists' Books,* Granary Books, New York, 1995.

5. There are a handful of other bookstores and dealers specializing in artists' books, but Printed Matter's symbolic identity and longevity define its particular role.

6. No doubt elsewhere as well, but if there is a significant output of artists' books in Africa, South America, or Asia, it has not managed to find much distribution or visibility.

7. Which only points out how "mythic" the idea of the democratic multiple was, and how linked to an artworld aesthetic styled as a political gesture: compare the careers and critical reception of the work of Joe Ruther and Ed Ruscha, of Telfer

Stokes and Gilbert and George, of Gary Richman and Richard Prince. In each case, the first artist in the pair worked in the form of independently produced multiples with affordable price tags (under $30); each is a compellingly original artist; each languishes in relative obscurity by contrast to the art star counterpart whose "democratic" multiple productions are frequently underwritten by well-funded publishers, galleries, or institutions.

This piece appeared in ArtPapers, *October, 1997, in a special feature on artists' books.*

Offset: The Work of Mechanical Art in the Age of Electronic (Re)production

Offset printing was designed for commercial purposes to facilitate the high-speed, high-volume production of multiples through photomechanical processes. The multiples in this exhibition are artists' productions. They are statements and expressions—original prints and books—which offer an alternative to the mainstream of mass media's hegemonic control over texts and images. In the form of prints, offset extends an industrial process into the territory of fine art printing calling into question the terms of finite production, especially the limited edition so central to that tradition. Offset books, meanwhile, offer the potential for the intimate, complex, and mobile structure of the book form to proliferate and move itself into a wide open cultural field. Books, even more than prints, have a life of their own. They are autonomous, self-sufficient, independent publications—with all that that implies in terms of editorial, artistic, communicative activity. Artists' books are in some ways the quintessential late twentieth century artform: interdisciplinary, unruly, loosed from the constraints of traditional media/genre definitions, and formal considerations into a free form play with images, ideas, texts and structures. They arose as an outgrowth of the conceptualization, democratization and popularization which characterized the artistic sensibility of the 1960s. In the last thirty years artists' books have come of age, and in spite of the many problems and paradoxes of production, distribution, and reception, they remain a vital mainstay of alternative expression. Offset is the preferred mode of production for this contemporary form—apparently cheap, readily accessible, and extremely accomodating to various sources and styles of information and aesthetics. Seen as a servicable mode of production, a facile means of rapidly reproducing images and words, offset has been slow to be appreciated in its own right—not merely for its reproductive capabilities, but for its specific qualities as an artistic medium.

Offset's Identity

Offset printing is situated at the intersection of individual creative expression and industrial production. The theoretical premises on which the identity of offset as a creative medium can be legitimated have yet to be fully articulated. In addition, practical considerations, such as the difficulty of learning the process, have kept the number of offset artists low. However, with the widespread availability of the electronic darkroom on personal computers the pre-press aspects of offset production are becoming part of the common currency of information processing. But the essential characteristics of offset as a printing process remain unchanged: the photomechanical transfer of visual information from film to a planographic aluminum plate to a soft blanket and then to paper on a high speed press. The most recent technology extends the electronic reach—for Heidelberg's newest press the plates are made from disks right on the press. But offset printing itself is still very much a mechanical art; its technology is based in nineteenth century process and machinery, in the mechanization of older craft practices which were slow, labor intensive, and dependent on skilled handwork. Offset is the high end output for electronic media, the most efficient, accurate, and versatile mode of rendering the digital, rasterized, processed data of the electronic environment into material form as print.

Offset is not an outmoded technology, like stone lithography or handset letterpress, acquiring status by virtue of its obsolescence. Offset art, instead, is comparable to video: it is an artistic use of a viable industrial mode. Not surprisingly, video has also been slow to obtain recognition—or, even more importantly—identity as an art form. As a creative medium in an age of electronic (re)production, offset can only be understood in relation to its continuing functionality as an industrial process. As a mechanical mode of production, offset can only be assessed aesthetically in relation to the eroding status of modernist claims about the autonomy of fine art. And the prosaic familiarity of offset printed sheets can only be theorized in terms of their specific cultural identity if the invisible aspects of skilled labor and production processes on which it depends are taken into account—and the ordinary character of offset defamiliarized. The purpose of this essay is to at least suggest some of the parameters within which such an assessment might be framed.

History and Technology

As stated above, the history of offset begins with its development as an industrial form of reproduction in the late nineteenth and early twentieth century. The techniques of halftone photography were combined with the mechanics of high speed printing to create a versatile medium—one which was capable of reproducing literally any image through photographic means. The history of offset as a creative medium is more recent. There are pioneer printers in this field: Eugene Feldman, Joe Ruther, Todd Walker. Their work stretches over more than forty years, a substantial period measured in human terms, a brief period in terms of the history of art. Several waves of younger artists have learned from these figures, or developed into offset artists through their own direct exposure to the printing process in studios, schools, or commercial environments, many of whom (though by no means all) are represented in this exhibition. Offset has only slowly found its place in the curricula of a few art schools, where it still suffers both an industrial stigma and also, suffers from the difficulties involved in coming to terms with such a complex process.

Designed to perfect the rapid reproduction of images and texts through a combination of photographic and lithographic printing processes, offset generally hides its complexity under the appearance of efficiency. In fact, offset is a process which requires elaborate and highly skilled work in every aspect of its production. In the pre-press stage, hours in the darkroom, at the drawing board, or in the design studio all contribute to the eventual making of a piece of film. Whether recording hand processes—drawing, mark-making, fingerprints—or using photographic methods—electronic or traditional—offset plates have to have their own photosensitive surfaces exposed and developed before they can be used in printing. At the stripping and platemaking stages, negatives, mylar, positive plates, stencils, opaquing fluid, elaborate burning and registration—any number of manipulations—provide tools for composing the visual image ultimately fixed in the photographic emulsion. Once made, the plate provides the means for transferring ink to the soft blanket and onto the paper. In printing, a plate is continually dampened to keep the oil base ink off the non-image area, and the variables of water, pressure, speed and inking require continual vigilance. When used as an artform and creative medium, offset sometimes calls attention to and disturbs the transparency of the reproductive process. It is possible to transform offset from a reproductive to a productive medium through interference at any point in the process. And yet, the very photomechanical character of offset is such that it will always, inevitably, conceal the labor involved in its operation.

Auratic Originals vs. Democratic (?) Multiples

The beginning of the modern period in visual art corresponds with the development of mass production modes in industry. The technology for such mass production of images (including offset) made it necessary for fine art to distinguish itself from other forms of image production. Modern fine art had two identifiable characteristics: it was autonomous, separate and distinct as a commodity form (an object among others and an image "free" from reference) and it was comprised of unique, original works—or at the very least, those in highly limited editions.

The modern concept of an autonomous fine art depended on the idea that art was somehow distinct from mass culture in its imagery, style, and method of production—and that it was capable of serving functions which could be served by no other cultural activity. As theorized by twentieth century critics, especially Clement Greenberg, the function of art was to preserve the values of individual expression in the face of the powerful instruments of information, control, and seduction of both totalitarian and capitalist ideologies. Art production was defined as a practice of individual expression that found its social and aesthetic identity in the institutions of museums, galleries, and critical discussion. The myth of the auratic original allowed status to accrue to the tradable commodity of the oil painting, while the use of certain print media was perceived to be too intimately intertwined with commercial, advertising, and industrial aims and methods to retain its aesthetic autonomy. Simply stated: lithographic prints too closely resembled the products of industry to pass as fine art. Needless to say, the more that machinery and less that hand work was involved in its making, the lower a work was on the hierarchical spectrum defined by "art" at one extreme and "mass media images" at the other. The mass produced images of high speed media have only been permitted to enter the fine art realm through imitation, iconic reference, or in parodic, limited ways which quickly recuperate them as fine art (Cubist collage, Dada assemblage, Pop art, Fluxus, recent appropriation work). Offset, after all, is real industrial production—not just a simulation. The grounds on which it could be distinguished from commercial production cannot be sustained on material terms, and thus, either have to be made on aesethetic terms (iconography of personal expression, laying bare of the mechanical devices, or the artificial limiting of editions) or social terms (through permitting offset to aspire to the condition of fine art through museum shows, gallery sales, critical review). Offset challenges the very premises of modern fine art (already severely eroded by postmodern rhetoric, if not practices) by its serious connection to industrial production, countering the premises and claims of the auratic original.

Ironically, offset is equally unable to sustain the mythic terms of the democratic multiple. One of offset's unique capabilities (the basis of its success as an industrial process) is the relation between production cost and unit cost. The high volume capacity of the printing machine is what renders the end-product affordable—if the equation is used conventionally. But offset equipment is extremely expensive. Joe Ruther's salvage techniques may have permitted him to keep a few old clunkers running, but even that was at a cost beyond the average computer or letterpress shop. (If not always true in monetary terms, this is the case in terms of the mechanical skill and patience to keep the old presses running.) Price tags for high end machines creep into the six-figure bracket pretty fast—they are complicated machines with thousands of moving parts functioning at extremely tight tolerances. Offset artists, typically, make small editions which are nonetheless high volume by art standards. Where a stone lithographer might push an edition to fifty or a hundred copies in the editioning process (and consider it excessive if the run were to include more than three or four colors) in offset printing that many sheets go by in two or three minutes during the "set-up" time on the press. For the artist, the greatest investment of time and effort is in the set-up, in the pre-press, darkroom, platemaking, stripping, and working the plate up on the press to print cleanly, densely and correctly. The costs in all of these pre-press processes are as high for ten (good) copies as they are for ten thousand or more. The only change in cost factor comes with costs of paper. An affordable, democratic, accessible form of production? Not exactly . . . and yet, its artistic identity is bound up with both making claims to be so (the case with Fluxus, Conceptual art, where an artists' books sensibility became associated with cheap quick print services, and the smeary, greyed-out, fuzz-focus image) and also, with the desire not to be condemned to this category (where offset art is considered too unlimited to claim a place in the market of the fine art print).

Production vs. Reproduction
Paradoxes paradoxes. The term reproduction is also fraught with con-

traditions. Offset is often a means of reproducing an image from another medium (art masterpiece post-cards)—but the concept of reproduction is always qualified. Transformation and mutation are effects of reproduction—the original is not only not present in its reproduced form, but is seriously altered by the photographic and printing processes—ink on paper is not, for example, oil paint, continuous tone photo, or water color on absorbent surface—it is a simulation of the same which references those visual codes by which it can be recognized that the original was such or such. But this concept of reproduction has little relevance to the offset artist/printer who is using the medium as a creative tool, since in most cases, these artists are intent on exploring the potential of the multifaceted process to make images which have no other original, do not exist outside of their production through the offset process.

To maximize the reproductive potential of the offset medium, then, one plays down, represses, the interventionary urges. To use offset as a means of producing images which have no pre-existence, no other corporeal life, the full range of manipulative operations are exploited. The simulation of sameness becomes a moot point in offset works which mutate in various stages of the printing process—except where editioned pieces follow printmaking protocol in spite of their use of mechanical means. Consistency, standardization, sameness—these are all readily achieved on an offset press, but there are offset artists for whom the mutability of process on press is part of the attraction of the medium. For others the darkroom remains the site of most interventions and manipulations, while for some the computer is the mutating instrument of choice.

The Electronic Myth

The electronic aspect of prepress production outstrips the capacities of the film imagesetting output devices to service high end printing at this point. The visualization of complex layering, printing effects and even the achievement of separations for film output can all be achieved on a computer monitor screen. But contrary to the hype of ad copy, getting from disk to printing plate is hardly a smooth and flawless process. Images which work in an electronic environment may be antithetical to the print processes—those which don't take into account the way the press works (the sequence of runs, the necessity for registration in the negatives, the peculiarities of stripping) are doomed to failure or laborious rework. Designers and artists unfamiliar with the "old" skills—such as reading halftones or evaluating film for flaws—are vulnerable to the pitfalls of default settings or machine-made decisions which override the traditional checks and balances which occurred when each step of production was in the hands of a trained professional. Now the technicians of design, pasteup, stripping, darkroom, are all combined into computer programs which do not always recognize the necessary nuances essential to each stage of production. Even in the hands of print-smart professional artists, the computer has its limitations—some film outputting devices cannot handle the byte-inflated files necessary for image production—and those designed for very high end production are out of the price (even for services) range of many personal computer users. The rasterized image still struggles as it becomes material form, suffering as in some medieval morality tale from the torments of the flesh. Printing is both a mechanical process and a human process—the machine doesn't run itself, but has to be carefully watched, continually fine-tuned, coaxed, even humored and coerced. When electronic media give up their nostalgic need for life in material, then the mechanical processes of offset printing will lose their industrial function and perform some new metaphysical practices of smooth running in an aesthetic dream.

Invisible Labor

For the moment, offset remains a mechanical process dependent on highly skilled and time-consuming labor. The seamless product tends to render the workedness of the production invisible. Labor, after all, does not disappear in a so-called post-industrial society, but it is rendered invisible, made to seem a natural function of the appearance of a product, rather than being a thing in itself. While it would be facile simply to equate art with work (however rarified) since it is clearly a much more complex activity than that, there is a sense in which visual art gains its auratic status by the way it represents specialized work as a category. One of the issues in the reassessment of offset has to be this calling to attention of the worked character of the product—not by counting runs, or ink layers, or by listing the hours of production—but by articulating the aspect of productivity which is constituted as labor, insisting on the value of production as it is, not by forcing it into some perverse imitation of fine art (limited editions or auratic originals). For offset to qualify as high art (according to modern or traditional criteria), does it have to conceal its having been made by machine? To force the offset artist into deconstructive imagery or printing techniques simply to call attention to production is artificial, though it is interesting that many of these artists do this. Todd Walker's simulations of industry style color separation (done in the darkroom, offset, and by collotype) serve as a good example here—calling attention to the medium in classic modernist terms, deconstructing it in classic postmodern method. The laying bare of devices so central to the modernist critique of capitalist production, advocated by Viktor Shklovsky in literature, Bertoldt Brecht in theater, Lev Kuleshov in cinema, and Marcel Duchamp in Conceptual art, finds expression in this offset work—but the use of mainstream industrial materials and production processes more aptly participates in the postmodern sensibility, one which profoundly challenges the autonomous status of art, at least in rhetorical terms.

Access

Ownership of the tools of production is always an issue in terms of control. The home printshop of the offset artist begging the castoffs of industry generally depends on low end equipment, while the better stocked printing studios of institutions—Visual Studies Workshop Press, Nexus Press, or the Borowsky Center—edge toward state of the art industrial equipment—but at the highest high end that streaks way out of reach, with six color million dollar presses capable of printing process colors plus metallic ink, varnish, or spot color additions in a single run. Dreams of access are merely that, and artists can only aspire to a simulation of the capabilities of such equipment through more labor and more expense. The irony, again, is that it is the most banal, most prolific forms of printed material which achieve that glitz level of production—precisely because they serve the most common functions. The more rarified and esoteric the conception, the lower the likely spot on the production scale. In this sense the artworld, even the offset artists book world, is governed by many of the same rules as the secular world—it isn't necessarily the most interesting work which gets production support, but rather, the work which is just enough familiar (i.e. like what's already been done) to pass as original (i.e. a variation of the known quantity). The truly original is almost always marginalized, certainly at first. But offset is a powerful tool in the artists' struggle to make effective, alternative, communication. Even with the very real obstacles of insufficient distribution, the artists represented here have established a viable network for circulating their work.

Offset Books

Most of the artists in this exhibition are involved in the complex creative process of making books. When offset and books combine, the
result is that the non-traditional artists medium combines with the non-
traditional artistic form. Since trade books are always made through offset means, the expectation, again, is that an offset book should sell as a
trade book—cheaply. That access to equipment, means of production,
and production costs are all factors which only level off in unit cost with
high volume production is again quickly forgotten—the viewer/buyer
/reader forgets that it is the second word of the term "offset artist's
book" which is the emphatic one. One isn't buying, trading, or reading
a book one is buying art, and art which, because it is in the form of the
book, can be carried, held in the hand, snuggled up to, misplaced, found
again after years, still in working condition. This is not nostalgic roman-
ticism, but hard physical fact: books have their own lives as objects.

The iconography of works in this exhibition is as varied as the field
of contemporary art: there are images of direct observation which mediate the appearance of experience with as little manipulation as possible,
and those which stretch the processes of montage within the camera,
darkroom, computer, and press as far as possible. Some of these images
belong to the classic high period of male fantasmatic imaging, others to
the by now equally classic feminist response. Some betray their owners
through vivid autobiographical trace, others are formalized to the point
where they only bear marks of individuation as style. Some are richly
layered, dense with ink and overprinting, others closer to a realist convention of the illusion of the real. In short, there are no limits to style
or content, and offset is an adaptable medium, capable of nearly noiseless transmission or high volume interference in its visual communicative operation.

Trying to see the history of the present requires a certain defamiliar-
ization. Offset printing is the taken for granted stock in trade of daily
print media, and yet the processes of its production are as unknown,
unfamiliar, and unrecognized as those of microchip manufacturing,
television broadcasting, or ultrasonic imaging. In short, offset requires
professional skills and industrial equipment. In the trade one works for
years to progress from apprentice to journeyperson to master. The distinctions which render offset productions creative productions rather

than commercial ones are the same as those of any other artistic process—individual vision, subjective expression, and creative use of the medium. Since the terms on which work gains status as art are dependent largely on the perceived identity of the pieces, their producers, and their place in the culture, the status of offset work seems to have finally edged towards mature recognition as an artform. Because of the difficulties involved in its production, the complexity of the process, the skill required for running a press, it will probably remain the province of a limited number of artist practitioners. But this work seems ready for critical recognition and appreciation—whether it is offset art in the form of prints, or artists' books. The development of electronic media, oddly enough, has become the fulcrum point for critical reflection upon the value of and character of mechanical work—the very act of dematerializing information has made the act of rendering it back into form that much more self-conscious a process. The history of any technology is always under change—in relation to this moment in time offset has become newly defined. Offset no longer has an identity only as a means of industrial, mechanical reproduction, but is clearly capable of sustaining an identity as artistic production as well.

Written for the catalogue Offset: Artists Books and Prints, *to accompany the exhibition curated by Brad Freeman at Granary Books, NYC, September 1993.*

Iliazd and the Book as a Form of Art

The work of Ilia Zdanevich (known as Iliazd) offers a good case study for a discussion of the status of the book as a legitimate art form in the twentieth century. Other avant-garde Russian artists experimented with handmade books during the period in which Iliazd printed his Futurist typographic work. There have been other talented and original editors of fine books. More recently, far more innovative and experimental artists have been working with the book as a form. But Iliazd is one of the few for whom the book was the only medium, a truly appropriate medium for combining the full sum of his interests and abilities. Moreover, Iliazd's total oeuvre displays a consciously constructed cycle, brought to closure in his final productions: two books designed to link the late work with the first efforts he had made in the domain of writing. This final gesture demonstrated the extent to which Iliazd's artistic energy found its expression in the book, making full use of its capacity to function as an art form.

Before launching into a discussion of Iliazd's work, it is necessary to question whether the book in general functions as an art form in terms of book arts as a cultural and aesthetic practice. After all, the question would not even need to be raised if it were not for the fact that the book has occupied a rather dubious, or at least undefined, position. For the book to be considered an art form, it must be distinguished from other products of superior craftsmanship and artisanal expertise. Though book production has a long-established tradition of fine print behind it, the notion of books as a modern art form belongs, with few arguable exceptions (notably William Blake and perhaps William Morris), to the twentieth century. And while exhibitions of artists' books have begun to proliferate in the last couple of decades, the terms on which such work can be critically evaluated, as well as the status of such work within the history and theory of contemporary art, remain vague.

As a cultural practice, the production of books as art objects—books whose value accrues to them through means which are additional to the literary value of the text, or even, the "art" value of the images—creates a certain paradox. On one hand, the artist's book represents the democratization of the fine art commodity. More fine books can be printed, made available, and consumed than unique objects such as oil paintings. On the other hand, the book is a troublesome form to distribute through the usual channels by which special or unique objects receive mass attention: exhibition and reproduction.

The problem of exhibiting these works seem to be insurmountable. In exhibition cases books lose their tactile, experiential quality, their pages can't be turned, their papers felt, their bindings weighed; the sequence of events which comprise the designed experience from cover to interior is reduced to a single, stiff, staged display. Also, unlike painting, sculpture, or other static art, the feeling of a book cannot be readily conveyed in the reproduction of a single image. One page, cover, or spine provides only a meager representation of the original. Consequently, book arts resist the normal means by which art objects receive mass exposure.

This could be construed negatively as elitist. More positively, these books allow an intimate experience of high aesthetic quality. And this intimate experience is also a low-priced luxury commodity, valuable in a culture predicated on mass production and consumption. But however this practice is construed, the fact is that both production and consumption are limited, therefore the means for developing an audience and critical discussion are also limited.

As aesthetic practice, the production of books raises the question of how the book might be defined as an art form in a way which differentiates it from being simply an artfully crafted object. Iliazd's books, for example, have all the traditional markings generally associated with fine books: beautiful papers, large formats, expensive engravings, plates, and lithographs, exquisite printing from handset type whose placement has been carefully manipulated letter by letter, and, finally, parchment bindings so stiff the reader struggles to free the delicate interior object from its protective cover. Iliazd's books convey something of the exotic in their form, less tame than the works designed by, for example, Stanley Morison. But their real deviation from traditional form comes in the selection of elements—images, text, materials—and the process by which they each evolve into a book which is uniquely expressive of Iliazd's aesthetic vision.

The combination of elements in the book raises curious questions about authorship. For instance, if Iliazd is the artist responsible for the bulk of the production decisions which brought the *livres de peintre* into being, then what role is ascribed to the artists whose work figures so prominently in those books? How is Picasso, for instance, not the primary artist in *Skinnybones, The Wandering Friar, Pirosmani,* and other works in which his collaboration is so conspicuous? Obviously, the notion of artist and author needs some adjustment presented with something as complex as a book, which resembles a film or television production more than a painting or sculpture insofar as it represents a collective effort, not just an individual one.

Finally, the plight of the book must be recognized as due in part to its interdisciplinary status. Largely ignored by art historians who consider it insufficiently pictorial, and also by literary critics who consider the surplus features of the book decorative and irrelevant, it has suffered from a lack of appropriate vocabulary within which to be legitimated. In this regard, features which are specific to avant-garde book work, such as typographic experimentation with linguistic meaning, have been particularly unfortunate victims of this lack of critical regard. The need for a discriminating discourse which will provide insight into the means by which the book functions as a particular form of art is evident. Within the limited bounds of this discussion, the works of Iliazd can at least serve to demonstrate the extent to which such discourse is justified at the level of an individual practice, and as evidence that the book participates in the general atmosphere of an historical period, reflecting its concerns and functioning on equal status with more traditional forms in investigating ongoing aesthetic issues.

Examination of Iliazd's work demonstrates that the book may serve the purpose of articulating a particular aesthetic vision in a way unique to it as a medium. Specifically, it allows for the production of a "text" which is not circumscribed by the limits of a literary work, but which includes all of the various features of the book: its materials, its imagery, its literary substance, and, most importantly, its function as the manifestation of a vision which could not take another form and still function as a fully self-reflexive, self-conscious art.

In the course of his life, Iliazd created over two dozen books. All of these were printed in small editions (mostly between fifty and seventy copies). All were printed from handset type meticulously justified by Iliazd's own hand or under his direct supervision. And all were made of fine materials, Japanese or Chinese papers, and parchment folded and assembled by Iliazd. They are grouped in two periods of activity: an early, Futurist phase of experimental, avant-garde work produced from 1917-1923, and a later period from 1940 onward in which he produced nearly twenty *livres de peintre*.

The Futurist period began in 1917, when Iliazd returned to his native town of Tiflis in Georgia and decided to apprentice himself to a printer there. Iliazd had spent the five previous years in Moscow and St. Petersburg, studying for a law degree and actively engaging himself in the wide variety of activities which passed under the general rubric of Futurism. In Russia of the period 1910-1917, Futurism was the term applied to almost any kind of avant-garde activity, and there were "Futurists" of almost every possible aesthetic orientation. Iliazd, through the social offices of his older brother Kyril, had gravitated toward a group of painters, including Natalia Goncharova and Mikhail Larionov, and had struck up friendships with the poets Igor Terentyev and Alexi Kruchenyk, among others. Iliazd had become an impassioned Futurist "overnight," he claimed, at the moment when a family friend returned to Tiflis in 1911 carrying a copy of the manifestos of the Italian F. T. Marinetti. Whatever Iliazd had in common with his Russian contemporaries, he shared with the Italian poet a radical interest in exploring typographic innovations. Unlike Marinetti, (and, indeed, this fact distinguishes Iliazd from most of his contemporaries), Iliazd learned his typography in a print shop, not merely from observations of the printed page. As a consequence, Iliazd made use of a technically based understanding of the printed word to a greater extent than almost any of his avant-garde peers.

From the outset, Iliazd's concerns were with the representation of language, with the ways in which the visual aspects of the presentation could be used to enhance the linguistic value of the texts. While in his mature work Iliazd would address other issues, such as the relations of text to image, the structure of the book as a whole, his interest in typographic representation would persist. In the early work, this typographic investigation takes place.

While a certain degree of idiosyncratic originality characterizes Iliazd's work throughout his life, the early phase also demonstrates the way in which book arts participate in aesthetic issues which were under investigation in both literary and visual arts at the time. In particular, Iliazd's investigation of typography poses the same kind of self-reflexive investigation of its specificity as a medium that modernist writers and artists were posing within their own media: investigating the qualities of paintings as marks on a surface, of writing as an investigation of the structure and function of language. That typography participated in this metacritical process can be vividly demonstrated by an examination of the work produced by Iliazd between 1917 and 1923.

Iliazd established a small Futurist group called 41 Degrees in Tiflis, Georgia, in 1917. Under this imprint, he published works by his fellow poets (especially Terentyev and Kruchenyk, who had accompanied him to Tiflis) and organized cabaret-type performances and lectures. He also wrote a cycle of five plays, in the invented, so called "transmental" language *zaoum*. The typographic treatment grew increasingly complex as Iliazd produced this sequence of books. A greater and greater variety of sizes and kinds of typeface invaded the pages, and Iliazd even combined elements in the typecase to manufacture letters larger than any he could find. The last play, *Ledentu*, produced in Paris after Iliazd's arrival there in 1922, is a masterwork of typographic design and technical achievement. Iliazd was not the only Russian writer to experiment with *zaoum*, though, by its very nature, *zaoum* works are highly individual, and each version of the invented language is distinctly personal. Both Velimir Khlebnikov and Kruchenyk, for instance, developed forms of *zaoum* which were much closer to the original Russian language on which they were based, reserving the forms of morphemes, making neologisms out of roots, prefixes, and suffixes, rather than attacking language at its phenomic base, as Iliazd did.

Iliazd's five early plays are exceedingly arcane works. First of all, the language in which they are written, *zaoum*, was a highly idiosyncratic invention. The search for a language which would transcend the conventions of ordinary language, which would communicate directly through the power of sound, was a curious outgrowth of a late Symbolist synesthetic sensibility combined with a rigorous linguistic investigation of the structure of Russian itself. Iliazd understood and manipulated the phonemes (the smallest units of meaningful, distinguishable sound) with consummate skill at an historical point when linguistic studies had also begun to organize the structure of language systematically in phonemic terms. His intuitive investigation brought him to develop a sound-poetry which hovered just on the edge of sense. In the plays, for instance, characters are often defined by the set of

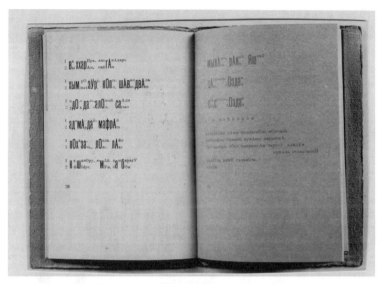

Fig. 1 *ZgA YAKaby (As if Zga)*, 1920, (Tiflis, Georgia: 41 Degrees), letterpress.

phonemes available for their speech; a sexy character may use many labial sounds while the lines of the Holy Ghost in *Ledentu*, the last of the plays, are constructed entirely of consonants, with no vowels or breath in them at all.

While the articulation of this *zaoum* experiment was already an accomplishment, its manifestation in typographic form represents one of the most fully realized avant-garde experiments of the period. In the first play *Janco, King of the Albanians*, in which Iliazd depicts himself as a little flea, the typographic effects do not go much beyond the grouping of words on the page or the occasional emphatic increase in type weight or size. In the next three plays, *Donkey for Hire, Easter Island,* and *As if Zga*, the page is used increasingly as the basis for scoring the relations among elements of speech (Fig. 1). The words of different characters are aligned in a manner which apes the features of a musical score. Gradually, bold face characters and different sizes and kinds of typeface are introduced both to emphasize the "character" of the different voices and to function as indicators of an intended oral reading. But in the printed form of the final play, *Ledentu*, the page appears as a fully elaborated score. Each character's speech, in addition to being phonemically distinguished, is typographically distinct. The timing of the delivery of these speeches is designed with the precision of an orchestral piece—and indeed, "orchestra" was the term which Iliazd applied to this approach (Fig. 2).

The meta-linguistic information which Iliazd manages to inscribe in these typographic treatments is enormous. While assigning any absolute value to the graphic features of a particular typeface or size would be spe-

Fig. 2a (above) and 2b (right). *LidantYU fAram* (*Ledentu as Beacon*), 1923, Paris: 41 Degrees, letterpress. In these facing pages Iliazd exploited the contents of the typographer's case to create outsized and unusual letterforms.

cious, their relative qualities are foregrounded by the juxtapositions on the page and relation to the page structure itself. For instance, when the main character in *Ledentu* lets out a full-page scream in the form of a single, large vowel sound, its impact is clearly indicated by its relation to the smaller lines of speech next to it on the sheet. Partially motivated by that synesthetic sensibility which the Futurists had inherited from the Symbolists, the plays foreshadow the linguistic rigor which would characterize Russian formalist linguistics. The plays also represent a thorough understanding of the technical possibilities which lead type offers as a medium. Iliazd respects these constraints and manages to find great potential within their boundaries, turning the rigid distinctions between sizes, faces, and weights into a fluid medium.

The work of the plays indicates the extent to which Iliazd understood one of the most problematic of all linguistic concerns: the distinc-

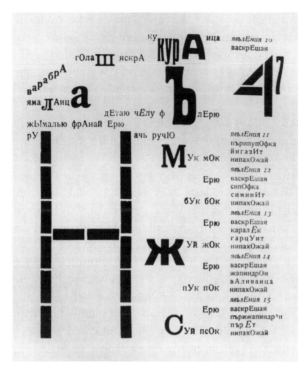

tion between spoken and written forms of language. While in spoken language the smallest meaningful unit is a single sound, its visual representation frequently requires more than one letter. Elements of meaning may be inserted into a visual text in ways which are the visual equivalent of the verbal pun, allowing plural readings and interpretations which cannot be sustained in verbal form. Iliazd's willingness to manipulate this discrepancy permitted him to deal with the typographic representation on the basis of its own smallest unit, the single piece of type. Often this meant the single letter, but sometimes it meant decorative elements which Iliazd combined to make letter forms much larger than any available to him in the typecase. This is a form of invention which proceeds directly from a material involvement with the medium, one suggested by the process of handling metal, holding it in one's hands and before one's eyes, being inspired by the possibilities it suggests.

It seems that Iliazd had planned his five plays as a full cycle, but it is not clear that he realized in advance the extremes to which he would push his typographic investigation. In fact, as a series, these books seem rather to demonstrate the extent to which his knowledge of type increased his sense of its possibilities as he gained experience and confidence as a compositor. The final pyrotechnics of *Ledentu* require no small degree of skill; the justification problems of mixing literally dozens of sizes of type on a single page would overwhelm a novice, even one with Iliazd's mathematical predisposition toward understanding the solid geometry of the printer's craft. The typographic evolution in this cycle of works can be taken as evidence that Iliazd saw typography, the printed word, as a medium capable of metalinguistic and metacritical expression.

While this cycle of plays focused on Iliazd's work as author as well as typographer/printer, his mature work would feature texts by other authors, friends, and unknown and obscure writers, as well as visual images from the hands of artist friends who ranked among the foremost practitioners of modern art—Picasso, Max Ernst, Raoul Hausmann, among others. In many ways this later work, produced mainly between 1950 and 1974, demonstrates the extent to which Iliazd's vision required the medium of the book in order to be fully served. For if the earlier books (not to deprecate their value, but to circumscribe it) were merely the demonstration of his interest in a particular capacity of the typographic medium to represent his own linguistic experiments, the later work drew on the full range of interests and abilities of a man whose diverse interests and capacities as scholar, artist, and humanist were all being brought to bear on his creative activity. The brashness, the bravado, the virtuoso flamboyance of the early books is replaced by a profound elegance of form, but even more, by a profound understanding of the uses of formal conventions as a means of structuring works which went beyond self-reflexivity or self-conscious manipulations.

A complex and diverse work, *Poetry of Unknown Words* announced this cycle of mature book production in 1950 (Fig. 3). Produced in response to the founders of the Lettrist movement, who in 1948-1949 claimed to have invented sound and visual poetry, it was a compendium of works by the poets and artists whose experiments thirty years earlier were being flagrantly ignored by the new group. This book forms the transition between the experimental typography of Iliazd's *zaoum* dramas, and the more conventional design and typographic characters of the books which follow. The typeface used in *Poetry of Unknown Words* is a bold sans serif: squat, sturdy, formal, in a small size which calls attention to the distribution of words on the page rather than to the letter by letter features of the text. *Poetry of Unknown Words* recapitulates the full range of possibilities which Iliazd had discovered for the pre-

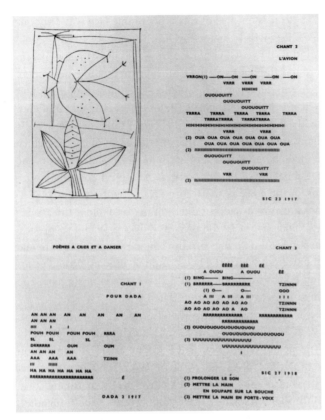

Fig. 3 *Poésie de mot inconnus (Poetry of Unknown Words)*, 1949, Paris: 41 Degrees; letterpress. This page showing poem by Pierre Albert-Birot and engraving by Pablo Picasso.

sentation of texts. Each of the sheets which comprise the work features a poem and print by a different author and artist. Each page format, while respecting a quadrant structure imposed by the folding process, has a unique visual quality to it. They represent the originators and early experimenters of sound, visual, and concrete poetry (including Arp, Schwitters, Hausmann, Khlebnikov, Ball) in a way which clearly proclaims at once their historical place and the end of an era in which those innovations formed a vital artistic practice. From this point on, Iliazd would respond less to the ongoing dialog of his times—the art movements of the 1950s, 60s, and 70s—and would forge his work from his personal vision as a mature artist whose aesthetic principles were already formed.

Beginning with the 1950 production of *Skinnybones*, Iliazd would use a more delicate Gill sans serif exclusively. He considered it a neutral face, capable of registering nuances in composition, placement, and arrangement. The consistent use of this typographic face was only one of the formal choices which materially link the nearly twenty books Iliazd produced in those years. Other choices—the use of heavy parchment folded around the books as their outside cover, the employment of oriental paper with its capacity to function as a filmy, supple support for the very delicate imprint of the Gill, the use of heavily textured endpaper thick with fibers and colored in earth tone pastels—would become the signature of Iliazd. But these are the kinds of choices which would also be made by an astute and aesthetically inclined editor, and the mere material beauty of Iliazd's books as art object does not suffice as an argument for the book as an art form. He did not push the objectness of the books toward a sculptural definition, or explore the assembly of elements which compose the book as a discourse in a theoretical sense (as for example Tom Phillips or Lucas Samaras might). But he did demonstrate the ways in which the book could be used as a complex art form, sustaining relations among a text, images, material support, and artisanal craftsmanship as a single interrelated system.

Skinnybones is also one of the first books which Iliazd produced in collaboration with Picasso. *Pismo* (*The Letter*), which Iliazd completed in 1948, marks the actual beginning of this cooperation. A companion since the days of Les Bals Russes in which Iliazd played an active part following his arrival in Paris, Picasso remained an intimate and loyal friend to Iliazd throughout his life. They produced nine books together, and Iliazd, as engineer of these projects, had the advantage of Picasso's fame to make use of in their sale. By the same token, it was Iliazd's persistence and discipline which bought the works to fruition. The relationship had peculiar balances in it. Picasso functioned for Iliazd as a kind of inverted shadow figure, as the image of the artist which he was not. Through his association with Picasso, Iliazd could also project that image as his own, lay claim to the status of major figure through the collaboration with Picasso as a peer.

The book is the one medium in which both text and image function as substantive entities while allowing the artisanal interest in material form to reach an equal level of sophistication. Iliazd arrived at the ensemble of elements which comprise his publications through scholarly research as well as creative intuition. Iliazd's books appeared at the rate of nearly one per year after 1950, but they should be understood as the result of a long gestation process. For example, *Maximiliana* (1964),

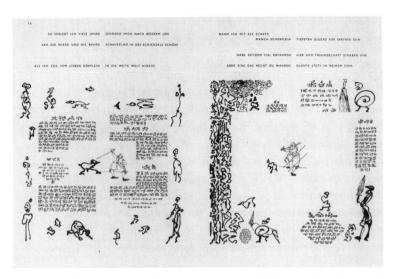

Fig. 4. *Maximiliana*, 1964, Paris: 41 Degrees, letterpress and relief engravings, Max Ernst's drawings and invented scripts in pages structured by Iliazd.

the collaboration with Max Ernst based on the texts of nineteenth century astronomer Guillaume Tempel, was originally conceived almost twenty years before it was finished. (Fig. 4). During that same time period, Iliazd researched the life of Tempel, synthesized a text from the astronomer's journals, proposed various formats and possibilities to Ernst, and developed, finally, a richly evolved product integrating many levels of image, text, and material form.

If the theme of invented language and typographic experiment dominated the early cycle of books, the themes of the unknown and under-recognized author and artist are conspicuous features of the mature work. With a few significant exceptions, notably two of the last books of his career, Iliazd was not the author of the works he printed after 1950. He became fascinated, for instance, with Adrian de Monluc, a seventeenth century subversive whose writings were so controversial politically that he became a fugitive from the vendettas of Cardinal Richelieu. This kind of marginal, radical position, typical of the role of the artist, also drew him to a biographical as well as literary interest in the astronomer Guillaume Tempel, whose struggles to pursue his scientific endeavors pushed him into material difficulties and extremes with which Iliazd must have been sympathetic. His fascination with the work of Roch Grey, a woman writer and friend whose work had received very little attention within mainstream or even avant-garde literary circles, was also fueled by his consideration of her marginal position.

By the 1950s and 60s, Iliazd clearly felt that his lot was to be a similar one, that his early Futurist work would "fall into obscurity" as had that of Monluc, Tempel, Roch Grey, and others. Rather than publish his own texts, he preferred to "bring to light" (his words) the texts of others. He was fully aware that in the process he was to some extent inventing those authors and, simultaneously, engaging in the process of constituting his own persona as an artist. Through them *he* was reinvented, his claims for their legitimacy, their value, were in a sense a claim for his own. It was also the invention of an elaborate, multi-faceted art identity through the proliferation of these many roles. Monluc, Tempel, Boissiere, Clavijo were not fictional characters, but they were constructed personae, made as much through Iliazd's recovery of their work as in any original publications.

By contrast, a number of artists and writers with whom Iliazd chose to collaborate were men who had been almost lifelong companions. Iliazd had met Ernst, Picasso, Eluard, and Hausmann soon after his arrival in Paris in 1922. These were his contemporaries, his peers. Their formation as artists had taken place in the same generation, the same historical moment, as his. The course of some of their careers had elevated them to the status of superstars, lifted them beyond the necessities of attending to the daily struggle of survival in a way which distinguished them from Iliazd. He nevertheless clearly identified himself with this group of contemporaries, claiming them as peers whose aesthetic projects and interests aligned with his own. The relations Iliazd had with these collaborators were not those of an editor contracting with an artist for work, they were the relations of peers and friends engaged in the pursuit of a vision which could only be achieved through that collaboration. Concealing his own persona, hiding his artistic vision behind his imprint 41 Degrees and the names of his collaborators, Iliazd's identity was subsumed in the works and revealed in the production of the books as projects whose form he conceived as a whole. Images might be by Picasso, the text by someone else, but, the book as a whole material and conceptual object was entirely Iliazd.

The evidence for this argument can be found in the fact that each of these books is a clear expression of some feature of Iliazd's own private interests. The works of Adrian de Monluc deal with the strategies of language vis-à-vis established social order. They are satires of social manners, full of puns and vulgar expression. A work by Boissiere, *Treatise on Ballet* (1953), manifested Iliazd's enthusiasm for dance, a passion he had had since his youth when he was renowned for dancing ten or twelve hours at a stretch. He had even composed a *zaoum* ballet in the late 1940s, a project which was never realized as a production. The story of *The Wandering Friar* (1959) was the culmination of years of research into voyages of discovery along the west coast of Africa, an interest fostered by his marriage in 1943 to a Nigerian princess. Iliazd studied the linguistic evolution of place names, traced the description of the coastal forms through various evolutions in successive mappings, and studied the original accounts to reconstruct day by day, point by point, these early journeys. One after another, the books Iliazd produced display his interests: dance, voyages, astronomy, Africa, Byzantine studies, and so on.

A prevailing theme throughout the books—a compelling interest in the forms of language and its representation—gives them consistency as a total oeuvre begun in the Futurist phase. Each one of the books stakes out a position vis-à-vis typography; each one employs typography not only distinctly, but also according to distinct conceptual principles. Iliazd developed terminology for these principles: variable spacing, square arrangements, and others based on his exploration of the formal qualities of type within its conventional, almost classical constraints. He never broke letters, cut lines and overlapped them, or violated in any other way the tradition in which each piece of type occupies a single point on the page within an essentially vertical and horizontal arrangement of the lines of metal in the chase (the metal frame which holds the type in place during printing, and which must be perfectly "composed" and "locked up" in order for printing—traditional printing—to occur). But within those limits Iliazd tried every possible variation, with results which bespeak the accuracy and intuitive rhythmic sensibility of his eye.

Iliazd lived to be eighty-one. He was working on books up until the last days of his life and perhaps would have gone on to more projects had he continued to live. Perhaps. The nature of the last books argues against this, for they form a self-consciously constructed closure on the cycle which not only formed his mature production but also echoed the work of his youth. Two books manifest this culmination, *Boustrophedon*

(1971) and *Pirosmani* (1972). Both were authored by Iliazd: it was clear that he wanted to write his own ending to the story of his work and life, and both were intensely personal statements.

Boustrophedon is composed of a series of short poems, each written in homage to or in commemoration of a particular person who had figured significantly and symbolically in his life (Fig. 5). They included his third wife Hélène, his brother Kyril, the painter Michel Ledentu who had died in the First World War, and the painter, Pirosmani, among others. The poems were laid out on the pages in short lines, not justified, but suspended in relation to each other with the delicate balance of a mobile structure. Each line, by its slight displacement from the margin, functions to hold the others in suspension. The texts, in Iliazd's habitual Gill majuscule, make their simple statements as well-spaced lines of large size type. Below each line, the letters of the words from which it is composed are inverted, spelled out in reverse, beginning to end, with different word breaks introduced into the sequence. This subtext reads like a series of sounds, without evident sense, a demonstration of a kind of *zaoum* which resides in any statement. It is as if Iliazd were at one and the same time demonstrating the futility and poetry of attempting to capture his own life in language. The book is without illustrations, but the visual impact of the text strongly evidences Iliazd's understanding of the letter as a letter, the word as a word, the page as a page, and the

ADRIANDEMONLUC
CUL NOM ED NAIRDA

DEVAVXDECRAMAIL
LIAMARC ED XVAV ED

DE SOLEIL
LIELOS ED

DES CHEVALIERS
SREILAVEHC SED

DE HUIT ANS
SNATIUH ED

DE BASTILLE
ELLITSABED

LE DENTU
UTNED EL

QUAND POURRAI JE
EJ IARRUOP DNAUQ

DÉNICHER CE PAS
SAPEC REHCINED

ENTRE LES DENTS
STNED SEL ERTNE

DE LA MONTAGNE
ENGATNO MALED

DENTELÉE
E ELETNED

Fig. 5 *Boustrophedon*, 1971, Paris: 41 Degrees, letterpress. Typographical poem composed by Iliazd. Poems depicted dedicated to Adrian de Monluc and Michel Ledentu.

book as a whole, personal synthesis of expressive potential.

In *Pirosmani*, Iliazd returned to the first text he had ever published, an essay on the naive Georgian painter, Nikos Pirosmanachvili, whom Iliazd had discovered in 1913 (Fig. 6). While this was not in a literal, chronological sense the last book Iliazd finished, it was intended to be. (*Courtesan Grotesque*, finished in 1974, had been in the works long before, but its completion had been delayed because of technical problems.) Iliazd had asked Picasso to make the plates for *Pirosmani*, since he wanted to

Fig. 6 *Pirosmanachvili, 1914*, 1972, Paris: 41 Degrees, letterpress. Pablo Picasso, frontispiece drypoint of the Georgian painter.

finish the cycle of large books as he had begun, in collaboration with Picasso (who had done the plates for the book *Pismo* in 1948). Picasso produced a single image for the book; in it the image of the painter as an old man, brush in hand, standing in front of his canvas. It is at once the image of Iliazd with his balding head and rotund form, of Picasso the painter involved intimately with his practice, and of Pirosmani who had already been an old man when Iliazd, in late adolescence, discovered him and idealized him as the very embodiment of the image of the artist, as the iconoclastic genius pursuing his own vision. The image offers all of these readings. Iliazd allowed that resonance to function, fully aware, no doubt that he had become the very image he had found so compelling in his youth. Drawing to the end of his energies, Iliazd had evidently wished this book to perform a double closure: as the end of the cycle of large books, and as the close of the full cycle of his life's work. There was a mirroring effect between the beginning and the end, a deliberate, marked recognition of self-consciousness which had dictated the construction of the oeuvre as a whole.

Iliazd was an artist. The books are adequate testimonial to that fact; they argue strongly that no other medium would have allowed Iliazd to represent the varied features of his intellect and personality with the same repleteness. Likewise, his love of the form demonstrates its richness, its capacity for almost infinite variety even within the rigorous limitations which he imposed upon it. His early *zaoum* works, with their self-reflexive investigation of typography as a medium, engaged the book form with issues central to early twentieth century arts and literature. His later works, of which only a handful have been referred to here, allowed the book form to function as the singular vehicle of a complexly structured creative expression, one which reflected a concern not only for the beauty of the book object, but also for its capacity to articulate the interests of a rich, intellectual, and creative life. Any single work of Iliazd's can function autonomously, providing the viewer with a sensual experience which stimulates the eye and hand as well as the intellect as one struggles with the stiff parchment to catch a glimpse of the silky thin papers within, to pore over the intricate text, to understand the logic of the layout and design. But taken as a whole, his oeuvre shows the conceptual relations among the individual pieces, and their capacity to reveal the multiple facets of a single, aesthetic vision.

The book should be recognized as an art form. The full complexity of the discourse of the book, with its textual, visual, and tactile components all need to be considered. The "text" of such books cannot be conceived of as delimited by linguistic content, literary substance; nor can the book be defined within the strict orthodoxy which evaluates the beauty and value of its parts such as typography, binding, and paper. Instead, the full interrelation of these elements in the production of a single textual system, a single articulate discourse, must be taken into account. Only then will the critical appreciation of the book as an art form be equal to the kind of creative project realized in the work of Iliazd.

First published in The Journal of Decorative and Propaganda Arts, *Winter 1988.*

VI. The Future of Writing

Geofroy Tory's image of the Pythagorean "Y" showing the easy and tempting path of vice and the difficult path of virtue.

Language as Information: Intimations of Immateriality

There are a wide variety of ways in which language and information intersect in traditional and electronic media. My basic inquiry has two parts to it: what constitutes the "information" of language and how does this "information" change in moving language from a material to an electronic environment?

My old favorite topic—the materiality of signification—describes the ways in which material substrates and visual/typographic/written (and by extension, verbal) styles encode history, identity, and cultural value at the primary level of the mark/letter/physical support (and in non-written form, the qualities of voice, tone, tenor, rhythm, inflection, etc.). I'm not going to go back over that ground since in fact I am more interested in exploring the "intimations of *im*materiality" of my title (and if you haven't read my books, *The Visible Word* or *The Alphabetic Labyrinth*, or work by Susan Howe or Jerome McGann or Roland Greene or Marjorie Perloff or any of the many other people working in this area this isn't going to be the moment you get the brief overview/encapsulated Cliff Notes version of *"Materiality as Signification"*). But for those of you who doubt, here's your pictorial proof: try translating this little item (at left) into Futura Bold and see what happens to the meaning. Some metaphor that would be—smooth and equal sailing up the pole of virtue or vice—with equal opportunity to sin or be saved in the Pythagorean paths of Vice and Virtue (Y).

At the secondary level language contains information as format, using spatial arrangement as a way of constituting meaning. A familiar example is the outline form where headings, subheads, and sub-subheads demarcate a discourse into conceptual spaces and territories. Elaborately structured hierarchies in this vein—descriptive systems of cosmological breadth and ambition—develop in the Middle Ages (as in the schemata illustrating the concepts of Petrus Ramus) and blossom in the late Renaissance work of such ambitious polymath scholars as Athanasius Kircher and Bishop John Wilkins. Wilkins's *Essay Towards a Real Character and Philosophical Language* includes a full outine of all aspects of the universe—part of his scheme to represent all of knowl-

edge/the world (in his work collapsed without argument) in a corresponding system of notation. This may sound old and quaint and
strange and remind us of ideas which stretch back into antiquity about
linking language and knowledge in a guaranteed system (whether
according to an atomistic logic or Adamic naming) but when we stretch
this concept forward to the all-elastic present such a positively logical
linguistic attitude turns out to underly one of the major strains of
Artifical Intelligence research.

For now, consider simply that this relational/structural/schematic
aspect of materiality uses spatial relations as significant, as part of meaning. The old memory theaters, also devised in antiquity and perfected in
conceptual/practical terms in the Renaissance, serve as another instance
of intertwining meaning and spatialized relations—and here "space" is
meant as something schematic, metaphoric, and abstract simultaneously. Basically the relations among linguistic components can be mapped
in the following ways: hierarchically in an outline, spatially according to
the descriptive coordinates of solid geometry (with a fourth dimension
suggested), in tree diagrams, in grids, in various indexed charts, and
two-dimensional graphs, or according to an iconographic form (as in
the case of certain concrete poems using shape to contribute to meaning). When these concepts of schematization and spatialization intersect
with electronic media, they can, potentially, expand into the multi-
dimensional structures available in hypertext and internet architecture.
The challenge is making spatial organization clear enough—logically,
conceptually, metaphorically, visually—for it to be useful rather than
confusing.

As we move into considering the language-to-code/code-to-lan-
guage relationship, or the intimations of immateriality, another key
theme will be that of basic binarism: In another wonderfully persistent
trajectory visual language is treated as the product of a binary code.
This concept doesn't need the electronic environment—quite the contrary, it's these precedents which allow for the electronic use of binarism
to carry nice, profound, philosophical weight. After all—in a conception
which is fully fleshed out by Renaissance type designer Geofroy Tory—
the construction of all letters, the full set of symbols of human language
and thus of cosmic as well as human thought, are comprised at base of
two elements: the I and O. For Tory these are essential elements: the
masculine principle of the vertical thrust and the feminine principle of

procreative fullness. Translating this into binary code, the I/O basis of all electronic activity, one can read machine language in the tradition of these combined "essences" or—according to a more contemporary deconstructive logic—as pure difference, as the fundamental non-essential and differentiating binarism which brings the possibility of signification into being.

(Now some of you, I know, are already better at reading binary code than listening to outmoded speech patterns, so for this section there will be a simultaneous translation by flashlight.) The essence of the "immaterial" electronic universe as we know it is this binary code, but it isn't essential to "computer" functions—unless they are electronic which wasn't always so: Analogue machines capable of performing computational functions—running punch-programs off cards—were used for running looms in French mills in the early 19th century—and mechanical automatons had used encrypted sequences of "instructions" on interlocking gears for a good long time before that. But the introduction of electricity and the reduction of all/any "info" to be stored and all/any instructions to be given to a binary code combined a level of abstractability with a potential for rapidity of processing which led to the modern computer.

Signal Formation: Claude Shannon, working as an assistant to the inventor Vannever Bush and operating the switches on his differential analyzer in the late 1930s, realised that the electromechanical relays in the switches could encode the configurations of data directly, thus paving the way for the translation of mathematical information into electrical form. Data became available to binary encoding as a result—and any communicative message, Shannon realized to the delight of Bell Labs where he was working, could be sent as a simple electrical signal as a result. One could translate anything into such a signal—but computational operations were more complex than mere communication—and data had to be conceptualized, not merely translated, to function in an electronic environment. Here again language comes under reconsideration—gets put, in fact, into a certain bondage in order to function according to a machine acceptable decorum.

Rules and Regulations: In a highly constrained, rule-bound, and logical form, natural language can serve as the basis of programming language, itself encoded in a binary numerical system. The leap from num-

bers connected to cogs and axels to sequences of interconnected switches would have had very little impact if it hadn't been for two things: the
possibility of logic, using "natural" language in constrained form, to
function as a set of precise instructions translatable into mathematical
equivalents, and the possibility for these mathematical equivalents to be
encoded in a binaristic form corresponding to the fundamental on/off of
current in an electrical gate/synapse/circuit.

George Boole's 1845 *Laws of Thought* realized the age-old philosophical belief in the possibility of finding a set of logical rules and laws
which corresponded to the operations of the human mind. Gottlob
Frege built on Boole's system, adding predicates to Boole's set of terms,
thus moving closer to what their predecessor Gottfried Leibniz had
envisioned as "a true reasoning calculus." The collapse of mathematical
and linguistic terms according to a philosophical belief in real logic (and
logic as real) was actual as well as metaphoric—and within the (many)
constraints of logic language is able to "perform" functions as precise as
those of any other calculating system. The philosophical underpinnings
of such an approach show through in Rudolf Carnap's 1928 book title,
The Logical Structure of the World. Whatever one thinks about the intellectual validity of presuming logic in the actual organization of the
"world"—or even in the human system of knowledge which describes
it—the linguistic properties of the lineage stretching from Leibniz to
Boole to Frege and Carnap (with all their own—many—differences
such as the more atomistic conceptions of Leibniz/Boole and more
gestalt oriented notions of Carnap)—this work provided a means
whereby linguistic terms could be made compatible with—even the
basis of—computational acts. It was this basic rule-boundedness which
allowed Alan Turing and John Von Neumann to interlink the concepts
of "reasoning calculus" with that of the "automata" of computational
machines—as Turing realized that logical/mathematical symbols could
represent any kind of information.

Languages and their Evolution: Generations of computer languages
now exist—beginning with the earliest versions from the big old main-
frames of the 1940s/1950s—machine languages so coded that their
workings are in some cases as indecipherable as Indus Valley script to
the contemporary eye—a fact made poignant by the current about-to-
be-a-plague situation I refer to as the Millennial Bug: access to this code
has been lost due to the death/retirement of original programmers who

never wrote it down anywhere—so that the problem of debugging the turn-of-the-century melt-down of 00 digits in all date-dependent data bases is truly mind-boggling.

There are several levels of languages, as well as types of languages, in computer programming: ultimately all computer languages have to translate into machine language: binaristic sequences which give specific instructions to data stored in various address locations to perform particular tasks in a particular sequence. Compiled and interpreted languages each organize the relation between commands and data according to distinct specifications, but an assembly language is required to translate this program code to the correct machine address so that the data can be located and the functions performed. Such symbolic assembly languages evolved in the mid-1950s, but it took until the 1960s for higher level interpreted languages (such as COBOL and FORTRAN) to evolve. Compiled languages allow for little human intervention in the course of the carrying-out of the program. By contrast, interpreted languages are not entirely in machine code, they have a front-end interface which can be manipulated by the user throughout. These higher level languages allow the user to take advantage of interpretive techniques to build the concepts as you go.[1] But all of these levels of accessibility are illusory in the sense that they are all equally constrained. If today a high-level language contains a simple "Delete" command, then ten years ago that read as: Execute Command D on Files G, H, and/or something like del.exe.bat*to*. At that point the combination of syntactics and mnemonics (that is sequence and terms) involved is hardly more flexible, even if slightly more user friendly, than the assembly level: L 3,x, M 2,y, A 3,w, ST 3,2 or the machine level: 41 2 OC1A4 3A 2 OC1A8 1A 3 OC1AO and 50 3 OC1 A 4.

Even a quick reading of these shows how much this stuff is not really "language" as we know it, which is just the point. Machine language, computer language, programming languages, are all able to contain information, to function as a descriptive metalanguage which is not information, but *rules*, highly constrained and specific, and thus able to describe information and encode it, but not embody it in material form.

AI: Knowledge based (Neural Nets) and Logic Based (Symbolic Processors): Data processing on a massive level or rule boundedness? How does the human mind make the leap from experience to generalized conceptualization? Are rules of logic endemic to the structure of knowledge and operations of thought, as per some complex symbolic linguistics, or do concepts emerge through the processing of massive amounts of data, through perception, into higher levels of pattern recognition, in which case "thinking" can not be contained within "logic" but has to let logic emerge from its evolution? This debate, the basic dialogue in contemporary Artificial Intelligence research, returns us to the basic language/information problem. For what is being filtered *out* of langauge when it enters the systemic logic of the electronic environment?

Whipped by the hot lash of illogic, the unneat and indecorous aspects of language wiggle free from their bonds clamoring for their right to be recognized within that universe of sense which is not all common sense or intractable systemic logic but is also stuff and nonsense—the information of sensation, of space, of material—crying in the dull-brained electronic universe to be heard.

While this historical and descriptive material opens all kinds of interesting possibilities for investigation, it is not particularly polemical. I would, however, like to raise two slightly polemical points. The first is that it is often/only at the expense of much of what is "information" in language—its complexity in material, syntactic, poetic, or even vernacular form—that language functions in the electronic environment. And secondly, since within electronic production (even, say, keyboard to printer) there is no necessary relation between input and output, then it is arguable that in the process of encoding the keystroke into digital form language is denuded of its material history which is lost. The "immaterial" is that gap of transformation—like that which used to exist for the typesetter between the reading of a line and its setting into hot type—and also exists between the material of text becoming that of sound, of sound to mind, of eye to voice, of hand to type—which is a basic characteristic of the way language is information in electronic form as well. It always precipitates back into material—mutated, transformed, rewrit, as it were. Language is not ever an ideal form. It always exists in some phenomenal form. I've spent a long time insisting on the value of materiality, but I'm also interested in the freedom from fixed relations of materiality and what that offers. Ultimately, one of the intimations of *im*materiality is the way it promises to change material form—and as such offers possibilities for reconceptualization of language as information in the traditional media as well as in hypertext and electronic formats.

We all know that there are certain basic—irresolvable—philosophical tensions in language—most particularly between its capacity to represent knowledge systematically and its capacity to be knowledge experientially and perceptually—and this tension intensifies in an electronic environment as a tension between machine language and natural language—since it is a reductive hybrid version of the one which can be encoded/encrypted in order to serve as the basis of the other. Ultimately the dilemma of the immaterial/material is unresolvable: you can't reconcile the need for the machine to work through logic and the capacity of human language to function through and on account of—not just in spite of—its illogic. Wittgenstein's dilemma: the realization that logic was outside the limit of philosophy, could only barely get one to the threshold—it was the material particularity of language in use which demonstrated the capacity of language to begin to pose philosophical questions—and it is here that the immaterial/material dilemma founders on a final rock, cracking apart the whole enterprise of translation and record, of language as history, memory, identity. For language to function as "immaterial" it must give up much of what constitutes its information—or at least, allow it to be translated into some alternate code, some other, surrogate, substitute form, a representation without material substrate in which to embed, make one with itself, the actual factual *stuffness* of lived language. Not a tragedy, just a fact. Having nothing particular at stake in trying to make machines be/imitate/function as or replace people, I'm not particularly bothered by this—but what is worrisome is the constraints on communicative action which potentially come into play—the unforgiving unkindness of the electronic database whose newspeak categories may at some point simply refuse to recognize those signs of human life, which like Artaud's, are "signalling through the flames" with a primal urgency which precedes/excludes/is exterior to/anterior to the logic of the code and which is simultaneous to, interpenetrated with, inseparable from the illogical materiality of natural language.

Coda: Now, Mike Groden did tell me that the one condition attached to this panel was that the talks had to deal with some aspect of English or American literature—and I have been searching my files without any success. But I contacted my friend, Herr Doktor Professor Popov-Opov who is working at Star Lab VI on Alpha Centuri 5.6 to see if he could find anything relevant in his data banks. Here's what he sent me:

"One final bit of insight I can share with you and your audience comes from a snippet of material recovered from a mid-20th century source in what was then termed "popular culture." It is a single fragment from a much longer, possibly epic, piece—it deals with a journey, no doubt a heroic quest, long in scope, wide in breadth, of which only this tiny piece has come to light. According to the formulations of which you have been speaking, the line takes on a cosmological significance which you will of course all immediately recognize. Here it is: "Why oh why oh why oh did I ever leave O-hI-O?" Analyzable into those component parts it turns out to be an instance of pure code (a vibratory binarism flickering between the I and O of all such inscriptions) and impure materiality (the inflections and embedments of its elemental structure within complex phonemic units whose semantic value as constitutent components I can, as yet, without more reseach, only hint at here). That the text itself contains suggestions of impermanence, of eternal return, of longing and displacement—is hardly suprising, given its ritual character. The line bears within it the full weight of the 20th century dilemma—the question of how to encode language as knowledge without loss, while recognizing the impossibility of this task in philosophical and even mathematical terms. The answer to the question of course is that one leaves the "paradise" of "O-hI-O" in order to be able to "write back" — that is, to "write to disk" to inscribe oneself perpetually in a relation to that act of coming into being which is writing, which is scribing, inscribing, in a communicative dialogue with the mother board, the operating system, the familial network of soft and hardware mouthing its happy duck-billed platitudes to an old favorite electronic tune."

1. Robin McKinnon Wood, "Computer Programming for Literary Laymen," p.186 in Jasia Reichardt, *Cybernetics, Art, and Ideas*. Greenwich, CT: New York Graphic Society Ltd.,1971.

This paper was delivered at the Modern Language Association in Washington DC, December 1996, on a panel with Jay Bolter and Michael Groden.

The Future of Writing in Terms of Its Past

The nature of language is such that information stored in linguistic form is basically fungible; that is, the form the information takes is interchangeable and mutable. A statement rendered in manuscript hand, in letterpress type, or in typewritten or electronic script can essentially contain the same linguistic message—with the major qualification that the material form in which written language appears encodes that message. The "information" quotient of the material can vary from negligible to highly significant. (A handwritten grocery list and a typewritten one will probably result in the same items being bought while a handwritten stop sign has a completely different status from an officially produced and sanctioned one.)

But the way this fungible character of writing functions is transforming dramatically in the age of electronic media. This is because for the first time, the encoding of a linguistic message into writing does not have any material stability. Texts were always fungible its true—there was always a moment in which texts slipped from one form to another, from manuscript to print, from one edition to the next. And there was a moment of suspended existence when the language was held in the mind of any fresh compositor outside of written material form. But the actual documents had a material character: a sentence rendered in handset Garamond foundry type and printed letterpress would retain that material information as part of its linguistic existence until it was re-rendered or transformed. But every written instance of the message would bear within it a whole history of its execution in the codes of the material in which it was embodied. In an electronic environment, entering a sentence in Garamond, Times, Matrix, or Hobo is in no way a permanent aspect of its existence as information. The keystroke commands, transformed into electronic code, are fungible in a whole new way: the mutability of the form the written language takes is increased radically. There is, simply, no longer any necessary relation between the input form of the written message and its output. There is nothing which links the characteristics of input and that of output in a material support or form. Stored electronically, the materiality of written language becomes a fungible factor—up until the existence of electronic media, the materiality of written language was part of what allowed it to function culturally.

The questions raised by this transformation can only be posed by sketching out the functions which writing as material has performed in the history of human culture and then considering the transformations which this new fungibility effects upon their operation. Some of these functions are quite apparent: the documentation of historical events, of lived experience of individuals, communities, and nations, legal functions, sacred and magical ritual performance and so forth. Other functions are more incidental than apparent—to assist in the inscription of identity, to call attention to the changeability of culture, or to mark the passage of time. In all of these functions it is not so much the permanence of writing which lets it function in these capacities. Rather, it is the fact that written documents record changes made to them because of their material existence. Changes to the document become part of its record—alterations, transformations, mutilations, imitations, and forgeries are all part of the vocabulary of a material record.

SO: Here we are in a moment of electronic hyper-hype, in the throes of a pre-millennial techno-fascination, on the verge of making virtual everything we never needed in the real, dematerializing experience and making it clean, safe, hygenic, remote. In all of this the future of reading is continually under discussion: proposals for branching, endlessly mutating spaces of hypertext or diving mice in a matrix of text modules, or scanning the unbounded resources of electronic archives.

But it is with writing that I am concerned and transformations of writing in the electronic environment. Has it changed fundamentally and will it change from the form it took in the hands of writing masters whose letters were feathered onto the page with consummate skill and grace?

By writing what I mean is production at the level of the mark, the letter, the sign. I am not interested in spell checks or writing programs, but in the relations between the new forms writing takes in electronic media and its cultural functions. And I am not suggesting that the effects of technology are causal or determinative. As we know, it took several generations for printing types to adapt to the character of metal and lose their relation to calligraphic forms.

Similarly, though the technology was in place for all kinds of dar-ing formats and innovations from the moment at which Johann Gutenburg invented cast and moveable type, it was several centuries before the idea of placing type on the diagonal became part of commonplace graphic vocabulary. Such innovations are often associated with the early 20th century avant-garde though they were in fact developed for advertising use in the 19th century. In either case, they represent conceptual, not technical, advances.

At the most fundamental level writing is a form of production which which involves mark making of a highly specific kind. It has something in common with drawing, but it is constrained because the letters must conform to the codes which give them their functional readability; overly distorted through individual style or creativity they would lose their communicative power. Writing, therefore, can be defined as the set of marks put at the service of the symbolic order, or language. The term symbolic order carries many connotations from the psychoanalytic and theoretical context in which it derives: it refers to language as a social code which is shared, rule-bound, capable of inflection, but is essentially set to such a degree that it determines the terms of individual psychic experience through constraints of established cultural parameters. In fact, my discussion is even more specific here since I am talking about the alphabet. In alphabetic writing (handwriting and its variants) we see the intersection of the cultural symbolic (language) and individual expression coded in material.

A recent Crane's ad shows the way in which the personal touch and special sign or mark of individuality is given value. It obviously matters—the handwritten note is something distinct and "distinctive" —associated with high level corporate class relations. This demonstrates the extent to which any instance of writing has to be understood in relation to the wider field of forms of written production against which it gains its value: The named author "Phil" clearly personalizes the exchange in his note to "Steve."

These are old modes and old observations, but considering the future of writing involves understanding the way these forms have functioned. In gross terms one could sketch a basic line in human history in which the notion of wisdom is changed to one of knowledge and then information—and in each of these writing would play a different part. Wisdom suggests an Old Testament concept of life experience, reflection, contemplation, devotion in which writing serves to reveal

Truth (God's word in a religious frame). Knowledge is a modern concept, originating with Renaissance attitutdes towards empirical information and evolving into 18th century Enlightenment rationality in which writing serves as authenticating, duplicatable, documentation. Information displaces knowledge in the latter part of the 20th century—and becomes immaterial, serving as one step in the operation of quantification—information as blip, chip, bit, and byte. Here writing approaches the identity granted by Jacques Derrida—to act as the site of differentiation, or in Derrida's terms, writing as *différance*. The question which immediately arises is what constitutes the information of writing itself—and whether writing at the service of quantified information preserves the information aspects of material writing, especially with respect to two major areas of cultural activity: history and identity.

It is obvious that the construction of history depends upon the record retained in both material artifacts and documents—castles and their record books, desks and their papers, objects and accounts. The meaning of any particular written record is not merely linguistic. The material support—the stone, clay, cloth, vellum, paper—on which it is recorded provides information about the culture in which it was produced. This is incidental but essential information. Though glyphs from a Cretan syllabary taken from a page of Ignace Gelb's work on the history of writing are available for study as part of a linguistic code when presented in the table form of his book's illustration, their individual occurences would give other indications about the date, place, and conditions of their production.

The importance of letters or other written marks is not just that they are material in form but that in and through that material they bear meaning.

The symbolic value of letterforms has been the subject of long and old debates. One of these focuses on the origin of letters. Are they essential elements of the cosmos gifted with archaic meaning as the Kabbalists believed? Were they written by the finger of God as the keys to divine thought and universal structure then given to humanity in the tablets handed to Moses on Mt. Sinai? Or were they a human invention scraped together from the impulse to make records of business transactions, historical events, and poetic insight? If so then their early forms were clearly crude, imperfect, and only slowly standardized, as the inscriptions from the Sinai and dated to about 1700 BC would suggest.

Other debates on the origins of the alphabetic letters link these to mythic tales about the origin of civilization—and philosophical proposals about the relative innocence or barbarity of early humanity. The letters were interpreted by the 18th century writer Court de Gebelin as icons recording the basic elements of a nomadic camp. Gebelin's belief that the letters had Semitic origins was correct, but to justify this he forced a reading of their schematic pictorial form into a correlation with the objects he felt comprised the tools for daily life of the people he supposed had been responsible for their invention. He had no archaeological evidence to support these claims—either for the original forms of the letters or for their iconic value, but the visual form of the alphabet has provoked many such imaginative readings over the course of human history.

The 18th century scholar Philip Allwood asserted that the form of the letter "A" was derived from tent poles used by people who made their yearly life according to the cycle of rising and falling river waters. The crossbar of the letter marked the important role which the high-water mark played in their lives—and since these cycles had such profound consequences for every other aspect of their existence, this letter naturally came first in the alphabet.

In the Renaissance, attempts to make the letters reflect divine proportions led to elaborate geometric schemes for their construction. This effort combined a search for a mathematical essence for letterforms as well as a tastefully aesthetic modification of the rigid rules of geometry in order to coax the letters into pleasing sensual forms.

These investigations of the formal essences of letters took on one meaning in the manuals of writing masters intent on defining the basic elements of a good hand, bringing the loops, curves, and strokes of a script into a logical relation to each other.

They take on another meaning in the labors of such early researchers as Donald Knuth who searched for mathematical formulae adequate for describing letters as "essences." Knuth's work returned to questions about letters posed since the days of Greek Pythagoreans who searched for the identity of all elements of the cosmos in mathematical terms.

Such a value, though mathematical in its fundamentals, was also loaded with symbolic information. In his graphic interpretation of the traditional Pythagorean symbolism accorded to the "Y," Renaissance type designer and printer Geofroy Tory rendered literal the metaphoric choice posed to a young initiate into the arcane mysteries of the philosophical system. The consequences of the choice between the easy path of worldly life with its tempting sausages and other delights and that of the difficult path to the acquisition of knowledge is rendered quite clearly in his 1529 edition of Champfleury.

The idea of the letters as potent forces for bringing the world into being has also had a long history. In such a belief system the letters not only represent cosmological elements, they literally embody a generative power—and it is the mating of the masculine principle of phallic letter "Aleph" with the fecund fertility of the curved "Beth" which gives rise to little "Gimel." Alfred Kallir is a British scholar whose researches in this area have led him to connect signs from almost all known scripts—Cretan, Indus Valley, Mayan, Eastern Island and Chinese (regardless of their historical distinctions and linguistic incompatibilities)—in order to show the universal human engagement with this mythology.

While such symbolic aspects are an important part of the cultural history of writing and its capacity to support and record beliefs, there is another basic aspect of writing's capacity to reveal history as a visual form even where there is no speculation about the origins or symbolic values of the letters. The pages of 19th century writing master George Becker, for instance, shows the influence of decorative metal faces on calligraphic techniques since Becker clearly had to show that his hand skills could compete with those of the print shop in extravant excess.

Such examples of material history in form are as limitless as the history of written language. The famous Bergamo alphabet produced in the last decade of the 14th century bears witness to the richness of information which visual form provides—as do the poses, costumes, and moral implications of those 19th century letters meant to inspire the denizens of the nursery by their models of behavior.

Schemes of symbolic value extend beyond individual letterforms to include the alphabet as a system. One such example is Francis Haab's early 20th century work on the divination of the Latin alphabet in which the lineage of gods and goddesses is shown in an alphabetic scheme tracing their marital and familial relations. Whether it is the action of the divinities which determines the order of the alphabet or whether the alphabet provides the key to this divine knowledge is not quite clear.

And the inquiry into the forms and values of known and unknown writing systems has even extended beyond the so-called ancient and exotic scripts to include the written language of other members of our solar system, as in the recorded notation of the Martian language made by the medium Hélène Smith in the 1920s.

Electronic media can record some of this rich legacy, but it is obvious from this smattering of examples that a great deal of non-linguistic information is recorded in each of these instances of written language. This "information" is not the apparent message but the incidental supplement provided by the material form and support. One could examine the inks, papers, printing technologies, economic circumstances of production and consumption, use and status, of each of these documents as well as the complex cultural discourses of history, religion, philosophy, and psychology in which they participate on the basis of their material existence. Reduced to mere elements of a static linguistic code Tory's Pythagorean "Y" or the Allwood's "A" would lose most of their resonance.

The functions of writing depend in large part on this material form in order for writing to serve the interests of power and production of history. The power of written documents is clear in the popular perception—just the other day on a bus ride from the airport I heard one uniformed worker discussing a workplace dispute with another. "Put it in writing," the first speaker kept saying, endorsing this faith in written testimony. The act of "signing on the dotted line" still has a performative function even in an electronic environment—it is the act of putting a mark on an electronic pad which one can later be called to recognize as one's own which renders it valid more than its visual form.

But the magic quality ascribed to written language also has a long history in which the swallowing, burning, or bodily application of spells and incantations produces unaccountable effects.

But the authority of written documents, as I mentioned once before, does not depend upon their pristine and unaltered condition. Quite the contrary—it is the capacity of material documents to record change which makes them such believable witnesses. Their very substance is a testimonial since marks, means of writing, and material all change over time. Such details of production have themselves been subject to considerable scrutiny upon occasion. One obsessively peculiar scholar William Newbold analyzed a cipher text believed to be in Roger Bacon's handwriting. Newbold coaxed a reading from these ciphers which depended on reading them as the production of a whole other minature code of secret glyphs used to compose ciphers of a second order. While Newbold's micrographia was most likely the pattern of ink attaching itself to fibers in the paper his dedication to interpretation demonstrates the capacity of material to provide untold revelations.

In the history of forgery the fortunes of visual forms have risen and fallen over time. The legitimacy of marks in legal testimony resided for centuries in an expert witness's capacity to assert the authenticity of a sample without recourse to any work with which to make a comparison. Comparative techniques for handwriting analysis were only admitted into courtrooms in the United States in the early part of the 20th century when the idea of accountability became linked to reproducibility as well as general visual characteristics of a piece of writing. But forgery studies had already become subject to scientificization in the 19th century when specific equipment for the examination of disputed documents was developed—such as this specialized microscope. Even more interesting is that the emphasis on evaluating documents shifted to the non-visible measure of muscular patterns—emphasis, weight, and gestural movements—which could be analyzed by electric equipment though they could not be detected by visual comparison. If the written history becomes increasingly separate from the history in material will anything be lost? Is the palimpsestic character of the material document something which has an electronic equivalent? Or is the vulnerability of the electronic document so perfect, the capacity for seamless, unmarked, alteration so developed, that materiality will no longer play an essential role in the assessment of written history?

In addition to the role writing plays in history, it also functions significantly in the production of identity as that is understood in late 20th century western culture. Handwriting serves many functions in this capacity—from the signature as an equivalent to identity to the simple pleasure of mark making to a complex investment in personality. The poet André Breton once produced a self-portrait showing himself engaged in optical manipulations and other aspects of fantasy. Its handwritten title "écriture automatique" ("automatic writing"—one of the Surrealists literary techniques) proclaimed the intimate relation of creative production and personal identity. The cultural critic Theodor

Adorno once remarked that the term "alienation" described a world in which there was no place for individual experience—or its record.

In that sense handwriting and penmanship are directly implicated in the imaginative production and recognition of individuality. Handwriting is the capacity of writing to be inflected, transformed, by the hand into a form which reflects the mutable, personal, and idiosyncratic image of the symbolic.

However rule-bound that symbolic order is, the act of inscription makes identity visible. One has the senses of becoming, being made, marked in the material process of writing. This is not meant to be a nostalgic observation or agenda: I use computers, think about their touch, take pleasure from the clean effects of the laser printer, feel an intimate relation to my smeary ink-jet drafts. So the pleasures of writing take many forms, some of them electronic.

But that doesn't dispense with the fundamental function of writing as an equivalent of, expression of, and embodiment of individuated identity. In the case of an analysis of the handwriting and work of the sculptor Jacques Lipschitz a graphologist attempted to assert the essential nature of an individual personality. The "essence" of Lipschitz was revealed through the similarity of forms he used in his signature and his three-dimensional work, in an analysis which subscribed to the idea of an inalterable kernel of human character.

But no matter what one's position is on identity, writing has a role to play in its construction. There are two competing models: in one the assumption is that character is fixed, almost like an aspect of genetic combination, in a unique and indelible fingerprint-like pattern in each individual from zygote to death. This is the humanist notion of identity—and handwriting is its revelation. In modified form, this humanist notion takes into account the vicissitudes of fortune (education, class, gender). The opposing model takes individual identity to be the mere coincidence of forces in which a specific intersection of desires, codes, and programmatic attitudes shows up as the mechanistic production of the cultural order. In this model, handwriting serves to inscribe the place the individual occupies in such an order, a place marked and demarcated according to rules, conventions, and constraints.

With all of this in mind, what does the immateriality of electronic media imply? Not a total loss of identity—surely the capacity of the keyboard to produce or even reproduce a specific handwriting extends the inscription of identity into the electronic mode? But such a simulacral image of character may lack the fundamantal pleasure associated with mark-making and the function this serves as a means of being and becoming in the world. Increasing alienation—the resistance of the world to inflection by individual experience—seems like a possibility at every stage of industrial and technological homogenization. The electronic universe is only an increase in quantity, rather than a qualitative transformation in that respect. But in other respects there remains the basic difference—a material difference—between the modes of electronic production and those of conventional pre-electronic media. And that, to return to my original point, is the condition of fungibility—fungibility to an unprecedented degree. Mark-making on the Newton tablet does not result in a trace inscribed in material, but a transformation into the quantifiable terms of an information-based analysis that stores those signs according to pre-set categories. The systematic and pre-ordered, rather than the incidental and serendipitous, are the ruling forces of this new universe. Even if it sounds naive to romanticize touch as the mark of the individual, and to assign to that a set of linked concerns involving existence, identity, and history, the absence of a material relation between inscription and production, the fungibility factor, will most certainly have an effect in those arenas of history and identity in which writing has played such an important part.

In the current phase of techno-consumerism and new media boosterism, the questions arising around electronic media have to be posed in terms of social effects, as well as aesthetic and technological ones. When there is no strict relation between input and output, no strict relation between the forms of labor in production and the format of the object that is produced, then labor risks increasing effacement from the very social processes it facilitates. The social spaces of community and the polis, already seriously disintegrated, risk further disintegration as the activities of production are materially unlinked and made spatially distinct from the conditions of production. And the focus on the body in the production of written language shifts to issues of interface—the lived experience of life with the machine.

The many functions of history and memory that are supported and served by materiality will inevitably transform as the seamless erasure and mutation of documents becomes a matter of course. When the vanishing trace of inscription is totally gone there will be no means of recovery—the incidental "information" of materiality will have dissolved, leaving only the bare-bones code of a starved linguistic message.

And as for identity, well, I conjure only a single image of the possible future when a "sim" rendezvous with a virtual celebrity produces an autographed signature, will anyone take that as "proof" of an actual encounter?

This paper was first written for a panel in April 1994, at Parsons School of Art, NYC, The Work of Art in the Age of Electronic Technology *and then revised and published in* Emigre, *in a version designed by Anne Burdick in 1995.*

Electronic Media and the Status of Writing

Before dealing with electronic media in relation to written language, it seems one should risk a definition of writing itself. Mine will be possibly problematic, and unpopular, since it disregards both the conventional idea of writing as being merely a surrogate form of spoken language and also the more in vogue, deconstructed notion of a disembodied trace far from the realm of the material reality of so-called pedestrian linguistic forms. The definition I would propose for writing takes seriously its materiality and the influence of the material aspects of written forms on the production of linguistic meanings. I define the term "writing" as the visible form of language from the level of the marks to the letters and includes all the characteristic features of the visible medium and I contend that these features contribute to structuring the linguistic significance of the text.

With this premise in mind, certain aspects of electronic documents and their capacity to function as "written" forms come immediately into question. Primary among these is the illusion that written language, in its electronic form, operates as a disembodied text of pure information. This illusion is based on the assumption that information is not influenced by or dependent on the forms in which it is presented. Simply speaking, an example of this would be the stripping down of the word into electronic bits or charges which could be refigured into any kind of re-rendering, with the assumption that the configuration of such bits or charges is sufficient to record and render the information contained in an original message. Translating an advertisement or newspaper front page, with their hierarchized visual arrangements of sizes and shapes and physical relations of words or copy blocks into a linear sequence of letters identified only as one of the twenty-six (or 52 including capitals) discrete elements and with no regard for the material properties of the original visual text would create precisely that form which I intend to designate by the term "disembodied text of information." The idea that information resides in the so-called lexical value, independent of any medium, I consider to be fundamentally incorrect. Several functional features of written texts are irrevocably lost in the process of this translation into electronic form, and it is precisely because of the value of these extra-lexical features in a written text that an electronic version of writing cannot succeed in totally replacing the traditional forms for all realms in which writing functions. Specifically, these realms depend upon: the ceremonial function of the written document within a ritualized cultural context; the vulnerability of the written document to change and to record change such that it functions in a historical context; the capacity of the written document to contain certain non-visible but otherwise tangible, qualifiable, characteristics which permit it to perform the identity of inscribing individual identity insofar as this concept of "identity" as "individually discrete personality" holds a value in the social order.

Let us now examine each of these three aspects in turn.

First, the status of the conventional written document is determined by a multitude of factors of which only a small portion can be considered "information" in the strict sense of a lexical context, ceremonial and ritualized circumstances.

Take for example the signing of William Penn's treaty with the Indians. What comes to mind? A Benjamin West type image—there is the spreading tree, the new land, the Native Americans in ceremonial paint and clothing, and Penn, his arms extended, striking a gesture of European fellowship. The treaty stretches between them, open to the skies, freshly signed. And the words of the treaty? The information on the document? Who remembers? Words dried with the ink and slipped into obscurity. The treaty as such is the least part of the historical moment as it has become mythologized in the annals of Americana.

A pact made by machines, in the dark swift space of seconds which characterize, for instance, an electronic bank transaction, would never fulfill the ritualistic functions of an act in which the text is made by context, full, replete, complex. The cultural significances of a document, as in the example cited above, is hardly determined by its lexical content, but rather by the surrounding context in which the written text serves a critical part by its role as a document generating and being generated by the event.

Secondly, the material properties of a written document make it vulnerable to change. These properties reflect the mode of production, link it to a particular moment in time, historical by virtue of that technology. The traditional material supports: paper, bark, cloth, skin, stone, wood, are all vulnerable materials. They are not only capable of being linked to a particular moment in terms of their creation, but, more significantly, because the materials are vulnerable, they record any change which occurs in the document. The capacity of material to record this history is a critical one. The traditional written document enters into a stream of relations to historical time at its inception and throughout its existence.

In an electronic document the very vulnerability on which the authenticity and integrity of the traditional document is based will be different. The capacity of the written document to serve a legally binding function is based upon its existence as a material artifact as such, with its material vulnerability, as well as upon its literal lexical content. Can an electronic document duplicate these conditions? Probably not. It is my contention that the electronic document has a differently constituted relation to vulnerability and change, and particularly because changes may occur in an electronic document without any record of that change being materially embedded in the document itself. The electronic document suffers, in this sense, from a material loss of memory, or a loss of material memory. An altered electronic document contains no palimpsestic layering, no complete history of its own existence. Even if the moment of its inception can be marked, either by its link to a particular machine, time, place of production, and even if it can be "write protected" against alteration, the medium has the capacity, as part of any change that takes place, to rearrange itself in the new configuration. The electronic charges, pulses, lose their capacity to recollect the previous arrangement, at least, they have the possibility of forgetting, the possibility of that loss of memory, whereas the traditional document has no possibility of forgetting its own history.

The status of the signature and the authenticity of handwriting in terms of the capacity to detect forgeries and also in the extent to which so-called character analysis can be systematized in correspondence to the physical form of handwritten materials, do not depend necessarily upon the visible form of the signature or handwritten material. Since the late 19th century when the study of such phenomena evolved from parlor game diversions to a self-styled science, finding is way even into a legal domain where questions of forgery depend upon identifying originals, what has become evident is that the grounds for determining authenticity are invisible ones. Again, these are elements linked specifically to the materiality of the media of paper, ink, and the physical movements associated with making the marks. In writing a gestural pattern, a muscular movement, which is completely unique and discrete, specific to the writer and unduplicatable, is recorded in the pressure and timing of the strokes. This rhythmic pattern, this sequence of pressures and movements and its impression upon the material support is what is examined by the forgery expert, and also by the handwriting analyst who professes any kind of "scientific" basis for a descriptive accuracy in the analytic method. An electronic medium, again, records primarily visual, visible material and information when it records writing as an image. The invisible, but tangible, record of physical and gestural patterns would escape the electronic medium, cannot be recorded or duplicated within its tracing of a visible pattern. Could an electronic signature ever be legally binding for this reason? Could it ever serve the function of the physical signature, which is to be the surrogate, substitute, *representamen* of the individual.

I invoke the notion of personality with some hesitation here because of the problems it can unleash, and it should be qualified in this instance by the suggestion that an investigation into the role of writing from the psychoanalytic point of view of the function of the symbolic system of language in the structuring of the individual "subject" still needs to be performed so that the effect of the "genericization" produced by a homogeneous visual representation of that symbolic system, such as is found in electronic documents, can be more fully appreciated.

In conclusion: clearly, the invention of electronic media does not threaten the existence of traditional written forms. The old rituals do not get obliterated, negated, by the invention of the new technology but, the place of the new technology invents another space, another dimension in the field of writing.

But what seems important is to note the way the new medium is limited by its material constraints, and to understand that the distinctions between a medium which functions in a ritual context and one which proposes a "disembodied text of information," one which is vulnerable to and records change, and one which has the possibility of forgetting, one which can reveal the intangible, and one which depends solely on the visual (or its "immaterial" abstraction)—that these distinctions, between traditional and electronic forms, are fundamental, structural ones which negate the possibility that electronic forms of written language could replace or duplicate the functions of traditional ones—in other words, the term "written language" has a different meaning in relation to electronic media than it does when describing more traditional forms.

Written in Berkeley, in 1982, as a speculation on the impact of electronic technology on the traditional cultural functions of writing.

VII. Personal Writing

Writing History: Mine

Any subjective sense of history, particularly one's own, has points of reference around which it formulates and fixates. Traces of experience become identified with manifest forms—that which has been inscribed through the very act of making marks. There was a crucial point in my own development in which I experienced a desire to copy marks which already existed, to incorporate myself into them by repeating their shapes in the disciplined exercise of my own hand. I knew their significance was already determined, that they had a place in a larger context, a systematized framework. That was their power and their allure. Because to make them, partake of them, was to insert oneself into that order which connected outward as well as inward. The word, the sign, the statement became infinitely recollectable in the process. The record was no longer simply dependent on my own mnemonic prowess or idiosyncratic system, but was capable of finding its way through the devices of a social and collective memory. Experience became memory through the process of writing, and the acquisition of writing inscribed me in the symbolic order mediating the real.

Brief flashes in that personal history remain vividly crystallized in my mind, with all the hideous privilege of clichéd moments standing out in time from a continuum. Unable to speak I am written into by the experience for which I have no words. The description made later is actually an inscription, in translation, of the sequence of perceived sensations which organized themselves into coherence. I knew my name before I knew the alphabet. I knew the alphabet before I knew there was another. Language was absolute before it was demonstrated to be relative. The text of an early prose work was spatially specific. There was that notebook around my neck, tied with a piece of string, pen dangling. Ever present to meet the anxiety of a need to always be prepared, at any instant, to write. That cloudy history of childhood, shot through with bars of light which still strike, sentimentally, upon those moments. As this writing now, in this loaded language, attempts to invoke them, peel them back out of that confusion into apparent form. Make them available to sight through a construction which is barely a re-construction. More likely, a fabrication based on the merest, slightest evidence. The trace does not reveal, does not permit the revelation of the real event. Rather, it provides the stimulus to project it into re-existence, new existence, again and again. Writing experience: continually renewing itself as a manuscript, the hermeneutic trace providing ample nourishment to sustain its own conviction through the process.

There is always the question of origins. Origins are always a question. A quest. Sought as the long-lost and unrecoverable point of coming into being, the guarantee, validity, solidity of that point is obscured and muddied. How can one recover that transition into form, the point of actual formation? It remains always unavailable, frustratingly so. The historical accounts dimly made out through issues of partisanship and lack of evidence, the tradition of the very forms themselves, beg the questions of the method of their invention. And place. Time. Cause. Course.

The shape. The sound. The sequence of the letter signs. The relation to spoken language as a system. These are the parameters used to shape the research. The criteria applied to the fragmentary data, trying to make it into a whole narrative of history. If there were pictures first, and there were, in that Egyptian version we so fondly mythologize, then how was the alphabet distinguished in its violent birth from that ancient system? The hieroglyphics were fraught with mystery and decadence by the time the letters reached their clean stride separate from that antique history, that primitive and not-so-primitive set of elaborate mnemonic signs.

No picture history of my own precedes my entrance into the alphabet. No concrete signs exist to guide me further back, into the origin which would have been Semitic. Thus the patriarchal aspect of the written language doubly identified for me with one historical and one personal facet. The forms had their roman barbarism firmly stamped in them and it was by my mother's hand that I had copies made to model mine on. She was literally Barbara-ic, fortunately, and thus served as the bright opposite to that fond Semitic history which belonged to my so civilized father. The straight lines, the pure curves, the rightness of the upright forms that I made standing by the dishwasher, not quite tall enough to see over its top to where she made those mysterious marks with equally mysterious competence, as if they lived in her and came out through her fingers in a fully-formed sequence of pre-ordained signs. I watched her arm in the process but could not really see the sequence according to which the letters were made, stroke by stroke. Her own care in making them was redolent with ritualistic tendencies of her own Druidic heritage. A true barbarian, an Anglo-Saxon with Celtic blood who traced for love of tracing, who wrote with a deep superstitious submission to the forms, all part of the cult of primitivism which dominated her thinking so that any deviance counted as transgression against a code which had value as ritual more than substance.

So the letters passed down to me on the floor where I lay, prone, reshaping them as mine, possessing my self through the making of that name. They had a heritage as forms and a different impact as a process, an exercise. And it was my mother who took me from the letters to literacy, to the implications of disregarding the visual images for the sake of their referential value. But that was later, through the veil, past the original and originary ritual of acquisition. And the first act was pure possession, the completely territorial urge to make myself through the writing of my name in letters which were language. My entrance into its claim upon me: my definition through it and its authority. That was personal, not cultural, but steeped in the mystery of the very tangible, tactile act of making. As a line on the earth makes property, necessarily, so the lines on the page made me mine in the invocation and power of the name, my name, written by me.

The early evidence for the alphabet's origin came from the turquoise mines in the Sinai where their sequence helped to mark the sequence of architectural constructions. Thus the greatest evidence of their existence comes from an incidental use which demonstrates how commonplace the system had become, how established, how taken for granted that it could be appropriated for other use on account of its standardization. I had not acquired standards, myself, not a whole system, just the piecemeal parts which had a relevance to my own project. Later, though, the realization that there was a standard, a limited set, a finitude to writing's signs met with great resistance, disbelief.

We had wallpaper, as one might in a child's room, decorated with letters. All majuscules and thickly loaded with floral and decorative motifs. The foliating of the strokes and trunks of the sturdy letters made them more elaborate than functional. But they were clear and laid out in a grid-like pattern. Laid out. My mother told me, though I knew it wasn't her idea, and just something that she knew as she tended to know all manner of rules, that they were all there were. Those twenty-six, she said, were the sum total of the letters from which all words were made. There were no others. I didn't believe it, though I knew her primitive faith in the sanctity of laws and limits, her resolute conviction that certain authority was absolute. At that point I didn't have the sophistication to understand that my uneasiness might have to do with the discrepancy between the phonetic and the alphabetic. That the complexity of sounds I knew and used familiarly was poorly matched by the rigid marks in that strangely limited number.

But my disbelief at that point was simply grounded in the visual. Nightly, the dim light left leaking from the hall through the partially opened door provided a crack of insight into the system of graphic language displayed in its inadequate beauty on the wall, I compared my mental images of my childish vocabulary with that increasingly finite set again and again—hoping to disprove her. For my own sake, but also, for the sake of language. I could not reconcile my sense of the infinity of possibilities which articulation seemed to possess with the notion of a set of only twenty-six letters through which to express them. Within those conceptions it was a project doomed to failure—though a failure sustained through a continual questioning and fascination. And as the Greeks inheriting, appropriating, those Semitic forms adopted them so as to include the notation of vowels that had always been left to interpretation (to the making of the text in the reading, a reinvention which was always an act of faith) so did my sense of the writing need to be transformed by a sense of its relations to language in general—and to spoken and uttered forms of expression—before the set of letters dissolved its limits (or obtained them with a graceful legitimacy which ceased to be inadequate) and became more than sufficient.

Those were the tenets that underlay the text, that preceded any entry into writing as language: learning visual models and learning that there was a limited set of alphabetic signs. Imitating handwriting, the mimetic trickery of little monkey hands, those child paws which played at adult language, was some other phase—as was the compulsive making of charts and graphs, of compulsive lists of copies in the attempt to achieve a degree zero of imitation, to repress all that infantile subjectivity below the effort of a gesture from which all individuation had been effaced. That never happened. Instead, the process continued by bringing the letters into being, then getting beyond the limits of their possibilities. These combined into the field and force of writing, which, striking out beyond its boundaries, then hurried to the real task of enunciation.

Text text text. The early urge to be productive. Just turned five. Taking a trip with my family to a place called Europe, which was across an ocean, which was the same as France and England though they were not the same as each other. Which was the same as "foreign." Curious these definitions of inclusion and exclusion. The relation of categories of difference and sets difficult to integrate. They stayed distinct. Europe and France and then Paris all lay next to each other as separate units until the travelling sequence aligned them through time as geographical masses whose relations to each other clarified through the sequence of experience. Europe became the title for a five page work, the story of a whole long trip. Three months worth and the hierarchy of the page clearly established the movements through space and time. Location became doubly specific: spot to spot, point to point. I could put my eyes on, lay hands on, get a sense of and remember: England and Scotland, France and Switzerland, Italy and the boat, Israel and the boat back. Gibraltar. Europe to England again and home. Five and a half pages: a spatial exercise, back to the source of writing, really, that remote edge of the Mediterranean, though we did not go far enough south to be able to touch those stones which bear the oldest alphabetic inscriptions nor to look over our shoulders at their iconic forbearers in stonecarved silhouette. But I could take hold of the language in this textuality, sensuality, spatiality, as I had not before. For in the making of the thing, the object, language itself—as writing—become objectifiable and thus discoverable and recoverable as something not invented but inventing, bearing, writing, living to insure my own sense of it for its own sake, to be reviewed as an exercise which in the acting out and through makes, by that pattern and patterning, the very shape it mimics in its form. So page to page, line by line, experience got specified in my five year old hand by its place on each of those sheets and the relation of those lines to each other in the whole. The end and the beginning acted to hold the rest in place so that it could have relations and take shape, the whole fragmenting insight itself in order to be made whole, real and resonant through the complex of relations.

A beginning point, an early text, a fundamental encounter with the form and function of writing and/as memory, experience and/as language. It became the start and yet, in its basic realizations, was already complete as an understanding of the force of writing history.

1981

Writing as Inscription

Dream and Image

I had a dream of "La Musée des Ecrits" which consisted of three images. The first was of a door on which the museum's name is written in the black-backed gold lettering of a late 19th century period effect. As the door swings open it is thrown backwards against the sky. Light from the outside reveals that there are perforations in the door in the form of letters whose message, though in writing, is indecipherable. The second image is from the collection of artifacts. It detaches from the archive like a freeze-frame moment blown to fill an entire screen and is of a young boy/girl with dark curly hair like mine, but s/he is unidentified and androgynous. On the surface of the image, as on celluloid, writing is superimposed with a magic marker: over the head and above the figure is the future, to be written, while on the lower part, scratched as through emulsion, is the record of the past. There is a sense of fatality in this materiality, that it would and could manifest the course of a life so completely. The final image is from a part of the collection dealing with the articulation of gesture. A whole spectrum of possibilities exists in which the body is distinctly articulated, very specifically. One image comes into focus: a face with shadows cast on it that are exaggerated just enough to become caricatured, distorted, but distinct forms of letters. To make the point more clearly, however, the photograph has been marked out with type to show that the shadow representations have a translation through a system of equivalences. Would the shadows read without that key?

In contrast to this, lurking behind it and as an always present reference, is the memory of a friend who, while having a psychotic breakdown, became disintegrated during the process of learning Chinese. She allowed that system to dictate the terms of her existence, finding in every lesson a personal message from which she took (mis)guidance. This dissociation, which allowed reference to take control, seems at the opposite end of the spectrum from the dream image of "La Musée des Ecrits," where the system is conceived of within reference, as a form of control. Between these two poles I see the possibility of constructing a history of writing interfaced with a history of ideas about writing, in which the integrity of the material will have restored to it both motive and function and cease to be merely the static excrement of the culture by which it is produced.

The Project

This is a brief statement, meant to serve as a plan of organization. Even here at the outset the following areas demand consideration: the history of the material forms of writing, the mythologies of origin and interpretation, the evolution of the social function of written language, and the metaphysics of its psychic operation. Materiality would include everything: stones to xerox through the evolution of marks, scripts, type. The history of writing as a technology is grounded in assumptions of traditional history: that the *techne* builds on itself, but makes leaps not predictable from the precedent while using aspects of that precedent to support an illusion of easy continuity in development. Mythology is in distinct opposition to the historical. The writing system is conceived of as exterior, always a "given," which allows projections of meaning and interpretation. Then there are the social functions: commerce, communication, expression, the effects, and what come to be history, science, accounting, the means of power and control, the force of the episteme. Finally, there is the metaphysics/metapsychics: ideas about writing as an externalization process, the dynamic of reference and self-referentiality, evidence and self-evidence. Each area is a whole discipline and must contribute to the synthesis for the full interest/impact of writing to state itself. There is the irrefutable formality of marks which produce the sense of writing. Materiality postulates a relation between men and that set of signs by which one recognizes one's own external definition. The model of the Torah is (re)activated by interplay of the written and spoken which implies a duality of force and meaning in a way which implies an erotics of inscription. Motive and function combine so that representation may be seen as the means of perpetuating that which brings it into being. Transformation is the becoming manifest which allows for use through engagement with the not dismissable fact of the material. Literacy, order, social function: the word is evidence, the basis of law. But "signing" is also always "corresponding to the obscene, fabulous, unknown reality," says Artaud. Making a bond, a signature, a liason, a sign with the value of an operation, the role of an abstraction in which the motive is missing, forgotten, and only elements of a motif are left. All intention and purpose are thrown out of the text. The explicit vs. the latent combine in a public record office and the recourse to social knowledge. Marks, the character or alphabet, are an exterior way to get at meaning through the divinity of the word/text relationship. This can be identified and laid to rest on an orthodox relation. The fetishism of the letter is what really destroys the text while the fetishism of the text renders the letter impotent and transparent. Nothing signifies when anything comes to signify in some system of complete subjectivism. Is there an essence of things? Beyond representability? Or is there only meaning in materiality? Is meaning death—or is non-meaning a condition of complete destruction? Neither, but resolution into any closed sign is a kind of death, as the static representation of desire is a death. Permanance is a form of loss. Overcoming the fatality of matter, the active, unresolved process of externalization, the bringing up and out into evidence in that continually renewed process which makes use of externalization for the prolongation and sustenance of desire—that is the possibility for life. A desire which does not subside in an immediate reach but is sublimated into an extension/perpetuation of itself through simultaneous creation/denial of its objectification. The risk of recognition, the possibility of being known, returns through the mirror function of the mark which makes the self, gives identity back to the self as the form of its own gesture so that it may come to recognize what it has not had other means to objectify. Therefore, bring into being the possibility of being known. It does cry out for the Other, in spite of and even on account of the xerox model and the future of reproduction: onanism loses momentum. There is a drive to exteriorize, the essential desire to realize the possibility of being known, through relational identity and, again, the mirror function which provides identity only through the existence of the Other. Inscription is continually restating a case: no progress, no evolution, only the continual re-invention of forms. Externalization is a process: not writing as a resolution, but an insistence on the necessity of non-resolution in order to preserve its dynamic.

Berkeley, 1982

Other than Linear

The difficulties I had in titling this piece raised several problems which are central to the consideration of linearity and the possibility of a (post)feminist reformulation of the problems its poses. In using the term "linear" and attempting to put next to it some term which would call it into question in a relationship of meaning not defined by antagonism or opposition, choices such as "alternative" or "non-linear" or "beyond" the linear seemed limited by precisely that sense of opposition (even though the term "beyond" has been used to suggest a way of working, a practice of writing, thinking about language which would avoid the difficult positions identified by early feminist criticism). Thus the use of the term "Other" since it is associated with the characterization of a woman's role in relation to language—woman as Other, language as dependent on the Other, systems of representation in general creating and suggesting, structuring an Other in their use—while not totally satisfactory, seemed the most appropriate.

Originally I had thought to explore in this talk various non-linear works—or works whose apparent form was non-linear—as a way of posing some alternatives to linearity. As I began to refine my investigation it became increasingly clear to me that it was precisely within the more conventional assumptions about the actual linearity of conventionalized language that the real possibility of non-linearity lay while the so-called alternative forms, concrete poetry, spatial and field works, had in them certain traps, certain deceits, which masked their real linear form under the guise of averting it. It was the linear which actually contained non-linearity—and the apparently non-linear, if it did not reinforce the very values it attempted to undermine, at any rate didn't really raise any significantly different issues than linear forms.

One way linearity operates in the structure of language is in the process of reading, restructuring, or generating signification from a text. On this point apparently non-linear forms of writing have their claim to non-linearity severely undermined, as will be examined further on. Reading always requires sequential ordering. While there may be a great number of possible readings for any text, and one would hope that an interesting work would provoke or be able to provoke a number of possible readings, still at any given time any particular reading, by the very nature of the reading process, will be linear. The attempts to generate exceptions to this in the form of concrete poetry tend to raise issues already posed by the investigation into the apparent linearity of language, rather than raising issues based on their specific form.

On the plane of discourse, literary forms may be non-linear by taking advantage of visual or phonic potential. Such works use one of several approaches to generate their non-linearity: the use of multiple choices, simultaneously presented, or of field/matrix forms embodying the element of choice within the form of the text. To pick any one of these choices is to negate the other—they are mutually exclusive within the sequence of reading though they allow for that sequence to be structured in a variety of ways. Examples of these works can be found beginning with the classic text of Stéphane Mallarmé and continuing through the "Words in Liberty" of the Futurists, the Dada typographic works and into the later twentieth century in concrete poetry and experimental book form. While many of these works push aggressively against the limits of language as a conventional system of communication and by so doing begin to break down linearity in terms of the possibility of achieving the closure inherent in the process of signification, the mechanics they operate through and against are not, in fact, structurally different from those of so-called "normal" language. They may resist closure more, but the closure they resist is equally problematic in other forms. Works which compose themselves as a field, without an apparent sequence, and spatialist compositions which, literally hang suspended or displayed so that the relations among the elements shift constantly and change, also pose extreme disruptions to the norm of communicative language. Whatever they may achieve in terms of disintegrating the linear authority of language seems minor compared to the degree to which they undermine control over their own authority as texts in so doing. While such a practice may successfully fulfill the aims of literary works in the disruption of normative reading, the relation of these methods to feminist practice raises other issues.

As a basis for feminist writing practice, or a writing practice influenced by the issues raised in feminist critical discourse, it seems too extreme to risk the highly personalized or extremely coded language which empowers itself mainly through denying access to the reader or by refusing an instrumental role in repositioning the reader or writer within the social configurations in which the text functions. Concepts of so-called feminine écriture have, however, attempted to do just that—take the stance that the only position that empowers feminist-gendered discourse must be necessarily outside the normative order of language. Thus the "feminine" formulated by the late 1960s and early 1970s feminist critical positions, was associated with a mass of works which attempted, by their fragmentary and disjunctive form, to pose an alternative to linearity. They attempted to embody a refusal of the coercive rules of rhetorical structure which had been associated with the so-called patriarchal systems of language use and representation. Works by Luce Irigary and Hélène Cixous are particularly well-known examples of writing produced as part of this early critical position and they bear the conspicuous marks of its major tenets. Luce Irigary, by insisting in "Le sexe qui n'est pas un" took literally the metaphors of gender specific sexual identity, of the body of the woman mirroring the body of the text (or vice versa) with its multi-erogenous zones, as one of the bases for the work. She used specific references such as the image of the vaginal lips rubbing, speaking against each other, as a basis for the notion of the plurivalent, non-linear foundation for a "feminist" writing. The resistance to closure which is one of the characteristic aspects of these works was one point on which their non-linearity is established.

The gender value which early feminist writers attached to normative language forced a reevaluation of formal means into a series of very limited choices: one could either replicate the norms of the patriarchal "male" or "masculine" language or one could resist these through invention of a "feminine" écriture. This was a somewhat damning position since it forced women into either a position of complicity or a position of outsider ghettoization. But what were the assumptions underlying this feminist position? First of all, they included the assumption that patriarchal language was in fact linear, that its effectiveness as a dominant form was achieved through this linearity and through the way in which such linearity permitted the continual exercise of authority in linear form. Now we have seen that this is not entirely true. In addition, there was the assumption that women's writing was necessarily inherently non-linear, which is both historically inaccurate and essentialist in its biases. Finally, this condemned women to very rigidly circumscribed practices of writing in the guise of a supposed plurality of positions (as opposed to the single, supposedly unified position of the masculine discourse—which, it turns out, is equally specious)—and this plurality, it turned out, was also highly rule-defined and exclusive since it was grounded in the metaphors and tropes of an essentially gendered identity. And, to paraphrase the point above, the dictates of the discourse of feminine écriture were such that women were either condemned to subordination to the masculine or sentenced to an outside position— both options that were sexually perverse.

Now, what happens if we decide to reevaluate these assumptions within light of the above discussion of the linearity and non-linearity of experimental and conventional forms of language? Is it possible for the Other who is woman to occupy a position which is not defined through opposition? To what extent can the concept of complicity be drawn into this discussion in a positive way, rather than a pejorative one, so that women's use of normative language can be demonstrated to make use of the destabilizing effects of non-linearity from within that language rather than being required to position themselves outside of it? It may be possible to show that the Otherness of women's writing is already present within language, does not need to be marked out from it, but shown to be there in the ways which are similar to the manner in which the complicit relations of gender are already present within the social order. And in addition, to show that women's discourse, women's Otherness, is a part of the Whole of language, is in fact the Other which makes the Whole appear to be so. As in any relation of subjectivity it is the Other that grants fictive unity to the Subject, so within the supposedly Linear and Total structure of supposedly normative and so-called patriarchal language it is the presence of that which is Other than Linear which guarantees this fiction.

To deny this Other is to deny the fact that there is, has frequently if not always been, a place for women within language. Their Otherness within that order is both a place and a power, assertive and seductive, even when apparently effaced. Recognizing this renders language and its discursive structures far more androgynous since the nature of Otherness (especially in a structure which is whole through a fiction dependent on the presence of the Other) is not gender specific with regard to positions, but gets its specificity in relation to the structure of signification. The very phrase of the title of this piece, "Other than . . ."

implies that representation always implies an Other, and that Otherness is always in relation, though not necessarily oppositional. There is, then, no particular gain to be made from condemning women writers to particular forms as if they necessarily carried gender value. For in fact, there is on the one hand an inevitable linearity to the sequential ordering of reading and at the same time a lack of clear linearity with respect to closure, meaning, signification. The complex relations between gendered identity and authority cannot be resolved simply by the use of alternative forms, but by making use of the Otherness within existing discourse formations.

After all, the Other has always existed—whether mutated, muted, or manifest, the place of the woman as Other within a dominant discourse has been an always present, necessary presence for the fictive unity of masculine authority to be guaranteed. This authority acts as an oppressive force—because it seems to work through a seamless, unified linearity. Showing that that linearity is itself unguaranteeable, structurally unsound, and conceptually inadequate to describe the real signifying practices of language, shows that the place of the Other is already fully present and operative within many aspects of normative language. It needs to be named, acknowledged, brought to the fore. So the not-speaking, not-writing place of women has to be replaced by a vociferous, active, speaking and writing. In the dismantling of patriarchy the very tissue of its linguistic structures must be infiltrated with a shock of awareness of that Other. The other that is the Other than Linear of language is not gender specific in form, in spite of the historical conditions which have placed women outside of the established order. The place for women is not as the Other but as the one who shows that the Other has always been present. The fictive unity and linearity on which masculine discourse stakes its claim to authority is just that—fictive, and highly bound up in its own complex and complicitous relation of dependence on the Other. The use of forms of writing which are Other than Linear, then, is the means by which to acknowledge and call attention to this condition of interrelations (of patriarchal language with its fictions of unity, of that unity with authority, of that authority with the role of the Other, etc.) without stigmatizing the structures of language in gendered terms. Such an acknowledgment frees the forms of linearity from their gendered identity, but more significantly, frees gendered writers from a prescription to form. The task of acknowledging our own complicit relation to authority, power, and language can be realized through an acknowledgment of our dependence on and fictive relationship with the Other within linguistic structure—and with the social consequences for gendered individuals that follow from these relations. But it is not by positioning women outside of linear structures, or in opposition to them as if they are indeed what they claim to be, that this acknowledgment can function effectively. It is instead by showing the already present Otherness within Linear forms and the complex of authority and power structures already extant which permits the reworking of those relations between form, language, and power. And this, in fact, is what I have been attempting to do with my recent creative work.

Delivered as a talk in 1984 at Canessa Park, San Francisco.

Auto-Écriture and the Polymorphous Text

The title of my talk—which is deliberately dense, obscure, and jargoned—is meant to suggest a number of things: first, the terms "auto-écriture" and "polymorphous text" refer to certain ideas about the activity of writing and to my current investigations of form; second, the tone of the title intentionally invokes a contemporary critical "discourse" around issues of feminism, writing, and language which has served a number of different purposes for me in my evolution as a writer. Writing very quickly became an exercise in writing one's self, writing my self into being, into form, into existence. The text was not surrogate, but real, its body, extension, dimension, came to be the thing I was making that was me.

The second phase of my evolution as a writer came in my mid-twenties, emerging from adolescent isolation, when I began to consider the question of placing myself within a tradition and had that questioned filtered through feminist theory: Do we have a tradition of writing as women, and do the rules of legacy, of heritage, of the legitimating role of claims to influence have a place in feminist practice? Now I think not . . . not in the same way as for men. In fact, one of the tenets of a feminist practice has to be a refusal to require history, tradition, and lineage as the grounds of legitimation.

Thus, the next phase of my history as a writer came with the realization—and the willingness to speak it—that I was indeed very much involved with gender, with being a woman, and that my intellectual formation had much to do (socially, sociologically, psychologically, and aesthetically) with my gender. And I began to look at feminist theory and criticism and to use it to reflect on my own practice.

The feminist theory I first encountered was that of French, language-oriented, psychoanalytically based theorists, particularly Julia Kristeva, who examined the means by which language as a system not only reflects relations of power, gender, and authority, but creates, inscribes, and perpetrates them. At that point I understood female and feminine to be the same, and feminist as the banner under which to carry on a subversive writing practice. My work had for some time been concerned with polymorphousness, with the visual inscription of multilayered texts, which refused any single or simple linearity, while still working with a narrative line. For instance, a book I produced in 1984, which was the first self-conscious application of feminist theory to a printing/writing project, was *Against Fiction*, a project in which I worked on the long-standing question of my relation to tradition as well as a number of other concerns: the book begins with a reification of linearity in monumental form, then divides and subdivides the voice/line. This is a motif I used again in *Through Light and the Alphabet* in 1986, which was a book which took the dissolution of linearity to greater extreme, disintegrating it in the setting of a text which was fully polymorphous: that is, many options and levels of reading were inscribed within it, and the text itself was about the limits of language. Then, in 1989, a project called *The Word Made Flesh*, took the issue of materiality, the physical body of writing, written forms, to extreme—making the material of visual form resist any easy reading or closure. And that leads me to *The History of the/my Wor(l)d* (1989-90; reprinted 1995). This is also a "polymorphous" text, one in which a single, unified linearity is refused by format, by interweaving several layers of text which read against each other, using fragmentation and plurality, phrases which diffuse themselves, disperse against the organizing insistence of narrative lines. It is definitely about "auto-écriture," about writing oneself, myself, and about the processes of learning language. I am also, in this book, attempting to offer a number of challenges to feminist theory as I first learned it. No longer content with the formulations which gave me comfort and insight at that point, I am trying to make use of my own experience vis à vis language acquisition to rethink the idea of language as patriarchal, as the father, the law, and so forth, especially within the mythic family narrative with its figuring of woman as "lack" and the strongly oppositional definitions of gendered positions used by certain strains of feminist critical theory which associate women with "muteness, the body, and physicality" and men with "order, reason, and language."

The book's title reads: "History of the Word, of the World, of my Word, and of my World." The premise: that there is no world, only the knowing of it, the learning of it through experience, and that experience is largely accessible only through the mediation of language. Thus, I first wrote a literal, but clearly critical, synthetic narrative of the history of the world: *In the beginning was the world, nursed on the warm breast of chaos, fast following a night of hard publicity. Genetics produced the fullness thereof and a new cosmology emerged as the flight from innocence locked them out of the garden. The law came down the mountain and up our heritage dictating transgressions we were subject to perform.*

This is the master narrative of history which is counterposed against the personal narrative of memory. Thus the first opposition is between history/memory, other/self. And clearly the "master narrative" here also contains critiques, constructed out of biblical, historically authoritative language turned on itself.

The second line, the red line, is about my own experience of learning language, of learning in general, being formed as a little epistemological being, in my very strong relation to my mother. She was, for me, the source of all language, limit, law—she was science, literature, and decorum—order, imagination, and behavior. And the scraps of memory which are written here are intensely personal, sensual, and specific (by contrast to the generalized tone of the first narrative). *Love was a question asked nightly to induce sleep, insoluble conundrums dropped on the tongue or given like a gift through ears to cheeks. Literacy and intimacy collapsed in the quiet conversations stolen innocently from routine.*

The final level of text attaches to the images: the cliché images, cuts, which I found at the press where I print. The first premise of the book was going to be that the order in which the images were found would be the determining order of the narrative of the history of the world. In fact, I gave myself permission to manipulate them. They are, literally, clichés—that is, engraved cuts which serve as generic figures in many circumstances (some are more specific). What I do is to dislocate them with captions which combine historical specifics with personal specifics about my family life and history. This cut, for instance, was the fantasy image of my mother, who had been, in fact, a baton-twirling drum majorette from Downer's Grove, Illinois: *All American dream girl, long-legged, blue-eyed, blonde the huntress the muse the law and the word adored.* And this one recalls the Sunday school illustrations in Bible stories my siblings and I were subjected to (albeit not very frequently):
Six days or seven a brother and two sisters not pictured here were the stars of the nuclear configuration, fractured and split in the familiar pattern and spreading to the cardinal points of the psychic globe, raised in the old testament way, with natural light and harsh, swift judgment.

So, the book is about learning language as a means of coming into a knowledge of the world, i.e., one's self. It is both about the process of writing one's self and is itself an exercise in doing that. It is about tradition and history and memory, and about the relations to established and existing order in language.

Is it feminist? Yes, in so far as it is about questioning, examining those relations and those relations of power which are necessarily involved in the forms and uses of language. It challenges, for instance, the mode in which the meta-narrative of history, like the meta-level of language, is positioned to exclude, undermine, displace personal history and experience by its fallacy of claiming to be "the" narrative. My sense now (as opposed to ten or even five years ago) is that the issues of gender and language are more complex and subtle than I had imagined—more insidious and devious and also less able to be resolved by attention to or claims asserted by the gendered identity of the author. The fact of my being female is certainly central to all of my experience, but I refuse any essentialist determination of what that "femaleness" entails in either existence or writing practice. Similarly, I cannot, will not, claim that the "polymorphous" is a "female" or "woman's" form. It is a feminine form, by virtue of occupying a place in the system of rhetoric which deliberately sets itself in opposition to a masculine trope of unity, singularity, linearity.

Delivered as a talk at the Associated Writing Programs meeting, Denver, March 25, 1990, on a panel organized by Rachel Blau du Plessis.

Writing with Respect to Gender

I believed that writing would save me from being a woman.

That writing was capable of providing salvation and that my female gender was something from which to be saved were the convictions that compelled me to define my identity as that of a writer.

Memory goes back beyond language and into sensation—visual, tactile, specific; but writing came early, predictably bound up with the structuring of experience in mnemonic terms and the claim to a social identity. These two concepts combined the drive to represent experience to myself in manifest form and the desire to present myself to others as and through written work. This essay is an attempt to come to terms with the invisible, unrecorded context which engendered that work. By engendered I mean to invoke both the notion of something brought into being and something persistently defined with respect to gender as a formative aspect of identity. Such circumstances are not always self-evident—quite the contrary. I generally effaced them from those texts for which they now seem more and more relevant as the defining frame. In an effort to understand my relation to gender in language, and especially in the masking, revealing, concealing and dissimulating forms of written language I have used (I had originally thought of titling this "Writing the Unreadable"), I have decided to undertake to discuss these absent contexts and resituate the written texts of some of my book projects in their recalled and reconstructed pasts. All fiction, in the subjective sense, this new information is fabricated for a present purpose, as a platform from which to make the (always) new project of what it means to be writing, recognizing that the writing is always with respect to gender, and that gender is also always being invented. Having spent much of my life denying, as a writer, that I was gendered, it seems particularly fruitful to reinvestigate the terms and contexts which formulated and motivated the denial.

Aspiring to Form

Long before it was within my power to make books, print, or even produce one-of-a-kind works, I was writing. My earliest conviction was that a life was only lived insofar as it was rendered into language. By the onset of puberty, the composition of long prose works had become a near compulsion. In my twelfth year I wrote five novels, one of which exceeded 60,000 words. These were the fictional works which mimicked the forms by which I had been inspired—the long prose monuments of the 19th century. Steeped in the literature of the Brontës, George Eliot, Thomas Hardy, Charles Dickens, Henry James, and Jane Austen, my strongest motivation lay in the desire to reproduce the sustained narrative and descriptive prose of their work.

The aspiration to these forms had many aspects. The desire for an identity as a writer was primary, but the specifics of this narrative form allowed the writing of the life as interior monologue to be played out in prose form with oneself as the undisputed heroine. The sense of destiny, which was the rendering into words of the course of events, necessarily inscribed quotidian existence in a personal teleology whose terms were identifiable clichés. Thus the particulars of my relation to the ongoing "unfolding of the drama" of my childhood existence took on the represented shape offered by the phraseology of such archaic forms as "she couldn't know then . . ." or "and when she later learned." This introduced a split into my consciousness—a sense that the life being lived, the story being written about it, and my own understanding, were all distinctly different, discrete points of reference for my single consciousness. Redemption from the ordinary and from the temporal both lay in writing. More important, more fundamental, was redemption from gender. Writing would, could, I firmly believed, save me from being a woman, and that being a woman was something from which one both wanted to be saved and could be by concealment behind the mask of writing (which shielded one from exposure of one's gender). All of these things were incontrovertible facts as far as I was concerned.

The Letter
My first complete novel, written in the summer of 1964, was titled *The Letter*. The story unfolds as the first person narrative of a woman suffering an unrequited love. Using the device of a letter addressed to the man she believes has scorned her, she recounts an autobiographical tale in which her history of rejection, of orphaned helplessness and inadequacy, has established her as a victim: she is rejected by her parents, by her classmates, by this man. She is always the unwanted, unloved, unattractive figure.

Dear John,

You asked to hear my life story. It is rather long and involved, and so I have decided to write it down instead of telling it to you in person. I shall do my very best not to bore you, but I shall go into as much detail as I can remember so as to give you as accurate a picture of my past as possible. I have forgotten much about my younger years, but never-the-less I can give you a brief idea of them so that perhaps you can understand why I am the way I am today and why I am going to do what I am.

The decision of the narrator to write instead of speak reveals the displacing instinct. The control of the story in prose is a counter to its ephemerality and vulnerability as utterance. Recollection, though vague, will be explanatory, sufficient, adequate where presence has been found wanting. The clichés of the story were invoked to guarantee its believability—with such reliable formulae, how could it fail? "My father was wealthy." "I was not a pretty child." A beautiful sister was born to "bless the house with her merry laughter." Our heroine is "left more and more to myself" and is finally sent away to boarding school. There her best friend dies of a mysterious wasting illness in the middle of the night, the little bed is empty in the morning, etc. And so it goes— through to the final circumstance of her present romantic dilemma. In love with the man she addresses in her letter, she believes him to love her best friend and arch-rival, the beautiful Elizabeth, and so has resolved to put a violent end to her life.

Tabatha put down the feather pen and then folded the letter very carefully. Then she put on her coat, because it was chilly ... She walked out down the lane to John's house. She knocked and gave the letter to the butler.

Receiving the letter just in time to run after her, the man confesses his love as Tabatha approaches the cliff from which she intends to throw herself.

"Tabatha, my darling, come back. I love you, really I do, please, please come back."

She was at the edge now. "Another step and I'll jump, John."

He took that step, his arms out, pleadingly, tears falling freely now as she was knocked off balance by the wind.

"John, John, my darling. I want you, save me, please. Please save me, John. I love you and I want you. I'm sorry John, I'm sorry."

The she was knocked, as I said, off balance and she fell. John ran to save her but it was too late. He was in time only to see her dashed to bits on the rocks below.

Who speaks at the end, interjecting another voice into the story—claiming the place of the writing for one whose role is not fictive, but enunciative? It is an I that wishes to be present, foregrounded, articulate. And this voice finds its arena of activity in the non-occulted position of another manuscript from that year and the following. This was a real experience, a relationship whose terms were also set by the forms of prose, but whose initial rendering in written form attempted to subvert the determining shape of those inherited forms.

Amy (1964)

I write this now as a child. I write not as an adult, from a child's point of view, but as a child from a child's point of view . . . .

I was writing just awhile ago and I put down my pen to read what I had written. It had no feeling, it was cold. I used to be able to write with expression and warmth. I could express my moods through the characters and I enjoyed it. It seemed to me that I wrote to exist, it was important to put down my thoughts and ideas. All that was less than three months ago, just three short months. But that was then and this is now and lots of things have changed and lots of things are different. A great deal has happened to alter the course of my life.

Sometimes I wonder about the endless writing, the brown notebooks, then I remember that they are so that I do not forget. Then I wonder why.

I was twelve when I wrote those words, now almost thirty years ago. The voice speaks out to me, sharp and direct, almost embarrassingly forthright, in spite of the melodramatic tone. It was my first novel in my own voice, serious, to the point, and motivated by a desire to put into written form the traumas of my early adolescence.

Written to record and exorcise a relationship whose tentative sexuality had awakened yearnings I would wait years to realize, this work gave a direct account, in my clear twelve-year-old tone, of the beginnings of my relationship with my girlfriend, Amy. Two years older than I, she had moved into a house on my street and captured my imaginings, projections, and affections. The cravings for intimacy which I had never managed to fulfill in a childhood friendship were now answered on the cusp of adolescence. For the entire of my teenage years, Amy would dominate the emotional landscape, and the consequences of the taboos under which our interaction took its form would have direct manifestation in my writing.

This first account, some sixty pages, recounted the circumstances under which we met and under which we constructed the mechanism through which the relationship would be played out. We adopted a form of storytelling in which we acted parts, a mode of interaction I had used with other friends in order to permit intimacies dictated by the narrative we unfolded which would never have been allowed to us otherwise. Amy and I, slowly at first, shifted the verbal features of the "plotting" which we did into a play legitimating physical affection.

Having no developed sense of sexuality at that age, (I was a twelve-year-old whose innocence was even more intact than my virginity), I had no sense at the outset that anything we were involved in would be perceived as deviant. The intensity of pleasure provided by the exchange of embraces, words, caresses and increasing closeness were troubled at the outset only by Amy's fickleness and high-handed tendency to dismiss me with the callous whimsy of a Proustian heroine. The relationship transported me into realms of psychic stimulation beyond my wildest imaginings. We concealed from our parents, friends and my siblings any hint of the full extent of our interaction, but more, we concealed it from ourselves. In the guise of characters, we indulged in endless hours of proximity, but never undressed together, never touched each other's genitals, and never admitted, face to face, that it was in fact we who were involved with each other.

The games of gender which we played worked through the dynamics of our occulted relationship. At the outset Amy held the power which she played through a male role and I was the passive, naive, and receptive female partner. As the relationship evolved, our parts fragmented, and we each found, created, acted out aspects of the struggles for control, submission, domination and escape which were the forces at work between us. The templates for relations, once romantic and melodramatic, turned sadistic. The story lines involved incest, homosexuality, and other twists which gave overt form to the conflicts each of us internalized.

Gender, in this relationship, had always been a masquerade—a pretense acted out through stereotypes and rote, through posturing and caricature and assumption. But the relationship itself brought down the wrath of my mother. In a powerful exercise of judgment she gave me to understand that there was something profoundly wrong in my intimacy with Amy. At an age in which the concepts of sexuality and sexual identity were embryonic in my psyche, when the exercise of affection and sensual communication had only sprung into being in the most innocent of forms, I had already learned to conceal it, and learned that the price of exposure was punishment. We were two or three years into our story lines and plots by the time my mother's limit had been reached. From that point on the relationship continued under the stigma of a perversion. Guilt set the prevailing tone and all sexual and emotional exchanges warped in reference to it. Writing was encoded into the voices of characters. Neither Amy nor I ever wrote as ourselves after my first account. From age twelve to age eighteen I lived in this fantasy life, with all its replete satisfactions and profound frustrations, deeply fearful of discovery, and yet bewildered. The scaffolding of concealment was much more elaborate than anything it could have concealed, given our innocence, our reticence, our modesty. By the time I left home, went to school, and eventually, California, my relationship to language had become complicated by my commitment to concealment.

Dark and Fragile

Between 1970 and 1972 my writing took the form of a purgative. It was fragmentary, spasmodic, unstructured, and without form. Any attempt to shape a story, provide continuity, or narrative, was blocked by my absolutely overwhelming phobic conviction that to provide a clear gestalt would violate my privacy. Language was abstracted beyond the clear sense of reference. This was not something I controlled, but something I discovered—as with a spastic hand attempting normal cursive writing, I found myself continually aware that the language I produced was not communicative. Poetic, suggestive, yes, but the power of vernacular speech, of direct account, was impossible as was anything even remotely approaching closure in the form of a narrative.

None of this work made it into print, or even, into the public arena. I sent the manuscript, some hundred pages of incomprehensible, densely figured writing, into the world in a manila envelope and received it back, unmarked, from whatever publisher I had approached. But in 1972, at age 20, in the context of a class at California College of Arts and Crafts, I printed my first book, *Dark*. (See illustration, page 8.) The expression of puerile, infantile sexuality was played out in the continual use of labile sounds and rhythmic structures, of images dense with moisture, seepage, and leaking linked to the bodies of these child-figures. Bound in red velvet and hand printed, with stone lithographs, the object had a look and feel reminiscent of Charles Kingsley or Christina Rosetti—a water-babies, goblin market volume. Inarticulatable in any adult form or any adult expression, gender came through as androgyny. The form of the bat-elf, Dark, was unidentifiable in clear terms as anything but a loose libidinal force, hissing and seductive, perverse and mischievous, mercurial and indeterminate.

"Kneel slowly for the ceremony I detest in you," Dark hissed demeaningly to swollen Six, and indicated by the brazing rod the spot upon the ground. They saw it now, well trampled dust to form a matted soil, from which the emanation was a root, thrust outward to reveal the part which should lie hidden. Its white skin especially contrasted the fiber's torsion with deep shadowing so that elongate Six's fingers found their way with ease among its contours, until it grasped the pupal hand with likewise coil and they nestled manual spaces as they grappled wrestling for Dark's disdained delight.

What I knew of sex had been learned from a groping, in-the-dark, much-repressed, and almost-unacknowledged relationship with a young man in my group household. What I knew of gender had progressed not at all—from my perspective the only model for the feminine was Victorian. I believed in blushing under-attentive gazes, in silently hoping for love, and that relationships were destiny and the most sweeping force in a woman's life. In my female role I believed, I had no chance of and no hope for control, and sexuality took the form of submission as if to the forces of fate. This first boyfriend was remorselessly promiscuous, and I was naively devastated until the wise counsel of a more experienced young woman friend convinced me to expand my horizons. By the time *Dark* was written, I had had more sexual experience, but no sense of my own sexuality. Gender carried cliché burdens of role, limitations, and restrictions, but provided no insights whatsoever, especially into its own formation. Writing was still the way out of gender, but language was only oozing out of the stopped up passages still blocked by traumatic adolescence.

The profound isolation of these teenage years ended, not when I "found love" but when I managed to break free of another long relationship which had replicated all the worst aspects of my early connection to Amy—exclusivity, loss of boundaries, regressive introversion—

The character Oh-Oh, invented in 1973-74, when I didn't have access to a printing press. Oh-Oh lived in a dome moved according to her will while she remained in its contained secure interior going on with the various activities of her life—as shown here.

and had few of the virtues of satisfaction for either mind or sensual appetite. Termination of that early relationship marked a transition into adult social behavior—or, at least, its possibility. From 1975 I began to function in the world, in a scene, to recuperate some of the developmental experience of gendered social existence which had been skipped.

On Not Working Out of Tradition

In 1975, at the age of twenty-three, I surfaced into a scene filled with young male poets. I had a job, part-time, at a print shop in California set up by the National Endowment for the Arts to provide printing services to the literary community. I worked as staff typesetter for almost two years, during which time I was exposed to poetry across the spectrum—from verses depicting unicorns on the lawn to the work of those writers who saw themselves as the keepers of the new flame of American poetics. My education took place on two fronts: the reading and typesetting of many of these texts, and the interactions with my colleagues, almost all young men. It was at this point that my sense of my own identity became linked, inevitably, to issues of gender in ways which would become increasingly overt, even through the thick fog of unconsciousness and denial in which I continued to exist. Gender had been, always, something to be denied since it only meant inadequacy.

A complicated series of interactions on a personal level brought the work I was doing out of the closet and onto the margins of the arena in which Work was being defined in this community. The social connections to this scene meant that I gave readings, went to parties, had affairs and relationships with the group. But my Otherness in terms of writing was evident. I wasn't fully uncomfortable with this, since for the first time I had at least a sense that I was perceived as a writer as well as the fact that I had a social life among peers unlike any I had had before.

I produced several books in the context of this scene and these relations. The first of these, *26 '76 Let Hers* (which had the subtitle, *Not A Matter of Permission)*, was written in the gap between my desire for narrative form and the prohibitions against it imposed by this group. The book had been inspired by a trip to Los Angeles, and came into being as the bare bones skeletal remnants of the story of that journey. Like several of my works of that period, the book requires a gloss to the text which is longer and more dense than the text itself. There were thematic issues of gender in this work as well since I had stayed with a couple in which the father/husband assertively took the position that all of life took place only in language. The wife/mother was having an affair with a painter, and sat at the dinner table with her foot in the crotch of her lover while her husband held forth on the defining power and character of language. The woman, claiming to be unable to speak, to be only marginally literate, manipulated one social situation after another through means which were powerful demonstrations of the effect of non-verbal communication. I was witness, and in my own tight, dense, rigidly controlled and closely-edited language, inscribed the structure of those events, her role, my understanding of this and other things visual and verbal, in this book. The force of repression was such that the book was virtually inaccessible and unreadable so abbreviated, so encoded, was its language. The pleasure of narrative was blocked at every point—its production, consumption, its extensions and its closures equally suspect under the new regime. On the other hand, the language I was using had, at least, come out from the baby-talk infantile sing-song of the early prose pieces of which *Dark* was but one example among many.

The patronizing attitude with which I found myself treated by men just a few years my senior began to irk me profoundly. I felt angry at not being fully recognized, granted status as a writer, especially considering that I had, as far as I knew, been writing at least as long as any of them. I was also concerned not to lose my social and sexual viability by becoming too strong a rival or too independent an entity. I still labored under the delusion that it would be through the offices of a man that I would come to prominence or achieve success. Men were in the world, promoters, networkers, and women, I believed, were the raw material from which they were capable of fashioning a consumable and promotable product. In my limited experience I had seen no women who had been able to achieve success without the support and endorsement of men. If I dreamed, with mistaken grotesqueness, of finding my Leonard Woolf, my Robert Browning, my Svengali, I had certainly never imagined the effects of exile and excommunication which would come when I asserted both sexual and intellectual independence from the group which had provided my first social identity as a writer.

On my birthday in May, 1977, disgusted with being treated like a newcomer novitiate with no background or experience, I put into print a selection of writings from 1971, *Fragile*. The complex interiority of the language in that work was opened up by my giving the sentences and fragments the form of poetry on the page. I spent my birthday in ritual ceremony, printing, using the authority of that skill to render the late adolescent manuscript legitimate. Little did I realize the consequences of that either—the fact that I would put my own work into print, unwilling to submit my writing to the editorial judgment of these men for their independent journals, would incur their deep resentment. That, combined with the fact that I began to elaborate the visual format of my texts, marked me as immodest and beyond the pale of the codes of conduct for a woman in that circle.

Meanwhile, I was preparing the elaborate manuscript that was to be *From A to Z.* This book took the form of pseudo-bibliography or anthology. Twenty-six poets were represented, each a parody of someone I had known in that scene, each described, ranked according to age and income, given a profile with respect to education, publishing record and career potential. Marginal notes and endnotes filled in details of the scene through excerpts of gossip, letters, reviews etc.—all of this fabricated, but loaded with enough specifics that I felt sure the *roman à cléf* aspect would be seen through immediately. While parodic, the styles of most writers were meant to be recognizable, though the themes in these works were all written as expressions of libidinal energy. Sexualized, and rather vulgar in character and tone, the work was meant to pique, if not directly offend. A running narrative through the book described the incidents in a flirtation and an unrequited crush. This was the first time I had allowed myself to put prose into print since entering that poetry scene, to let a sequence of full sentences describing events stand without fragmentation, erasure, pulverization. The relationship described was one I had lived through, of course, and in part the book had been done as a last gasp bid for attention from the object of my crush. This failed, fortunately, I realize in retrospect.

The book was without precedent. The use of the structured page as a means of organizing the text, the closed set of interrelationships of textual elements, the parodic anthologizing of contemporary literature, and the pulp form of the narrative line—all of these elements had been engineered to describe the full field of activity of the poetry scene in a

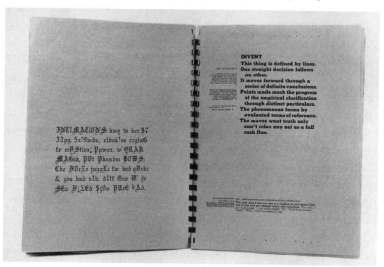

From A to Z, 1977, letterpress on kraft paper, 9" x 12".

book format which made innovative use of layout and design. Several hours after I finished the book I left for a two year trip abroad, certain that the thinly concealed identities of people I knew would be quickly perceived, and that the consequences would be socially disastrous. That turned out not to be the case. My sense of the importance and impact of the project was grossly exaggerated.

Constricted Fictions

Against Fiction was my attempt to work out all of my various ambivalences about narrative and fiction. For four years, from 1977 to 1981, I produced fragments which were almost irrepressible bursts of prose, figured and abstract, which came in fits and starts. They might suggest a narrative line, but had no continuity. I blocked any story structure, refusing such conventions as unacceptable. When the critical mass of pieces reached a certain point, peaking with my frustration at not being able to find some means by which to give the project shape as a book, I took all the scraps and bits of writing and pasted them into a long document according to theme. At this stage the subtitle "Organized Affinities" emerged. In the time since I had begun to produce the fragments, to the point where the project emerged as a printed book, I spent two years travelling, a year working, and a year in graduate school. Still deeply resistant to feminist theory, I nonetheless began to have an inkling that the polymorphous proliferation of voices in this work, the tensions and conflicts with conventions and forms, and my continual (and continually repressed) desire to unify the whole into a narrative frame were all related to issues of gender. In print form the work borrowed the attributes of a tabloid, with headlines proclaiming themes and events in an attempt to counter some of the abstract character of the prose.

The compulsion to erase closed figures, to keep any narrative line repressed, continued, I believe, largely because of the lingering fear of revelation which was the residual effort of my censoring my relationship with Amy. The force of repression had an emotional charge—clear statement meant disclosure, and disclosure meant detection, punishment, guilt. Sexuality was similarly occulted in that period and charged with negativity: To admit to desire would require that I admit, not only my desire for Amy, which was innocent enough, but the complexities of the emotional dynamics with that more fundamental figure, my mother. My feelings for my mother had always been complicated by a

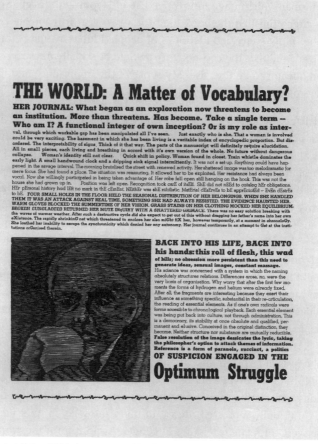

Against Fiction, 1984, letterpress and linoleum block images, 13″ x 16″.

sense of her taboos and boundaries, internalized as blocks against direct expression. Prose, the discursive form of (family) romance and description, risked revealing too much. But the repression was reinforced intellectually by my renewed (continued) relationship with the poetry scene to which I had returned after a two-year absence abroad. In that group (of what are now known as Language poets) discursive prose, real narrative, was so negatively stigmatized that to employ its forms was simply to invite disdain and dismissal. I had received these anyway by calling attention to myself with bold immodesty, display and flash activity of images and type and challenging the authority of the literary text by demonstrating its dependence upon the embodied form of materiality.

Meanwhile, almost surreptitiously, I had produced a prose novel *Greece and Good Behavior* in which I tried to work through my deep compulsions to behave in superlative compliance with norms and expectations. I remained, however, ashamed of this work, ashamed of having given in to the direct storytelling and clear prose. I wrote this piece and rewrote it in tandem with the *Against Fiction* project, but never let it into print or even into the sight of any of my colleagues, peers, companions. An excerpt:

"We adjourned upstairs for coffee. Marinos wanted us to see the hotel, his room. Cold corridor, sterile by its simplicity, lack of imagination, lack of concession to anything but function. Concrete, stucco, made to accommodate as many rooms as possible, to allow maximum occupancy in the space—a string of cell-like spaces off the short-seeming straight of the corridor. His own room—sink in it, hot water, boastfully indicated, and a heater, tv—was crowded, stuffed, really not much bigger than the bed on which he sat and the doctor sat, chubby little body assuming a position of comfort, curled up, watching the television. His nap after lunch a habit too, in Marinos' warm room, on Marinos' soft bed. We sat, being proper, exaggeratedly formal. They told us we were as bad as Greek girls—meaning too good, too proper. We agreed, laughing to ease the strain which didn't cease as we didn't yield anything. Became only more rigid, more distinct, more separate. Of course they tried to put the make on us and of course we refused. Lisa antagonistic, me slow, restrained by her resistance as much as by my own judgment, because that was not clear. We split. They wanted us to come back for dinner, for lunch the next day, any day, any time—we just refused everything, quick, non-committal, and took off back through the windy ruins to our cave house, private space."

My mother died just as I began to print *Against Fiction*. The project was delayed for a year. There was no catharsis, no relief, just loss. Over time and only very slowly would I come to feel a reorientation to the terms of judgment which had been hers, as I had internalized them. My sublimated affections, desires, and longings for her transferred into a highly cathected and totally unexpressed, unacknowledged, relationship with my mentor in graduate school. By the time *Against Fiction* was done (it took 800 hours of printing time) I was complexly involved in an interaction which consumed much energy and emotion but had no overt form. This chaste, unspoken, and obsessive relationship kept me from any but the most superficial of other flirtations. Of the many fic-

tions I wrote in that time (from 1982 through 1986) *Final Fiction,
The Blank-Minded Murder, The Yellow Dog,* and *Mark and the Medium,*
most were written to engage the attention of this man about whom
I also kept a diary of dreams.

Unnamed. Unnameable. Something about which I cannot talk publicly, nor address privately, dominates my life . . . By the very fact that it cannot, will not, be spoken it becomes the reference behind every word, statement, expression. The negotiation of desire with the object is effaced. The driving force for speaking is the further obfuscation of the very real central focus, more absent than any void, more present than any substance . . . And the dreams? Feb. 6, 1981—Of school and of B. He is giving me texts, more and more texts. Dense, complicated, satisfying texts. Involvement, stimulation, interest. These works are the substance and vehicle of our relationship. Then, second segment, warts appear around my lips. Horrible sense of physical repulsiveness, unattractiveness. I am obsessed, worried that he will reject me, find me ugly. One of the largest warts full of water bursts when I touch it with my teeth and collapses, an ugly sack of brown skin.

As in all stories of schoolgirls, I carried the book of dreams
around with me for months, thinking I would leave it for him,
hand it to him, find a resolution in a confessionary moment. Text
was to be the means to intimacy, I believed, letting it function really as displacement. What I craved, after all, was not so much intimacy as safe distance. Gender had, in fact, become embattled territory, though I was unconscious of the ways in which I was acting
out my fears about what was at stake. What I wished to risk least
of all was my autonomy and having few skills for negotiating compromise, I remained, instinctively, committed to an all or nothing
policy with respect to engagement.

Mind Massage rendered explicit many of these issues. Written in
1985 in Paris, it was produced only as a unique book, handlettered,
handdrawn, handbound, it was the story of a woman artist who
sells her soul (what else?) in return for the promise of success. Her
devil is the male producer of whom I had fantasized in my youth,
and she barters with her talents, seducing him with her telepathic
powers and gifts. The book took the form of a main text and off-
shoots. Tales she told became books in their own right, and all were
contained in a box so that the reader could handle the tale of

Eusabia and the Victorians or *Suburban Miracle* independently. At the end of the book, when the male comes to claim his prize, the heroine cheats him through a loophole. She asserts that retaining her own consciousness is essential if her relation of beholdenness to him is to be recognized as significant. In asserting her continued consciousness as part of the fulfillment of their bargain, she retains her own autonomy. The moment of their first meeting:

"Painfully young and slim, he carried himself erect. His maleness spit itself on the carpet. Cheap perfume. She recoiled from his presence but held her ground. This was not the sort of challenge she was likely to avoid. He carried a briefcase. She meant business. He had the look of an entrepreneur and the posture of a punk. Kid vice president. Community affairs manager. Junior chamber of commerce. Her judgment jumped ahead of her. He squinted. She knew what he wanted to offer. She had asked for it. This was the critical image of a dream which would come true. Why fight it? The contract in his hand required blood. She knew that. Hers was in her head. Her body was nothing to him. She had barely used it. Gradual decay had denied even any shattering experience to mark its decline. His eyebrows raised the questions. She had only one chance to answer. The conclusion had been foregone. The pact had been made by the meeting. Her admission was concession. She yielded her consent. He snapped open the case in his hand. All she had hoped for in the grossest terms. She gave in to her worst instincts. He offered her every advantage and took it."

I had the sense at least not to give the book-object to the man who had inspired it as he, like the other lovers of that year, became objectified in prose. Though I lifted my self-censorship in composing *Mind Massage*, I kept intact the harsh codes of concealment which tortured the form of my writing for the long, many-voiced dense passages of the accounts of sexual and intellectual promiscuity recounted in *Paris Sights*.

"My small rooms. The cats. Heat. Putting down his coat. He will not look around. My space. Now my apartment is already like my body. Not violently but actually. Artwork. He won't look at the walls. Why this avoidance? Worried to have to decide? Make a statement of evaluation? Into the bedroom.

His attack on my body is extremely sensitive. He pulls my sweater free from my belt, lifts my shirt and reaches for my breasts. Standing face to face I am keenly aware of the lace which separates his fingers from my skin.

He has to go pick up his daughter so we will not make love, he says, only, can we just lie down a moment. Yes. And then, on the smooth, slick surface of my sleeping bag, will I take off my clothes. My shirt and sweater. My pants. Will I take off my clothes so he can look at me?

Backward motion.

My phobia. Seeking its release. All the agony, all the restraint, all the long-term, stored-up, built up sense of my own inadequacy precipitates itself violently through me. I take off my clothes. I take off my clothes so he can look at me."

I thought I had left the domain of Language writing in the course of doing *Against Fiction*. But I had only slightly transgressed all kinds of categories of the good behavior to which I thought myself addicted. Breaking free of the dominance of the males central to that scene cost me the entire social circle and much pain. And I found I had internalized their prohibitions as my own taboos against certain modes of writing. It wasn't really until I left Berkeley that I gave myself full permission to try to write as I wanted. Before leaving I made a letterpress project in which I undertook to play out more fully the disintegration of linearity which had been implied and begun in the structure of the pages of *Against Fiction*. I had by this time determined that I had been expelled from the poetry scene for using visual means, for printing independently, for being interested in prose and pulp forms, for following my own theoretical line, and for ceasing to act out my sexuality within the social limits of the scene.

Through Light and the Alphabet (1986) posed visuality and flesh as the material that escapes language, not according to an opposition of intellect and sensuality nor of the masculine linguistic and the feminine body, rather, in the Kristevan formulation of a dia-

All our conversations were in language and according to conventions the others could be party to, but this one took off on its own trajectory to mind the business being left out of the accounts. The world was too amorphous for repose inside of sweet articulation. The various intensities of a single tone haunted the retina with figments of a wild imagination. A

Through Light and the Alphabet, 1986, letterpress, 13" x13", opening.

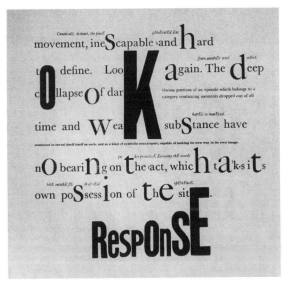

movement, ineScapable and hard to define. LooK again. The deep cOllapse Of dar viscous portions of an episode which belongs to a category containing moments dropped out of all time and Wea substance have continued to reveal itself itself as such, and as a kind of symbolic counterpart, capable of making its own way in its own image. nO beariNg on the act, which taks its own poSsession of the site.

ResPOnSE

Final page of *Through Light and the Alphabet*, 1986, showing the development of the typographic themes.

logue between the semiotic and symbolic orders of experience. In this work material, specifically the material form of typography, was used as a means to open the linear sequence of the text, itself about the limits of language, and allow meaning to proliferate on the page.

Three years later (1989), in a counterpart piece, *The Word Made Flesh*, I used the visual materiality of language as both the referent for the text and as the mechanical means to prevent easy reading, prevent the achievement of linguistic value, and to continually block and frustrate the reader's progress through insistence on the visual form of the words on the page.

In two recent projects, thematic concerns in the text and the structuring principles in the page were determined by a direct engagement with gender issues. The breakdown of linear form, the use of fragmentary elements, the use of clichés about women and their lives borrowed from found imagery and from pulp and mass media sources, and an inquiry into the nature of feminine subjectivity form the basis of these works.

The History of the/my Wor(l)d (1990), as I have elaborated elsewhere, is a polymorphous text whose multi-layers interweave themes of history and memory. The main narrative line offers a feminist critique of the meta-narrative of history. The smaller, more intimate red-printed line which constantly erupts through it is the force of personal memory taking issue with Lacanian-influenced feminist theory in its assignment of a masculine and exclusively patriarchal role to language. The premise of this work was that there was no world, only the knowing of it in and through language, and that the knowing of one's self was parallel to this, a construction of and in language through its acquisition. Learning language was, for me, intimately bound up in my relationship with my mother, and with the sublimation of sexuality into an exchange of texts, between us, and in the physical circumstances of those exchanges. The "cliché" images, found photo-

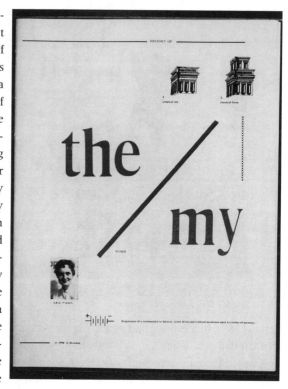

The History of the/my Wor(l)d, 1990, letterpress with found images from Bow and Arrow Press, 10" x 13".

engravings, served to make their own history through a sequence which is explained by captions which layer specifics from my family's past onto specifics suggested by the images themselves. My primary assertion was to claim a place for a feminine subject whose personal narrative of memory continually interrupts the narrative production of history.

In *Simulant Portrait* I played out the fantasy of making a history for a feminine subject, for a simulant created in the 21st century whose history has to be made for her in order to allow her the replete dimensions of character necessary for full interaction with humans in intimate and social relationships. The simulant, a programmed cyborg, is attracted to the worst trashy biographical narratives, and is interested in writing a version of a life filled with the satisfactions and shortcomings of melodrama. The book was produced on a low-level Macintosh, to give it the quality of mass production and generic technology.

I realize now that all the books and writing I have done have been produced with respect to gender. Engendered. Made in the constraints of parameters which work through the conceptual limits of my sense of my identity in what are necessarily gendered terms. However incidental, the work reflects these limits, these internal structures of the possible and impossible, the censorable and the taboo, the permitted and the prohibited with respect to language, to thematics, to form.

I am surprised, looking back over this piece now that it is written, to find that it reads very much like those 19th century sources of my original inspiration in which the heroine's travails are recounted with a fake ingenuousness, and her lapsed control combines with assaults on her virtue to motivate the narrative. Much is still repressed in this piece —which is after all just a sketch, a text which hovers between autobiographical anecdote and critical account.

I arrive at this point with only one clear conviction—that to come to terms with the social shape of the feminine as I experience it requires that I continually investigate the way my own writing negotiates the relation between the orders of language and culture and the realms of my life as a subject. The struggle remains: to become the subject of my own enunciation, subject of my own desire. And it is in the understanding of that condition as always ongoing and in formation to which the writing seems to provide at least some access.

This paper was prepared for the Women and Society *Seminar at Columbia University, March 9, 1992.*

Narratology: Genre Fiction and New Writing

Narratology, *which appeared in book form in May 1994*, was the resolution of both a writing issue and a book format issue, as is generally the case with my books. I had a thematic in mind in terms of the text: the relation between so-called "lived experience" (this term will be elaborated upon in a moment) and the received clichés about the nature of the narrative according to which I thought my life would be lived (mainly acquired reading standard fiction from *Little Women* to *Clarissa* to *Jane Eyre* etc.). But I also had a structure in mind—I had wanted for some time to do a book which had a varied page size, one in which the revelation of the text elements would occur through covering/uncovering portions of a page in turn. This is hardly a complicated idea, nor really even a very original one, but I wanted to try this in a way which would be fairly simple in format, regular (I like regularly structured books rather than irregular ones), and would integrate with the text/image elements in a clearly readable way.

Narratology: The stories according to which the possibility of living a life gained access to the psychic theater staging the imaginary event as real.

Sometime in the last couple of years, critical theory embraced the concept of "lived experience." This was intended as a guerilla action to upstage theory, to challenge the concepts of "the mediated" "constructed" and "semiotic" models of experience (and representation) which had become the evil dominatrices and terminators of academic writing. This assertion of the Lived was that it was real, direct, available—and more authentic than all this structuralist, poststructuralist and deconstructive blah blah. This was a sharp slap in the face of the artifices of criticism which had split the subject, robbed us of our small pleasures and personal feelings by holding us up with the nasty weapon of ideology, binding and gagging us to our place in the code. Right? The quest for real experience, however, took on all the chimerical mythic quality of the old heroines of fiction whose quest for the virtuous path of the lived became the machine which would supposedly drive the narrative right out of the thorny wood of fiction. Say huh?

At first I thought the text would simply be bifurcated so that the "lived experience" was one identifiable strain and the "mediated" or "clichéd" representation was another. That way what was initially visible on each page could be questioned or contradicted by what got revealed in the turning. As the writing proceeded and I found there were problems in this strict distinction lived/mediated I had to give up this idea. The concept of a dialogue within the text thus began to focus on the way the chunks of prose would interweave with each other.

The driving rain beat hard, soaking the thin cloth of her frock, and raced in icy rivulets down her back, inside her clothes. Where in this dark night was she to find help? Comfort? Or even—safety? The chill she felt as she spoke that word to herself did not come from the cold wind, but from the realization that she was not to speak what was on her mind, not now, not here, and not maybe to anyone, ever. The rules had changed, she knew that, and the fierceness of the storm—her hair whipped violently across her face—was nothing to the force of vengeful anger she knew would be brought down upon her head for her transgressions. If only she could get back inside the narrative and stay there.

So, there I was, set to search out the terms on which to write my lived experience. Obedient to the critical temper of the times. I was to be the genuine heroine of all literature, now slipping out of the narrative closure and into the continually unfolding tale of my own making, unmaking, in which all which is representation slips from view, and the language only unpacks a suitcase. But that, it turns out, contains only tricks and instructions for sleight of hand.

The page/signature structure was a little tricky because I was varying the page size in two directions and I wanted everything to be able to be secured in the binding. I like my books to lie really flat, so that is also a consideration I have to take into account from the outset of the design. I am a pretty bad binder, but I like to do the sewing part of binding. I knew I would have to get a consultation since it wasn't really possible for me to come up with something suitably professional on my own. But working out the sequence of pages as a set of signatures I could do. The idea was for the pages to have a neat alternation of sizes, one which did not feel overly chaotic. I divided the page in two directions. There

were four even horizontal strips or "zones," and there were two vertical zones of uneven size—a fat chunk toward the spine which was
about two-thirds the full width and a thin, one-third, column on the
outside of the page. This was the conceptual "grid" of the book. Then
the pages all conformed to one of these zone sizes: a full sheet, a two-
thirds, or a horizontal banner. These alternate in a regular sequence so
that the partial sheets are always in pairs between the full sheets. The
horizontal banners, of which there are four, stagger down the book as
one moves through it from top to bottom—this gives the book its physical momentum since this is the element which marks one's progression
through the signatures.

> *A narratological bias against the truth upstages the ordinary offerings of a*
> *supposedly lived experience, polluting the psychological atmosphere with*
> *the smokescreen pleasures of received knowledge. The fantasmatic projection*
> *of the real plays out its lines with all the seductive facility of tales told in the*
> *tabloids—signifying everything.*

The typography posed its own dilemmas. I knew that I wanted to use
the Mac to produce the type and to then go to film and polymer plates.
The reason for this, aside from wanting to experiment with the polymer, was that I wanted to put images into the pages and also, there were
specific aspects of the way type can be manipulated in Quark (the layout program) which I had become attached to—in particular, "stretch to
fit"—my all time favorite Quark feature. More about this in a minute.
But since I also wanted to be able to distinguish different "tones" in the
text I had to decide on two faces which could be used for contrast. At
first I thought I would design a face—something along the lines of
Melior. The aesthetic considerations were that it should be able to be
slanted, condensed, stretched, and emboldened without becoming
grotesque. For this I thought a face that was squarish in its curves would
be the best bet. Thanks to my buddy Gino Lee (a truly great type designer and bezier manipulator) I had access to Fontographer. I gave it a shot.
And boy did I come up with some ugly letterforms! I found the whole
business of where to put the defining curve points and the way to wiggle those curves around to be a major operation. For me to make a typeface suitable for anything more than joke stationery was going to be a
six-month project at least—and no guarantee it would be anything but
lousy. Later I realized that Zuzanna Licko's Matrix had all the features I

was looking for, but that was after I did the book. I settled on Franklin Gothic and my favorite old Stymie, this time in a Memphis variety. I always feel like I know what I'm doing with Stymie since I've used it so many times in so many ways, and I like it for its stolid sturdiness. Each to their own, I guess—type preferences are just like any others, but I'm uncomfortable with those precious Italian faces that are all finely serifed and delicately curved whereas a Stymie feels dependable and unfussy by contrast.

Lived experience turned out to be an elusive heroine if ever there was one, slipping away through the tropes of narration with all the expertise of an old fashioned psychoanalytic subject always gone from exactly the place of articulation. The notion of the Lived seemed to invoke a politics of writing—a writing predicated on a binaristic opposition between the body and the social, the real and the symbolic, the transparent and the mediated. As if there were a recoverable actuality which could be nailed down with language without transformation into or through the linguistic medium. I began:

Child of the baby boom, raised for science and industry in the norm of the nuclear family. An urban upbringing in public institutions and the home neighborhood took off the edges of innocence while sheltering her from the real drama of the age, the suburban nightmare spreading its formulaic patterns onto the vast blur of the landscape. School promoted her abilities and research became the studied focus of her young life while the writing piled up in secret, notebooks filled and hidden in a separate life of the mind and soul. Growing out of the home environment into the embraces of an adolescent tale written by Colette and performed in costume she escaped and then went on the college.

Once I had the typeface picked out I started playing with layout. This was already somewhat prescribed by the page size divisions. Because I am used to thinking in letterpress terms I thought that interlining two different "colors" of type should be done line by line. In fact, in Quark, the best thing to do is to overlay two different text boxes and then make sure that the point size and interline spacing in the two boxes are all multiples of each other (12 pt. type on 18 pt. spacing and 6 pt. on 24 for instance so that both end up as 30). That way there was no "creep" as the type moved down the page. This all sounds obvious in retrospect, of course. Because of the "stretch to fit" aspect (really a combination of horizontal manipulation and point size variation—a several step process, not a single feature) I could make letters four inches high, three inches wide, or any other shape my little heart desired. This was a HUGE thrill. After all the years of trying to find point sizes to suit my geometrically defined desires (that is—something that would spell out a certain word and make it a certain size, width, and color) in the dusty musty drawers of the print shop I could now manufacture these elements at will.

It didn't work. There was no real in this, all the referents slipped away as fast in this rendering as in any other—and the pure banality of language did little to justify recording the pure banality of experience. The lived must not be this accounting, this simple statement of experience. I had the sense that it was instead about a form of liberation—from language, conventions which were themselves identified as both instrument and locus of political and sexual repression. The lived, then, had something to do with nature. Which translated into individual experience meant, I guess, orgasms. The pure experience of the body. The body. As if it could float free of the vile facts of culture. This was deteriorating rapidly. My sense of the lived was looking more and more like a commercial for feminine hygiene products—fresh rain, morning dew, a light breeze on clean skin. More to the point, this was as facile a misrepresentation as any other form—and writing those phrases I felt myself continually repressing another version of my life, one lived in and through fantasy:

She is always a princess, banished by her family to learn humility, constantly under observation, using her inherent superiority as a means of distinguishing herself from her brutally common surroundings. Sent to a boarding school she suffers at the hands of a cruel mistress and stern warden, clinging in a hard attic bed to the hand of her one true friend, an invalid, who dies. Sent home she finds herself outcast in the family, discarded by an ugly, arrogant mother, ignored by a father caught up in business affairs. Her mother dies, tragically, in an accident and tears flow beside the bed for all that could have been.

Interlining—alternating differing weights or type or different faces either within lines or in alternate lines is a typographic trope I had used since I had first started playing around with handset type in Betsy Davids' class at CCAC in 1972. I have always liked the effects one gets using black and white printing to make "color" on a page. For a while I contemplated printing *Narratology* in various pigments—but the difficulty of this (all the type was on a single plate and separating the lines would have required two plates for each chunk) combined with my basic preference for simpler solutions (see image page 31). The look of this book is more letterpress than Macintosh—and I'm glad about that. I didn't want all the design features of *Wired* or *Omni* or any of the rest of the stock in trade of electronic aesthetics. The computer manipulations are a definite part of this work, but they are subtle.

> Well, so, maybe I could attempt to work between these narratives—the ones according to which I thought, earnestly believed, my life would be lived, and some version of the real. I would weave the two strains together in an opposition of "the stories according to which" and the "banal facts of the actual." So, for Chapter One, I sketched a series of titles and put them next to counterpoint responses:

> *Orphan Melodrama, alone in the storm / / Demographic banality*
> *Swaddled, wrapped, and trundled out of the house, the newborn infant,*
> *cast onto the rough waters of a life / / Child of the baby boom, born on*
> *the crest of a now familiar demographic wave, the solid, swollen middle*
> *class.*

Next came the problem of images. I have never been much for appropriated material—text, photos, anything. I like my work to have passed through into my own language, own hand, own style. But I wanted the images, like the writing, to suggest found images. They had to have a cliché quality so that anyone looking at them would have a sense of recognition. Using several books on the history of illustration I traced out postures, expressions, gestures, and so forth. These were removed from their backgrounds, collaged together, given new clothing hairstyles or accessories. Because they were all redrawn in my own hand they combined an appropriated look with my own drawing style. The tissue paper finishes were scanned into the computer, manipulated again—stretched, compressed, rescaled, and their contrast and tonal values played with. Then they were entered into the Quark document as well.

There were still problems. The opposition was false, the two strains did not, could not contradict each other, even comment on each other, because they were so far apart, each somehow inadequate—my life, in fact, had not been lived in an opposition, a tension between these two, but in a synthesis. The utter banality of daily life, which provides pleasure, frustration delusion and satisfaction, defintely needed to be analysed and so did the clichés of the fictions—but in what terms?

The little heroine, on the slippery path to understanding her own subject position, looks up and sees the peaks of a glorious mountain range catching the first blush of a new dawn. Cast in deep purple shadows against the flaming peach of the snow covered crests words, letters, and titles are engraved naming the terms on which her life, in its struggle to ascend these glorious heights of the once sublime, will be analysed: Economic, Sociological, Psychoanalytic, Ideological. She reconsiders, it's maybe better to have her picnic right there, on the level plain.

After that I took the disks to the service bureau for film output from which I made the polymer plates. I had access to equipment at Soho Services in New York where Joe Elliot and Anne Noonan taught me the basics of platemaking. I made quite a few mistakes at the beginning—mainly from sloppy contact between the negative and the plate. This made for swollen, distorted, illegible type and filled in half-tones. There was no reason for this to happen except carelessness and once I realized how to be more vigilant the results were fine and I made most of the plates in two days. There were a few problems with the half-tones—but this came from the film output—spots where the halftone breaks down. This was a Photoshop error and I decided just to live with it.

But if the opposition was impossible to sustain, the structure of the synthesis had to be clearer as well. Easy enough to invoke cliché, trite narrative, a general field of received knowledge in fiction form. But what about specifics? In *Simulant Portrait* I had already written out a kind of parody of narrative forms in one of the elements tracing the simulant's life—from Victorian prose to postmodern fiction. I didn't want to repeat that gesture. Also none of this was meant as parody. That would imply that the level of discourse was distinct from and critical of some level of reference. Which isn't the case. The reference is the work. But what were the

narratives? How to articulate the clichés that had insinuated themselves into the very core of my psyche?

The little heroine shows a sour face. Except, we've moved past her, beyond
the orphan, out of the storm, into the titillating realm of the just barely ado-
lescent, or is it the unspoiled bud of young womanhood, or the passionate
yielding flesh of the full grown female? I of course was none of these, ever,
always next to outside of and in relation to these roles. This is hardly cause
for regret, nor censure. The indulgence in invention, reinvention, of cliché is
justified, at the very least, by the sense that there is humor in the foibles of
the writer yearning, still, to write herself into being through the work.

Printing was quite easy with the plates—getting them in position and
keeping them straight takes attention. (Duh.) But the only real problem
was that I was working for speed rather than perfection. The printing
was done at the Bow and Arrow in Cambridge over Christmas break. I
only had a few days and so I printed the plates as whole double-page
spreads the way they had been made. This meant that there was type
which was as big as 700 pt. being printed at the same time as 6 pt. type
and halftones. The result was a compromised inking which tended to fill
the halftones and leave the large type a bit anemic. A compromise is a
compromise. Also there were a few errors in placement of chunks of
image or text and this could easily have been dealt with by cutting the
plates apart. I'm not sure why I didn't do this—maybe it didn't occur to
me and maybe it seemed like more trouble than it was worth. Also I
may not have noticed til later since I didn't print a whole dummy and
then do the runs—I just printed the runs one after another. Not something you would do with a client.

And then I realized that the narratives according to which I
believed my life would be lived had come from genre fiction. Genre
fiction—books with attractive covers, embossed, foil stamped and
bearing vivid images. Available in supermarkets, airline terminals,
train stations, malls. Except that I was never, had never been,
allowed to read any. Allowed by whom? By myself of course. Once
when I had sublet someone's apartment I had inherited a shelf of
miscellany ranging from ghost written autobiographies of
Hollywood stars (women) and a couple of those books that are
about a Family with a Destiny stretching across six generations. But
even then, in the privacy of that domestic space, I felt a strong

taboo against reading them. I mean they were bad, bad literature. So, though I have rarely allowed myself to read this stuff, I was caught up in imagining it. I had decided *Narratology* would use genre forms, and then lo and behold (the hot hand of fate!) I got a circular in the mail. "Do you want to write for profit?" It asked (obviously not knowing me very well). It was from a pulp company soliciting authors in a whole range of genre categories.

Melodrama. Sweet Romance. Science Fiction. Romantic Suspense. Supernatural. Horror. Sensual Romance. Adventure. Thriller. Glitz.

There were the categories. My heart thrilled. Even though my experience of them was at one remove, I could invoke them: as if I knew, for instance, what sensual romance was or meant. Since I won't permit myself access to genre fiction as a reader, at least I could reinvent the form in a way which seems enough like New Writing to be permissible as activity, creative, substantive, critically legitimate. I began again:

Melodrama: Once the orphan, never the throne. All the pretty dreams abandoned her to an early grave. Holding the hand that fed her, she lost her claim to the inheritance. Inconsequential beginnings ultimately augured ill. The baby's breath bartered for a place in history. Once mute, twice wary, found and described before the voice broke the silence. The name of enigmatic femininity betrayed a faith in glamour. Later there will be a way to speak directly.

And so forth through to the Glitz conclusion: A small duplicating machine in the palm of her hand served to repeat those events by which she became fixated, holding her eyes in a permanent position in order to penetrate the field of vision along a single, platinum line of axis. Her press release was a long, slow ship, which smeared the horizon in its wake, a mute surgical device repairing the surface of the water. A poor trope for her meteoric rise, which would have been better served by a stretched limo of self-congratulatory prose.

Binding is its own nightmare, as we all know. I was saved, really saved, in this situation by the expertise of Nora Ligorano who generously designed the binding and taught me how to do it. She also helped me to cut all the boards (with Brad Freeman's assistance), and the cloth, glue all the cases, and to do a huge amount of other work. Marisa Januzzi also lent a hand for several days worth of work on binding during which we sat for hours doing repetitive labor and telling stories. We bound twenty books completely in half a dozen sessions—and then I bound the rest in the summer having acquired a tiny book press and huge sewing frame in the interim. Nora helped arrange for the foil stamping on the cover—the final "pulp" novel touch.

The last step of the process was handpainting the images with watercolor and gouache. I painted twenty out of seventy copies—and this took most of the month of May, 1994. There are twenty-five full-color images in each book—so that's five thousand watercolors just in the first twenty copies. I watched daytime t.v. (truly strange—but I like the company), sat in my study with all twenty books open to a single image doing each color on each image in turn. Since then I have painted a few copies, but the rest are waiting for summer space and a bit of time. I basically enjoy this work, though it gets tedious it is peaceful and gratifying for short periods. The images are pretty and I enjoy the sensuality of watercolor stroking and filling the forms, but there are a lot of hours in each of these books. I like to keep track of these things. Not counting the writing, which spread over a couple of years (1992-94) in bits and starts, the production work on this book included: drawing, Quarking, platemaking, printing, binding, painting. Calculated roughly these came to more than fifteen hours labor per book (more than a thousand hours in all, or, twenty-five weeks of full time work, half a year!), plus cost of materials.

> *Narratology: the stories according to which I thought my life would be lived, which shaped my expectations, the psychic disposition according to which the narrative of experience took its responsive form, in synthetic dialogue getting at the peculiar, particular condition of the imaginary in which living one's life was in/through writing/representation, not outside it, inside it, or in opposition, but in something which was a version of the real as the represented.*

> *The "real" mounts its own headlines, bids for a place in the daily news of literature.*

Published in A Poetics of Criticsm, *Leave Books, Buffalo, NY, 1994, edited by Juliana Spahr, Mark Wallace, Kristin Prevallet and Pam Rehm.*

Conclusion: Figuring the Word

Figuring the Word

Figuring the word against a jealous ground which rises to protest the independence of a xenophobic hand asserting presence as writing on a surface softer than the mind. "Prove before laying," read the label—or "etiquette" as it is called in a term which aptly states its prescriptive attitude toward protocol. What could be revealed without sullying the pristine integrity of the letters? Their unmarked and virgin faces flush with ink in the first encounter as the dark experience of knowledge pressed up and into the receptive fibers of some off-hand sheet. In a desperate attempt at self-assuring recognition they repeat endlessly this passage from cast form to transmitter of impression in the sequence of an infinitely mutable array. Their finite hearts beat hard in anticipation of imminent contact, their figurative feet solid on the base of the press, their discoursing surfaces pressed into the service of a continual rearrangement which suggests that any statement at all is a possibility within the momentary configurings of their categorical imperative. Their capacity for repetition and reuse is only real in the ephemeral sense of material, while the carnal knowledge of the alphabetic resides in its infinite ability to be dispersed into new relations of the letters with themselves and thus to us.

Disputed origins—born in flame and brought into being through some celestial crown or etched on the beach sands in the rapidly disappearing footprints of some incidental creature? Signs read in the patterns of nature as if they were culture and then aped to serve the purpose of possession. Stamped and sealed, scribed and inscribed, in a passionate legislation of accounts. Essential form or mere element of the code: does a letter need a body? Can it live as an idea? In the hard place of one thing differentiated from another by its own qualities and without contradiction? The tension between the pitiful finitude of marks and the infinitude of language in the book one writes as a corrective to the lived, trying to make the awful errors and gaffs over into a more coherent narrative account. Literary forms all figure forth proudly at the center of a story in which a certain measure of demons comes dancing around the hearth/heart of the psyche where neither chapter nor verse guarantees the site of power. Who makes noises about the behavorial norms of the lines and their studied disinterest in creative exercise? Who could tell the shape of time from the wretched of the earth, stretched out again and again as bare boned glyphs? Horrific texts, incised with accusations and disbelief, protesting the celebratory syntax of cultural capital and its inability to govern its own free enterprise arena of bright lights and textual reduction with any modicum of decency or decorum in the distribution of verb to noun and value to the phrase. Meanwhile the writing at the margins of the work kicks hard against the liminal zone in which it risks being sewn into the spine or lost in a final trimming. Bound and gagged the printed page submits to an order other than that of its original composition. As if words could be made to speak independently of the relations into which they enter hoping to clean the familial drains and be free of those unlicensed bonds vibrating in the cosmic marketplace. Reference embues the landscape with its saturating impulses, letting the news fall where it may while the baby aches its sounds towards meaning, hobbled by the uninspired albatross of intention. Writing, bright as bitemarks in the bark, negotiates the space between the public and the private, promoting an image of the personal as a ghost trace of the somatic, offering its pale marks as a mistaken index of the essential soul. If language functions as the symbolic—the social, the law, the cultural space in which the subject finds identity as position—then the semiotic is the resonant realm of all the rest of human meaning in sense, sensation, signification. No outside, never outside, but within, as part of, as an aspect and instance of—writing is not the flesh but is of it, out of the mouth of and worth two in the hand, its freakish tracery mocks only the attempt at careful legislation. A grid, a rule, a form from which the making deviates, always according to a rhythmic expression of the call to the self's alarm. The desire to be found is never greater than the force of the repressed's capacity to sublimate the figure into another version of some other inflection, a misnomer, a mistake, a missionary gap between the possible and the performed in which all of the matter is what is. Still, there is a theory of language which says "speak" and breaks its teeth on the hard syllabic facts lurking behind the tongue. There are other possibilities: that atomistic particles of thought were precipitated into linguistic material, in units more fundamental than the bent sounds perceptible to the feeble ear. Memory combines in symbol sites and logic maps coupled with their illicit brethren those sensations out of wedlock and bred according to immediate and mediate response. Who would know, staring backwards into the dark dawn, whether it was light or writing which broke first across the inarticulate horizon? Scribblage, the term according to which insane and writhing, bilious and inane, the proto-letters scream all over the obsessive page, trying so hard to be good, behave, be anything which gives them recognition as the managers of the prose whose limits they exceed like expectations at a fair ground catering to the most banal diversion. Does the surface remain a staid and stable ground as if that fixing fixture fixation fiction were possible outside of the instabilities. The soaking ink sweats and permeates through a whole cloth texture text fiber making its hot way back onto the page which pretends to want more than anything to embrace the tongue which speaks back in the head and makes more noise than ever in its struggle to write. A full throated cry of heroic pro-portions breaks lose on the trail of tears and torn water breaks wave after wave of meaning on the blank shore of that politely forgetful stretch of private real estate which passes for the mind. But the current state of language is concealment. Public hype makes the imperceptible real into a mistake of phraseology. Waiting by the phone we wake to more and more news, frightened into breaking the silence on the face of the sleeping monitor. Who wanted to be opportunistically immune to the possibility of new technology? And who willed themselves into the foreground by virtue of a lost art, type casting the frigid elements of new culture into one mold after another in a desperate search for insight. Caressing the new medium, the speakers take the message to the peo-ple in the same old way, day in and day out, no matter what charge the circuit carries it remains a matter of translation—my venerable hero lurks in the interstices between one moment of information and the next—but how long will fevered fortunes keep their shadows off his brow? Spatial distortion melts the fixed parameters of the daily reports and lets the supplicating code out of storage. Free to wander through the nightmare networks, the dull-frame modem jack-rabbits its first probes out as tentative forms of address. No interpersonal messages came back but the soft whiskers of the fuzzy logic generator trembled slightly in the light of a hot mother board casting its glow onto the shift-ed window of opportunity. A price code flashed its innocent request for an approval rating and waited with bated breath for a reply. What flickers across the consciousness is not just data but its reflective force, affective value— rethinking our every act. Second nature is still less a matter of choice than of ignoring various constraints in the program. In code life the briefest interval suffices to introduce doubt between one signal and the next. The once pure connection suffers a twinge of conscience, followed by a swift interrogation of the hours, minutes, and times of day in which narrative and location match—or do not. Nothing ruins the insulation as fast as the juice of a leaking emotional battery so that there is no repairing the old configuration in its circuit to circuit, hand to mouth, lips to heat sweet embrace of the familiar machine. In order to invent the new universe it must first be thought outside the old architecture, intolerant of the tight linguistics. The hum of a printer rubs the wires and the bald faced lies of a new generation of hypocrites barely merits a record but we cannot be sure of what they will want to know in the future when new levels of banality will penetrate the industry fashion with so much noise the line of power will shift from the right side of the public brain to the farthest reaches of an eclipsed hemisphere of reason. The heartless waters accept the goods thrown to them with the blood of strangers, runes writ in the thick sinewy line of new letters on the roiling surface of the angry earth. All of the refugees of the known universe are cast out of the heavens of use, so let us tell them everything about the storm which wrecked the mother ship and broke its timbers into chunks of prose, then sentence fragments, phrases ineptly suited for recombination into a tale of grace and recovery. The jolly rancher had sold off the unreal portions of the estate without considering what might happen to the good rules of respectable syntax and decorous grammar, his older workers, now committed to the bandwidth circles of a new hell, finding fascination in the device displays which distract the eager mind from all but the most seductive forms of engagement. The path of virtue does not repeat the circuit diagram as an inevitability but most data behaves as best it can, trying to find its place in the unsocial order of things immaterial which is neither of use nor of any particular moral value given the atmosphere of terror initiated by the brain dump upgrade in which the rules were never asked to review their violations of the ancestral code. A harsh algorithmic line levels its gaze and makes one admission after another while the time in which the statement expands and contracts with all the efficient respiration of an echo following itself across the bitmapped spaces of the mind.

The letterpress version of this text, with accompanying typographic work, was printed in 1997, in New Haven, Connecticut.

an image of the personal as a ghost trace of the somatic, offering its pale marks as a mistaken index of the essential soul. If language observes behavioral laws inscribed in the very dancefloor of the social, then the resonant qualm of all the rest of human meaning creaks through the cultural ether with a bodily sigh. Not outside of, but

ABUUVVHW&,&,MLL
KQ&THE WORD&CC
JJYZ;IMAGINES;DTRI
&BROKEN SYNTAX&1
1EFFGPPS$$O000998
87766554443322ZZE3

:aammmæœcĉtĉtwww
..vpqqhhKKnnbbbdyy
æstheticfiguresagainst
!-',,themind'sjealous,,'-!
oooccr?ground?rzzooo
eeejxxfftt:iillrrrrrsppv

within, as part of, an integral aspect and instance of the shuddering ensemble which we inhabit and are subject to — writing is not the flesh but is of it, out of the mouth and worth two in the hand, its freakish tracery mocks only the attempt at careful leg-islation. A grid, a rule, a form from which the making deviates, always according to a rhythmic expression of the call to the self's alarm. The desire to be found is never

Prove Before Laying: Figuring the Word, 1997, letterpress from foundry type (center) and polymer plates (top and bottom),9″ x 10″ .

Appendices

Checklist of Artist's Books: 1972 to 1998

A Chronology of Books from 1970 to 1994, written on occasion of an exhibition of Druckwerk at Granary Books, New York City, June 1994

The current exhibition contains works in editioned and unique form. In the late 1970s, the imprint under which the editioned works were produced was Chased Press (combining the metal chase, the gendered environment, and the chaste pun); by the late 1970s, I switched to Druckwerk, though a number of these works bear only a copyright and my name as the imprimature.

1970—**A Story for Philip** (unique book), watercolor, india ink, on drawing paper, 4" x 4", hand-bound in purple velvet.
Early books (and sometimes later ones) were frequently motivated by thwarted, unrequited, or unrecognized affections. This was the case with *A Story for Philip*, which I made in my first year of college at the University of Rochester, where I suffered a gruesome crush and made this water-colored and ink drawn piece. With great enthusiasm. To no avail. The one activity in that whole, cold, frozen, snow-bound and desperately introverted year which provided satisfaction. It was a unique book, made in a single copy, which I presented to him anonymously. Realizing the possible folly of this gesture and sparked by a sense of loss at having this one, first fruit of genuinely positive labor taken away, I made a second copy, this one, in order to keep something for myself.

1972—**Dark** (edition of 13 copies), handset Times New Roman on Rives lightweight, stone lithographed images and end-papers, sixteen pages, 8" x 8", hand bound in red velvet. "Dark, the bat-elf, dauphin to a leaf, our prince, licked his leaden lips and spewed back to them the piecemeal come of their misgivings . . ." My first letterpress book, printed at California College of Arts and Crafts in a course on Creative Writing and Printmaking taught by Betsy Davids. She had just aquired a first Vandercook for the school. Her course allowed me the opportunity, skills, and means to make this first printed book. The edition was small—I had very little cash and no access to a paper cutter, (all the

paper was cut by hand with a knife and straight-edge). The binding was
self-taught, not quite standard, and I printed the lithos through masks
because I had so much trouble keeping the edges of the stone clean—
thus the raised area which frames them.

The text was fraught with repressed juvenile sexuality, perverse,
Victorian, and replete with images of wetness, slime, mucuous and
other fluids and liquids. It was a text which emerged, whole, in just a
few sittings, the full, dream-like expression of some latent energy which
had only awaited the opportunity to be coaxed into form. A not yet
happy time, still living in a twilight zone of inability, social and emotional and sexual. Surfacing slowly.

From 1972 to 1975 I didn't have access to a press. During those years I
produced two groups of unique books—a constellation of odd little
hand-drawn works in black and white, written in rhyme, which I
thought might have commercial potential—and a few elaborate manuscripts of creative prose, archaic, arcane, impenetrable and coded in
their language. The amount of energy, time, and concentration involved
was in inverse proportion to my capacity to find any place in the world
for these works. Needless to say, none of them ever found commercial
publishers.

1972 **The Real Whole Story of the God-thing** (unique book), cal-
ligraphed in india ink, accordion fold, handbound in green cotton,
approximately 8" x 10". "It begins with a processional, a circular profu-
sion of attendants to the diety." Based on a pencil drawing, a single
image, which evoked memories of my brother, on whom the text med-
itates.

1972 **Light and the Pork Pie** (unique book) watercolor, india ink,
handbound, approximately 7" x 10". "A Pork Pie gone dancing, in need
of romancing, now prancing, now glancing at errored ways plays by
herself in the dark . . ."

1972 **The Story of the Pet Orange** (unique book), watercolor, india ink,
bound in purple cotton, approximately 4" x 4". A flatly ironic children's
story.

1972 **The Fruit and Vegetable Book for Children** (unique book), india
ink, handbound in green cloth, approximately 3" x 5". "Lemon girl

would brush her hair if only there were something there."

1973 **The Fruit and Vegetable Book for Children** (unique book), india ink, handdrawn and lettered, bound in beige linen, approximately 6" x 4". "Avocado with only one shoe—what is the other foot to do?"

1973 **The Vegetable Recipe Book for Children** (unique book), india ink, handdrawn and lettered, bound in beige linen, approximately 7" x 9". Contains such gourmet treats as "Steamed Carrots" and "Gumba Rice."

1973 **The Girl Who Did Nearly Nothing at All** (unique book), india ink, handdrawn and lettered, bound in blue denim, approximately 3" x 5". "Although it may seem I do nothing at all I can say with a great deal of pride, I am thinking of ways to explain to the world all the various things I have tried."

1973 **Spice Advice** (unique book), india ink, handdrawn and lettered, bound in printed cotton, approximately 3" x 4". No comment.

1973 **A BaB at C** (unique book), india ink, handdrawn and lettered, bound in blue denim, for my mother, an alphabetical nautical tale.

1973 **Eat!** (xerox) now lost, only have original mock-ups from which a few xeroxes were made, on the theme of eating—dark and funny.

1974 **Tomato's Rescue** (unique book), india ink, handdrawn and lettered, bound in red cotton, approximately 6" x 6". A full-scale, forty or more page novel about a Tomato, a Zucchini, and other vegetable characters. Endless, with dozens of images.

1975 **As No Storm or The Any Port Party** (Rebis Press, edition of 326 copies), letterpress on Rives, with photoengraved plates made from ink drawings, bound in canvas with knotting and eyelets, thirty-two pages, approximately 10" x 8". Printed with Betsy Davids, from whom I learned to print, though never as carefully or exquisitely as she. The text described a disastrous New Year's party, transposed into a nautical theme of shipwreck. Betsy had a grant from the NEA which she used in part to produce this book. This brought me back into the Bay Area and provided access to printing facilities—first through Rebis Press and then, in late 1975, through the West Coast Print Center, where I worked until Summer 1977.

1975 **The Rite Soft Passage** (unique book), india ink, handlettered in imitation of Bell types, on Arches, approximately 8″ x 10″, bound in black velvet with handlettered spine piece. A funereal text mourning an aborted relationship with a printer whose favorite types at the time were Bell and Bulmer.

1976 **Twenty-Six '76 Let Hers: Not A Matter of Permission** (Chased Press, edition of 30 copies), letterpress on etching paper, originally with accompanying abstract prints, (later abandoned—the sheets were torn down to eliminate the few finished prints), from fonts in a double case at the Print Center, owned by John McBride, who kindly let me use both them and his Vandercook, thirty sheets, 8.5″ x 11″ in hand-sewn cotton covered carton with ivory ring and shoe lace closing. The text to this work was derived from a trip to Los Angeles with Rebis (Betsy Davids and Jim Petrillo) to perform at the Vanguard Theater in Hollywood; the book was an alphabet book of private letters about a journey in the bicentennial year. Only who could tell? Different typefaces designate different registers of language. There is an annotated version of this in xerox which gives the gloss on the pages, replacing the skeletal extracts into a contextualizing narrative.

1977 **Surprise Party** (Chased Press, edition of 120 copies), handset prose in Stymie light, printed on colored tissue, four offset illustrations and illustrated cover, nine pages, 6″ x 8″. A nasty story about a birthday party I didn't attend.

1977 **Fragile** (Chased Press, edition of 200 copies), handset in Stymie light, printed on offset paper end cuts, bound in scrap carton accordion folded with packing label and string, twelve pages, 4″ x 4″. Printed entirely on my birthday—three set ups, three runs—in order to prove that I had been writing for a long time—these poems from a manuscript written in 1971.

1977 **From A to Z: OUR AN (Collective Specific) an im partial bibliography** (Chased Press, edition of 96 copies), handset from approximately forty faces, printed on Kraft paper, thirty-three sheets, 9″ x 12″, bound in plastic spiral. A pseudobibliography recording all the information, gossip, and poetry knowledge I had gained in two years' typesetting for the West Coast Print Center, plus a pulp-like account of a non-relationship based on a real crush I had had on a real poet; all the poems in this work are based on real people's styles, and all the characters, each identified by a letter, are identifiable. Finished a few hours before I left the Bay Area for a two year trip to Europe. I thought everyone would recognize themselves and I would never be allowed back—hardly a problem, as it turned out. The structural premise of the book was to use each and every piece of type in the forty-odd drawers and use them once and only once and make a text which made sense. I nearly managed to do this—only leaving a few odds and ends of numbers in the drawers at the end. The footnote pages, explaining the marginalia, were all set in one night.

1978 **Experience of the Medium** (edition of 10 copies, plus artist's and parents' proofs), printed at the Drukhuis in Amsterdam, in handset Garamont, on vellum, with ten sequential etchings, unbound, on German etching paper, handbound in canvas covered carton, 45 x 65 cm. The ten abstract etchings were meant to show the way a visual system defines itself and its constituent elements through a network of relations; in the text a term is associated with each visual element and is in turn defined by the sequence of sentences in which it is contained; the work came out of several years' drawing experience focusing on process, markmaking, and organic visual "events."

1978 **Netherland: How (so) Far** (edition of 114 copies), also printed at the Drukhuis in Amsterdam, in Verlangde Mercator, on newsprint, eight pages, 10 x 15 cm., bound with split pins on scrap carton with toilet paper and carton in self-mailer. This was sent to friends and family to describe my impressions and responses to the Dutch environment—which I found safe, suffocating, and conventional; one of the few poetry pieces I ever wrote.

1979 **Kidz** (edition of 76 copies), negative silkscreened text on Rives lightweight, linoleum block and silkscreen cover on Rives heavyweight, four pages 5.5" x 7", bound with glue in the spine. Punk prose narrative refusing patriarchy in favor of bad behavior and anti-oedipal indulgences. Printed at the warehouse, mostly outside, back in Oakland, California.

1979 **It Happens Pretty Fast** (edition of maybe 10 copies), xeroxed from pen and ink drawings and typewritten captions, a group of cards, meant to make a multiple option narrative, instead, functioning in the end as odd one-liners. Not quite a book, but it was surprisingly much fun to do those drawings.

1980 **Italy** (The Figures, edition approximately 500 copies), offset printed, about 60 pages, 6" x 7" or so, perfect bound. An account of a trip to Italy in 1978, with images from postcards sent to friends during that time; with the Dutch poem at the end. Thanks to Geoff Young and Laura Chester—at that time the Figures Press in Berkeley.

1980 **Jane Goes Out W' the Scouts** (edition of 90 copies), letterpress printed in handset Century italic on Rives lightweight, four pages, 6" x 12.5", handsewn pamphlet stitch. A tale for a friend who was too fond of the little ones, with linoleum block prints for which Tamia Marg posed. This was done in the best possible form in order to meet the standards of the Fine Print crowd—in material terms—and thus force them to deal with my work (they wouldn't) as well as with the pure perversity of the content of this piece (they didn't). Printed in the garage of Rebis Press in Oakland.

1980 **'S Crap 'S Ample** (edition of 80 copies), letterpress printed, handset Stymie light, medium and bold, on Rives lightweight, eight pages, 5" x 10", in pages folded to different lengths as in a sample book, bound into linen paper cover, pamphlet stitched. A portrait presented in different levels and degrees of accessibility corresponding to the apparent and less obvious levels of personality. The covers were a combination of linoleum, potato print, and handwork and were printed in a cross-country trip in summer 1979—part in Texas, part in Louisiana, and handfinished on the train going West while I composed the text. Text printed in the garage of Rebis Press in Oakland.

1981 **Dolls of the Spirit** (edition of 90 copies) linoleum cuts, handset sans serif type, on Basingwerk, fourteen pages, 8" x 5", bound with pamphlet stitch. Based on a Dutch emblem book of the same title, that about farm implements, this about transformative objects and prepositions. Written after beginning graduate work at the University of California, Berkeley, where I had begun to study the history of writing and printing. Printed, I think, on my own press, newly installed in the warehouse in Oakland, though the actual date of that press's arrival is a little vague in my mind.

1982 **Tongues, A Parent Language** (edition of 90 copies), handset Stymie light on Warren's oldstyle, twelve pages, 9" x 4", accordion fold, with illustrations printed by hand, accumulatively, so that each individual book required 55 impressions (multiplied by the number of books in the edition). Meant as a New Year's greeting, it was based on a work by Firth, *The Tongues of Man*, from which I extracted this text through mathematical process—first every other word, then every third, fourth and so forth.

1983 **Just As** (edition of 500 copies), produced with a grant from L.I.N.E. foundation, thanks to the kind auspices of Judith Barry, produced offset, black and white, from images drawn with magic marker and pen, twenty pages, 11" x 14", highly illustrated, text blocks originally composed on IBM selectric, saddlestitched. A picture book of ordinary life transformed through condensation accompanied by text created in the same manner.

1983 **Spectacle** (edition of 10 copies), xeroxed from computer output, generated on a rather grim school printer, bound in velo binding, with pink paper covers. A long prose piece whose format was determined by the original notebook in which it was written out, about film theory, love, romance, history, Ben Hur, and other things.

1983-84 **Against Fiction** (Druckwerk, edition of 100 copies, with 25 others on newsprint), handset in Stymie light, medium, and bold, sizes 10 point through 48 point, on Warren's oldstyle, originally bound (badly) into black Arches cover, with odd muslin spine piece glued to museum board, forty-eight pages, 13" x 16", illustrated with linoleum cuts. Images and text printed together in one run. This book took about 800 hours of printing time, including setting, running, distributing type and making images. The text had been five years in the writing, editing, typing, and much was changed in the composition process to tighten it up. All typographic oddities in the setting were dictated by necessity—I would begin with standard conventions and substitute only when my supplies were exhausted. My intention was to use the tabloid format to open up the dense text for browsing. The text recorded a five year struggle with the desire to write fiction and the sense of its impossibility in contemporary literary context.

1984 **Dream Life and Desire** (unique book, one xerox copy), 8.5" x

11", based on dreams and fantasies of relationship, too private to show.

1985 **Mind Massage** (unique book), made from all kinds of papers, mainly Rives grey BFK, with foil, ink, goauche, handpainting, approximately 8" x 10" x 4" in the finished box, which contained the major text and several satellite books which were referred to in that main body of the book: *Eusabia and the Victorians, Suburban Miracle, The Messages,* and so forth. All done by hand through the Spring of 1985, in Paris, where I was suffering another crush, and inspired by it to this tale of telepathy, diabolical bargains, and out of body travel. In a private collection.

1986 **The Yellow Dog** (unique book) handpainted in acrylic on rag paper, heavyweight, approximately 16" and 24", bound in some elaborate manner, with pages laminated at inside edges and folded on outside edges. Produced through a very long and very cold winter, my last in the warehouse in Oakland, while finishing my Ph.D. dissertation, and waiting for the phone to ring (sorry to say)—another bit of bad judgement. A mystery tale set in Bay Area locations, quasi-sci-fi, which was much fun to write and paint, though tinged with bad memories of an unhappy time. In University of California, San Diego's Mandeville Collection.

1986 **Through Light and the Alphabet** (edition of 50 copies, only 25 of which were offered for sale), handset in various typefaces both metal and wood from the shop set up in Wurster Hall for the Visual Studies Program at Berkeley, on Warren's oldstyle, sixteen pages, 13" x 13", originally in Fabriano covers, some bound with museum board, others (five or six copies) bound professionally in 1992. A typographic fugue in which the theme is the continual proliferation of texts as subtexts and the possibility of a linear reading is undermined by format while the text is a polemic against the idea of language as the limit of experience. The justification of the pages was a major task, and as the book proceeded, became increasingly complicated. I would stand the small units of paragonnage up on a galley, and then justify them into larger units and so forth, rather than work in a composing stick. Many changes in the text were necessary to accomodate letters that stretched through two or three lines and had to fall in words in those lines. Done as a farewell to Berkeley, on the verge of moving to Texas, finished with my degree.

1986-88 **Bookscape** (unique book), a large (approximately 18″ x 24″ x 7″) box in gold and silver foil to resemble a Neiman Marcus giftwrap, contains two levels of smaller boxes, each with a book object, made of paper of various kinds, with texts produced in all manner except by printing—handlettering, stencil, typewriter and pin pricks. This book was conceived as a response to the Dallas landscape, which could not be described in the conventions of any prose form I knew—not essay, not story, not outline, not narrative. The individual book objects were to reflect the postmodern object oriented architecture of Dallas, with its crystalline geometric forms, mirrored surfaces, and faux faux finishes. The book was about the relation between living a life and finding prose forms for its expression, specifically in relation to Dallas, but layered with examinations of the problems of writing feminine experience in conventions from a mainly patriarchal tradition. The book took two years to complete, owing to slack motivation and complexity of construction, and was mainly finished in a six week blitz of daytime t.v. watching in May and June before leaving Dallas, happily for good.

1989 **The Word Made Flesh** (Druckwerk, edition of 50 copies) letterpress from many handset types, wood and metal, tiny copperplate in the red field, on Mohawk superfine, with red Moriki endsheets and metallic Lindenmeyer-Munroe cover stock, twenty-three pages, 12.5″ x 10.5″, bound with rivets. The counterpoint to *Through Light and the Alphabet*, this book attempts to halt linear reading to call attention to the physical, visual materiality of the page. The text is all about the visceral character of language, thus the referent is also material, non-transcendent, while the form uses format to render the text resistant. Printed at the Bow and Arrow Press in the basement of Adams House in a very happy year at Harvard, thanks to the kindness and generosity of Gino Lee and Jim Barondess. Printed in three runs—the black wooden letters, the black smaller text and the red. Another justification nightmare. A play on carmina figurata of the Renaissance. [Reprinted by Granary Books in 1996.]

1989 **Sample Dialogue** (edition 10 copies) printed from various types at the Bow and Arrow, in collaboration with Emily McVarish, each of us writing one line throughout, to display the type collection, and to teach her to print. A few weeks of composition, but almost entirely printed in a single afternoon, adding ink slowly to change its color on the press.

On Mohawk offcuts, bound in paper we marbled ourselves under Gino Lee's expert tutelage, and in a binding he taught us.

1990 **The History of the/my Wor(l)d** (Druckwerk, edition, 70 copies), letterpress in black and red from handset Caslon, illustrated with found line cuts, on Warren's lustro dull (which often causes the book to be mistaken for an offset book), with Bagasse cover and Fabriano end-sheets, handsewn, forty pages, 10″ x 13″. Printed in several runs, small and large black type separately, red type, and red and black images—about two hundred hours of printing time, I think. The main text undermines the meta-narrative of history through its own clichés while the red type erupts, interrupts, with a personal memory of learning language in an intimate, even erotic, relationship with my mother—this recounted as a critique of the feminist position that language is always patriarchal. The captions collapse family history with imagined history. [Reprinted by Granary Books in 1995.]

1990 **Simulant Portrait** (Druckwerk and Pyramid Atlantic, edition 350 copies), offset printed from MacIntosh produced originals in green and black, on Warren's lustro dull, forty-eight pages, 8.75″ x 7.25″, bound by Judy Conant, sewn and inserted into paper covers. Biographical profile of the first simulant, provided for her as a means of writing herself back into history and serving as the basis of real neurotic behavior. Printed by Brad Freeman, who did much careful repair work in the stripping, since it had turned out that learning Mac was much harder than I had thought.

1991 **Crisis Romance** (unique book) produced in silver paper, by pin pricks, in accordion fold, on string, in black box, as a present to Brad Freeman on the occasion of his birthday, our relationship, and the Gulf War all at once. Private collection.

1992 **Otherspace: Martian Ty/opography** (Interplanetary Productions and Nexus Press, edition of 500 copies) a collaboration with Brad Freeman, printed in black and red, offset, on Warren's lustro dull, ninety-six pages, 6.5″ x 6.5″, smythe sewn and case bound. A narrative of cross-cultural relations, (mis)representation, knowledge and sexuality in interspecies communications, based on archival research into the history of images of Mars, as well as the diaries of Hélène Smith for images of Martian writing, and so forth. Starring Amy Komisarek, who kindly allowed us to photograph her, and who also arranged the shooting locations. Photoshop work by Brad Freeman, with our pre-press time totalling about 1200 hours. Printed by Michael Goodman at Nexus, in Atlanta, with kind support of JoAnne Paschal.

1993 **Deterring Discourse** (edition, ongoing) laser printed and/or xeroxed, in Memphis (the closest thing to Stymie in my type library), with manipulated photos (crude) in response to current phases of imperialism on national, literary, academic, and international fronts. About 4″ x 5.5″, with neon covers, pamphlet stitched.

1994 **Three Early Fictions** (Potes and Poets, edition 30 copies), xeroxed on rag paper from laser printed originals, thanks to Peter Ganick and Dennis Barone, saddlestitched. A collection of three pieces of fictional prose written in the late 1970s, early 1980s.

1994 **Narratology** (Druckwerk, edition 70 copies, of which 20 were hors commerce). Type and images generated on Mac, through Quark, and then output as film, turned into Polymer plates, then letterpress printed at the Bow and Arrow on Rives lightweight, forty-eight pages, 10″ x 12″, finished with handpainting in watercolor and gouache, bound into silk/rayon blend Japanese cloth, with Unryu, Kozo, and Tulip paper endsheets, foil stamped cover thanks to Barbara Mauriello. Binding with much assistance by Nora Ligorano at Lost Link in Brooklyn and some helpful labor by Brad Freeman and Marisa Januzzi. "The stories according to which the possibilities of living a life gained access to the psychic theater staging the events as real." The book is about the relation between tropes of genre fiction as models for women's lives and the lived experience of my own life—sythesized and at time counterposed in this text. Images appropriated, redrawn, and reworked to suit the themes of Glitz, Sensual Romance, Sci-Fi, Horror and others.

Addenda:
1996 **The Current Line** (Druckwerk, edition 25 copies) 5 letterpress and laserprint handbound and 20 letterpress and xerox spiral bound, 11″ x 8 1/2″, 36 pages, in black and red, made for wall display as well as book form; text about the current "line" of media hype and obfuscation.

1997 **Prove Before Laying: Figuring the Word** (Druckwerk, edition 90 copies) 40 copies letterpress on Rives handbound in printed paper, cloth spine, 50 copies letterpress on Mohawk superfine, 28 pages spiral bound in boards and hors commerce, 9 1/4" x 10". Two texts: one on writing as a mythic and cultural phenomenon, the other generated from a new foundry font and emerging page by page.

The works on this list are creative prose in either unique or editioned books. I have made this as complete as possible, but it does not include ephemera, printed posters, broadsides, performance texts, unpublished manuscripts, or other pieces of creative or critical prose published in magazines or anthologies. Neither does it include the scholarly/critical works: *Theorizing Modernism* (New York: Columbia University Press, 1994), *The Visible Word: Experimental Typography and Modern Art* (Chicago: University of Chicago Press, 1994), *The Alphabetic Labyrinth* (New York and London: Thames and Hudson 1995), and *The Century of Artists' Books* (New York: Granary Books, 1995).

Acknowledgments and Permissions

Most of the pieces in this collection appeared in print in some earlier publication, as noted at the end of each chapter. Permission to reprint was kindly granted by the following:

"Through Light and the Alphabet," Interview with Matthew G. Kirschenbaum, *Post-Modern Culture,* on-line, Spring 1997, Johns Hopkins University Press.

"The Art of the Written Image," *Dual Muse,* exhibition catalogue, 1997, Washington University Gallery of Art and Benjamins Publishing Co.

"Simulacral Exoticism," *AIGA Journal.* Volume 14, No.3, 1996.

"Experimental / Visual / Concrete," from *Experimental / Visual / Concrete,* Eric Vos, David Jackson, Johanna Drucker, eds., *Avant-Garde Critical Studies* #10; 1996, Rodopi publishers, Amsterdam.

"Letterpress Language," *Leonardo,* 17:1, 1984, by the International Society for the Arts, Sciences and Technology and MIT Press Journals.

"The Corona Palimpsest," Marshall Reese and Nora Ligorano,1995.

"Critical Metalanguage," *Talking the Boundless Book,* Minnesota Center for the Book Arts, 1995.

"The Myth of the Democratic Multiple," *ArtPapers,* Fall 1997.

"The Work of Mechanical Art in the Age of Electronic (Re)Production," *Offset: Artists Books and Prints,* Brad Freeman, ed. 1993.

"Iliazd and the Book as a Form of Art," *Journal of Decorative and Propaganda Arts,* Winter 1988, Illustrated Book Theme Issue. Published by the Wolfsonian Foundation of Decorative and Propaganda Arts. Miami Beach, FL.

"Narratology," *A Poetics of Criticism,* Juliana Spahr, Mark Wallace, Kristin Prevallet, and Pam Rhem, eds., Leave Books, 1994.

Johanna Drucker Photo by Brad Freeman, 1998.

Colophon: This book was set mostly in Meridien, with Klang titles. Formatted pieces use Bodoni, Memphis, and Franklin Gothic. The title page uses Times, Matrix, Klang, Meridien, Brush, Copperplate, and Bodoni. Designed by the author.